797,885 Books
are available to read at

www.ForgottenBooks.com

Forgotten Books' App
Available for mobile, tablet & eReader

ISBN 978-1-333-64464-2
PIBN 10530369

This book is a reproduction of an important historical work. Forgotten Books uses state-of-the-art technology to digitally reconstruct the work, preserving the original format whilst repairing imperfections present in the aged copy. In rare cases, an imperfection in the original, such as a blemish or missing page, may be replicated in our edition. We do, however, repair the vast majority of imperfections successfully; any imperfections that remain are intentionally left to preserve the state of such historical works.

Forgotten Books is a registered trademark of FB &c Ltd.
Copyright © 2015 FB &c Ltd.
FB &c Ltd, Dalton House, 60 Windsor Avenue, London, SW19 2RR.
Company number 08720141. Registered in England and Wales.

For support please visit www.forgottenbooks.com

1 MONTH OF FREE READING

at
www.ForgottenBooks.com

By purchasing this book you are eligible for one month membership to ForgottenBooks.com, giving you unlimited access to our entire collection of over 700,000 titles via our web site and mobile apps.

To claim your free month visit:
www.forgottenbooks.com/free530369

* Offer is valid for 45 days from date of purchase. Terms and conditions apply.

English
Français
Deutsche
Italiano
Español
Português

www.forgottenbooks.com

Mythology Photography **Fiction** Fishing Christianity **Art** Cooking Essays Buddhism Freemasonry Medicine **Biology** Music **Ancient Egypt** Evolution Carpentry Physics Dance Geology **Mathematics** Fitness Shakespeare **Folklore** Yoga Marketing **Confidence** Immortality Biographies Poetry **Psychology** Witchcraft Electronics Chemistry History **Law** Accounting **Philosophy** Anthropology Alchemy Drama Quantum Mechanics Atheism Sexual Health **Ancient History** **Entrepreneurship** Languages Sport Paleontology Needlework Islam **Metaphysics** Investment Archaeology Parenting Statistics Criminology **Motivational**

MOORESTOWN,

OLD AND NEW.

A LOCAL SKETCH.

By JAMES C. PURDY.

CHAPTER XI.
North of the Railroad, ... 1

CHAPTER XII.
Religious Bodies, ... 1

CHAPTER XIII.
The Schools, ... 1

CHAPTER XIV.
Societies and Institutions, ... 1

CHAPTER XV.
The News of the Day, ... 2

CHAPTER XVI.
The New Station, ... 2

CHAPTER XVII.
In Later War Times, ... 2

CHAPTER XVIII.
Old Houses and Landmarks, ... 2

CHAPTER XIX.
A Dish of Old Gossip, ... 2

CHAPTER XX.
Some Old Reading Matter, ... 3

CHAPTER XXI.
An Old Neighbor, ... 3

CHAPTER XXII.
Moorestown To-Day, ... 3

CHAPTER XXIII.
Moorestown in 1900, ... 3

Moorestown, Old and New.

Chapter I.

Introductory.

MOORESTOWN had its pioneer days as truly as Tincup, or Tombstone, or Chicago, or Denver, only longer ago. Not many of us stop to think of those days, however; and there is nothing in the present aspect of the place to encourage such thinking. The pleasant old town with its steady and comfortable solidity, and with the lighter elegance of its more recent development, seems to those of our day almost a part of the landscape itself; and to imagine the landscape a wilderness, with no Moorestown in it, and with only Indian wigwams to mark the site of the undreamed of town, demands a nimble play of the faculties.

Still, we all like to "think back," and it is sometimes a profitable as well as an interesting thing to do. The man who gives a sympathizing thought to the first settler riding his horse through storm and mud along a path of his own surveying, will thus better appreciate his own quick and easy trips in a comfortable railroad car; and the lady of to-day will find a new pleasure in her next shopping expedition if she has bestowed a sympathetic sigh upon her early predecessor, who had to make the thing she wanted " and make the thing to make it with." The citizen will take an added interest in the beautiful streets of his town, and in the cosy homes ranged all about, after he has tried to find traces of the abundant spring that is said to have first attracted white settlers, and induced them to place their cabins among the Indian wigwams on the ridge in Rodmantown; and we will all enjoy our holiday seasons the better for remembering that the old-time residents had their fun too, and that the mineral spring at Colestown attracted gay parties of pleasurers to the Fountain Hotel there.

And all the steps of progress from the old times to the new, if we could trace them, would be of interest and of profit. The advance from the Indian trails to turnpike roads, and to railroads; from the casual news a distant neighbor chanced to bring, to the frequent daily mails, and the telegraph and the telephone; from the wigwam and the log cabin to the elaborate modern home; from the horse-back journey to the stage-coach ride, and from that to the speedy railroad trip — all these things must interest each of us.

It is partly with the purpose of meeting and satisfying the interest suggested that this unpretentious little volume has been prepared. There has been no effort to make it a detailed and exhaustive history of Moorestown. That is a task which, it is to be hoped, an abler and more competent hand will accomplish some time in the future. Some little history there is in the book, but so far as the old times are concerned the aim has been to give reminiscences rather than history; personal recollections and traditions rather than official records.

But it is not alone with the old times that we are concerned. After all, the old times were but stepping stones on the way toward the new times; and if Moorestown had remained what it was a hundred or even fifty years ago, our interest in it would have been but vague and remote. It is the Moorestown of to-day that we care most for. Therefore the town as it now is, and the process of its evolution have been dealt with to some extent; and note has been made of the introduction of new elements and the growth of new influences which, working in connection with the old, have made Moorestown what it is—one of the most thriving as well as one of the most charming places of rural residence to be found within a long journey from Philadelphia.

Chapter II.

The Beginning.

THE first house in Moorestown was undoubtedly a wigwam. The town, as we know it, lies along a ridge a little South of the center line of Chester township. This ridge is about two miles in length, and its direction is a little North of East and South of West. The town, long and narrow, stretches from below the "Forks of the Road" on the West well up towards "North Bend" on the East; overlooking a lovely valley that borders its whole length on the South, and spreading out, in recent years, a goodly distance beyond the railroad on the North. Every one must appreciate the charm of the location; and the Indian had been gratifying his appreciation of it a long time before the first white man came to share the situation with him.

An abundant spring of good water existed at the foot of the ridge; south of where Elisha Barckalow's house now stands, on the South side of Main street, below Union street, West Moorestown. Tradition says that that spring, with its bountiful supply of pure and sparkling water, decided the location of Moorestown. The Indians understood its advantages and settled on the ridge in its neighborhood. As the squaws had to carry the water this fact would indicate that our red predecessors here had a tenderer consideration for their womenfolk than is generally supposed; or else that women's rights had thus early gained a foot-hold among the aborigines. Later, when the white settlers came in, the spring was a decisive influence with them also, and their cabins grew up among the wigwams on the slope near the fountain. The spring still exists but its ancient glory has departed. Its mission was accomplished long ago.

Just when these first white settlers came here, or who they were or whence they came, are matters that neither history nor tradition sheds much light upon. According to the law of primitive growth the navigable water-courses controlled the location of the first settlement in the region. Penisauken and Rancocas creeks were such water-courses, and the first English settlement in this vicinity was planted between the branches of the Penisauken; and all Chester township, including what are now Cinnaminson and Delran townships, was originally named Posomokin, or Penisauken, from the Indian town already existing there when the first white settlers came. The banks of the Rancocas gained their share of settlers not long afterwards, and the holdings of white men gradually extended along both streams. People are easily crowded in a new country. Where there is plenty of room everybody wants a good deal; and so the pioneers and their civilization are shouldered farther and farther into the wilderness. So the first creek settlements soon began to throw out off-shoots; but not, at first, into the interior.

Moorestown has no navigable streams, and so it had to wait for roads. The Burlington and Salem road, called "King's Highway," was laid out in 1682, and passed along the ridge on which Moorestown stands. With the road came settlers, and they appear to have come from the Penisauken and Rancocas settlements at about the same time, the Penisauken pioneers coming by way of West Moorestown, and those from Rancocas by way of East Moorestown, meeting and mingling after a time on the ridge in the neighborhood of the spring. The official records do not deal with these scouts who came ahead of the advance guard of civilization. Those who came later came with due regard to the formalities, and their names and the limitations of their holdings were properly recorded. But these first comers were "squatters," as are the first comers into all new regions. Their enterprise gave them the choice of location, and they sat them down where they pleased, and possessed such of the land as suited their notion. Afterwards, when an adjustment of titles became necessary, some of them formally secured their possessions, and others established squatter sovereignty elsewhere.

There are no log cabins left among the landmarks of old Moorestown. If there were they would be older than the oldest building now left standing here, for they would show the earliest order of architecture introduced by white men into these parts. In the course of time men generally contrive to command circumstances to some extent, but to begin with, the circumstances command them. The earliest homes in any community are of the kind dictated by the surroundings. On the great prairies sod-houses and "dug-outs" shelter the first families; in the depths of the forests log cabins are the obvious refuge. There was no prairie here, and logs were the available building material. The whole region, in the early times, was thickly wooded, and the settler had a very different experience to that of the "homesteader" of our day who takes up a claim in the treeless regions of the West. Here the axe had to clear the way for the plow, and the plow had to make a large allowance for stumps. In these days one has to take a long walk to get into the woods. In the days of old a still longer walk was necessary to get out of them. The clearing process would seem to have been a slow one; for even so late as forty years ago the forest still held to much of its ancient dominion, and people not much past middle-age talk of taking little walks out of the village into the woods in all directions.

As may be supposed there were a great many more logs than were needed to build the walls of the few cabins, and about the first busiuess enterprises we have record of were saw-mills and tanneries. Much of the timber here consisted of oak and chestnut—kinds that saw-mills and tanneries could make good use of. Grist mills were put up here and there; schools and places of worship were provided, and, with the agricultural beginnings already made, here was a civilized community in full process of development, and Moorestown had passed beyond its beginnings.

Chapter III.

After the Start.

ALTHOUGH somewhat bigger, Philadelphia is only a very little older than Moorestown. About 1682, the year that William Penn reached the shores of America, and the year before he purchased his town site on the bank of the Delaware, Thomas Hooten and his son Thomas located 600 acres of land on Rancocas creek. This was the year in which the "King's Highway" was laid out, and was a good time for real estate investments here. In 1689 John Hollinshead, already in possession of 1000 acres, had 150 acres additional surveyed for him. These two properties extended from Rancocas creek to near where the toll-gate now is on the Mt. Holly and Moorestown turnpike.

In May, 1686, when Philadelphia was about three years old, Dr. John Rodman bought 500 acres in what is now known as West Moorestown; and in July of the same year Thomas Rodman bought 533 acres in the same neighborhood. These were the two wings of the regular army of title-holders, advancing from the East and from the West upon the domain of the "Squatters."

The beautifully simple and direct way of doing things in those days would at first sight appear to have obviated all difficulties as to the ownership of real estate; but in reality the methods adopted had served to complicate matters, and the squatters had far the easiest time of it. In 1664 Charles II., King of England, had, by such means as satisfied himself, come into possession of the New Netherlands.

Of this additional American territory he, by Royal charter, dated March 20, 1664, granted an extensive tract to his brother, the Duke of York; and the Duke, with a generosity easily afforded under the circumstances, made a present of what is now the whole of the State of New Jersey, to a couple of his friends—Lord John Berkeley and Sir George Carteret. This munificient present was bestowed on the 23d of June, 1664, and to save the formalities pretended to be a sale; James, Duke of York, receiving the consideration of ten shillings lawful money of England, and bargaining for an annual rent of one pepper-corn. The two noble proprietors of New Jersey—or New Cesarea—granted a constitution to their province, and invited settlers; but troubles about titles arose, and some settlers who had bought land of Indians refused to pay rent to the new proprietors. An insurrection ensued; then the Dutch recaptured their old possessions, and after mixing things up somewhat, surrendered the territory to the English again.

All this raised doubts as to the validity of the Duke of York's title to the property he claimed, and he obtained a new patent. His governor under the new charter, claimed jurisdiction over New Jersey, holding that the two proprietors had lost their right by the Dutch conquest. This claim of his was finally negatived, but for a long time a troubled and unsettled condition of affairs existed.

Finally Lord Berkeley became tired of the real estate business, and seeing little prospect of profit from his five shilling investment, offered his share of New Jersey for sale. His interest was purchased by John Fenwick and Edward Byllings, two members of the Society of Friends, for one thousand pounds, and became known as West New Jersey. Fenwick came to America with his family, and settled upon his new possesions; but Byllinge remained in England and before very long, by reason of financial difficulties, assigned his property for the benefit of his creditors, William Penn and some other Friends being the assignees. In the adjustment of his affairs the assignees sold a considerable portion of his share of West New Jersey, the sales being to many different purchasers and of various extent. Those who bought became part proprietors of the future state.

A constitution was adopted, a formal division of the province was effected, and many immigrants, chiefly Friends, came in from England to settle. Commissioners were appointed by the new purchasers to examine and confirm titles; and it may readily be imagined that their task of adjusting and clearing the claims to ownership was no easy one, for King Charles' simple method of acquiring and conveying had resulted in a badly tangled state of affairs. The task was satisfactorily accomplished in time, however, and so effectively that the work done then has held good ever since. Under Queen Anne, after the transfer of the province to the crown by the proprietors on April 17th, 1702, there was no disturbance of titles; and after the colony became a state, titles seem to have been adjusted to the new order of things without any friction. It is claimed that all land belonging to the Indians was obtained from them by fair and honorable purchase, and that good titles were good by right as well as by legal observance.

The building of Moorestown, instead of beginning in the centre and spreading outwards, began at both ends and advanced towards the middle. There were two settlements, and neither of them was Moorestown to begin with. The one at the East was Chestertown when it had grown sufficiently important to have a name, and the one at the West was Rodmantown. Perhaps it would be more nearly correct to say that the place as a whole was sometimes called Chestertown, and that the Western end was occasionally spoken of as Rodmantown. Both names are easy to trace. Some of the more prominent and influential ones among the early settlers were from Chester, England, and love for the old home led them to transfer its name to the new home they had chosen. So the township in which they settled was called Chester, and the name was easily extended to the chief village within its limits. The extensive proprietorship established by the Rodmans in the Western part of the settlement, would readily explain the fastening of their name upon that portion of the village. It would appear, however, that the name was not generally adopted, or applied for any long time.

The aboriginal inhabitants whom the white settlers had for neighbors were one of the numerous branches of the Delaware tribe. They were friendly, as that term goes in describing the relations of Indians and white men, and for the most part they and their white neighbors got along harmoniously enough together. It would appear, however, that the red man did not forget that he was the first comer; and he had his own way of asserting himself as rightful lord of the domain, and showing that he regarded the whites as merely tenants at will. Whenever, for instance, he took a notion to enjoy civilized cookery, he had no hesitation in saying so; and the housekeeper of whom the demand was made was generally prompt in complying with it. It may not always have been quite convenient—indeed, there are vague traditions of instances when it was quite the reverse—but that was a condition of affairs that had to be accepted and made the best of; and the compromise was maintained unbroken.

Then, too, the Indians, when they had gathered a good deal of rancor toward the white men in general, sometimes worked off some of it on the particular white men hereabouts, and made life a somewhat uneasy, if not uncertain, affair for the time being. Various annoyances were visited upon the settlers; live stock was made to suffer; the people were made to feel apprehensive and distrustful; women and children were terrified; solitary riders had more or less unpleasant experiences in the woods, and sometimes word came of murders committed. It was the old, old story—old as the first contact of the two races—of wrong done and revenge wreaked. But here, so far as known, no serious wrong was complained of, and the minor annoyances and depredations experienced at the hands of the Indians seem to have been but the result of general irritation, while the usual character of the intercourse between the two races was amicable.

In 1758 the Indians here, in common with all those in the colony, released all their claims to lands and removed to the reservation of 3044 acres

purchased for them in Evesham township, in this
County. There they lived in complete harmony
with their white neighbors until long after the Revolution. Buildings of various sorts, including houses
of worship, were erected for them, and their settlement was called Brotherton. At length the remnant of the red men there removed to Oneida Co.,
N, Y,, where they had relatives whom they wished
to join. At this time they numbered only 63 adults
In 1822 they removed to Green Bay, on Lake
Michigan ; and in 1832 the last of the Indian claims
in this State was extinguised by the purchase of
their remaining fishing and hunting rights. So
disappeared, with their brethren, these earliest
inhabitants of Moorestown.

The purchasers of the Indian Reservation lands
in Evesham indulged their natural antipathy to
the tax-collector so far that they resisted the payment of taxes on the lands they had purchased.
They claimed exemption under the act by which
the lands were granted to the Indians, and the
Supreme Court sustained their claim. In 1814,
however, by some adjustment of the difficulty, the
payment of taxes began ; and in 1877 it was formally decided that the lands were taxable.

As has been said, saw mills and tanneries represented the earliest business enterprises here, always
excepting agriculture. Perhaps the first saw-mill
erected in this section was Matlack's. It stood on

Wagon Bridge Run, a stream that rises East of Moorestown and runs Southwesterly, about half a mile South of the Moorestown ridge, to join the North Branch of the Penisauken Creek; before reaching which it takes the name of Hooten's Mill Stream. The mill stood near the Elbow Lane Road. Hooten's saw mill, on the same stream, stood East of the Marlton Road. It was a very old mill when it was taken down in 1850. Another old saw-mill was Samuel Robbins' mill, on a stream that empties into the South Branch of the Penisauken. LeConey's grist mill now occupies its site. Another was Joseph Burroughs' mill on a small branch of the Penisauken. It has entirely disappeared.

As to the tanneries, there were many of them, some occupying positions in the town which it would occasion no small amazement to see so occupied now. One old establishment of the kind was located on the Main street, West of Union street. The buildings, greatly dilapidated, remained on the ground until 1879, when they were torn down. The property passed into the hands of Albert C. Heulings, and handsome residences took the place of the tannery buildings. When the tannery business was started there is not known, but the place was owned and operated by Thomas Bispham for some time prior to 1806. In that year he sold the property, and successive owners carried on the business until some time after 1820, when active operations ceased. The buildings, however, were left to cumber the ground until a few years ago, as already stated. This location is also memorable, in that tradition says that on it was the site of the hotel kept by Thomas Moore, the enterprising settler who gave his name to the town.

On the eastern portion of the farm of the late John Perkins, in the extreme western end of the village, there was a tannery which was burned down in 1820. George Matlack was the last to carry on business there. The old well used in the business was filled up not many years ago.

But the largest establishment of the kind here was situated in what is now the heart of the village. It was on the North side of Main Street, and occupied the ground on which the Methodist Church and two or three of the buildings below it now stand. It extended back to Second Street, and was for a long time actively operated by James Robinson, an English bachelor. This property also, was a part of the ground owned by Thomas Moore, but he and his wife Elizabeth sold it a good many years before Robinson got possesion of it. It passed through a succession of ownerships until 1793, when it was purchased by Robinson. After his death his niece, who had lived with him, returned to England; and in 1822 the tannery was purchased by William Boradaile and Samuel H.

Edwards. They carried on the tanning business for a number of years when they were succeeded by Isaac Saunders. He continued the business for a time, and eventually the property passed into the hands of Amos Stiles. Under his ownership the old business was not carried on, and the tannery went to decay. The old buildings were destroyed by fire in 1838; and after the death of Amos Stiles, in 1856, the ground was sold off in building lots.

Another industry, tributary to farming, milling and most other operations, was blacksmithing. Farming was not done by machinery in those days. There were no mowing machines, no reapers and binders, no steam threshers, no horse drills—only the simple appliances that took account of personal skill and strength as a principal element of success. Therefore the blacksmith was, to a considerable extent, an agricultural implement maker. An enterprise in this line was undertaken by Reuben Matlack, about the year 1780. He had been trained to the blacksmith's calling, and set up a sickle and scythe mill on the South Branch of the Penisauken, near where the Salem road crossed it. He fitted up his mill with a trip hammer, and for a time carried on the manufacture of the curved swords of peace quite actively. A difficulty arose, however. To gain sufficient power to operate his mill he was obliged to "back" the water of the stream to such an extent that the back water overflowed the lands of some of his neighbors; and that no wrong might be done he suspended his work for a time. A way seems to have been found of obviating the difficulty, for operations were eventually resumed. The sickle mill was afterwards changed to a saw mill, and in that capacity did good work for many years. The foundation of the old mill still remains, and upon it stands another saw mill, now and for many years operated by Asa Matlack, grandson of Reuben. The present mill was erected in 1814, and may itself be regarded as a venerable institution. Antedating it and the other early saw mills were the saw pits in which man-power took the place of water power, and two men, by the aid of a two-handled saw, worked up the logs into such lumber as they could.

Moorestown went early into the fruit-raising and gardening business, and the farmers here and in the immediate vicinity for years furnished peaches to the New York market. The peaches were carted from here to New Brunswick or Amboy, and taken thence by boat to New York. That was a state of affairs that could not be permitted to last. The farmers nearer to New York did not relish standing by and seeing the dollars roll past them towards this distant point. There were nurseries here as well as orchards, and the Monmouth county farmers supplied themselves with Moorestown peach trees. About 1830 they began to furnish the Jersey peaches required by the New York market, and that branch of the business here was killed. It was only a branch, however, and the fruit-raising and nursery business is still extensively carried on here.

The settlers, obliged at first to depend on distant sources of supply for bread-stuffs, took as early an opportunity as might be for obviating that inconvenience by erecting grist mills nearer home. There would seem to have been no grist mills erected in early times in the immediate neighborborhood of Moorestown, but quite a number were established within reach. **Walton's**, Haines' and **Warrington's** mills were all established at a comparatively early date. They were located in what is now Delran township, and all stood on a small stream known as Wright's Mill stream. Ideas as to "immediate neighborhood" differ, and the people of those days no doubt felt that their base of supplies was very conveniently near with the grist mills no farther away; and they would have shut up, as a dangerous lunatic, any one who had foretold a steam grist mill in the middle of the town, with wagons to convey the grain products to the doors of the purchasers. Such a vision of mad luxury would have been too much for them.

It is to be observed in passing that liquid comfort was looked after as well as solid nourishment; for Wright's Mill Stream, besides doing service for the grist mills, had on its banks Hollinshead's distillery and Garwood's combination enterprise of saw mill and distillery. And there were other distilleries hereabouts, in different directions and at various distances. Local option was the unwritten law of those days. But the option of most localities was in favor of having whiskey and kindred fluids within comfortable reach.

In those old times, as in the still older times, "Adam delved and Eve span." Homespun was the principal wear; and "store-clothes," except for "quality folks," were rarely seen. The men raised the flax and sheared the sheep; the women spun the fibre and wove the cloth; and after the cloth was woven they cut it up and sewed it into garments. There was a trade in flourishing existence then, the artisans in which would starve to death now. Men went about from house to house combing wool and hetchelling flax, making them ready for the women to spin. Another queer custom that is now obsolete gave an added interest to life then. The families received professional visits from the shoemaker, just as some families now receive professional visits from the dressmaker. The Crispinite came with his full equipment of tools and materials and staid until he had cut out and made up such shoes as the family needed, or could afford. At some houses he came once a year and made two pairs of shoes for every member of the family—one pair for "common" and one pair for "best." We may be sure that neither pair was of the tooth-pick or the high-buttoned type; but such as they were they had to do the owner until the time came round for the next annual manufacture. It is to be hoped that the shoe-maker was always of a genial and sociable disposition, for his visits were depended upon more than almost anything else to drop the ripple-making stone of gossip into the quiet stream of rather isolated home-life.

They were a robust, hardy, enterprising people, those early settlers here. They battled against obstacles right sturdily, and encountered hardships with a cheerful spirit. Indeed they seem not to have known that there were hardships, and regarded their Jersey home as a kind of earthly paradise, where life was easier and more bountiful than elsewhere. Some of their business enterprises were on a large scale; and the manner in which they were carried forward to success would be creditable with the facilities of to-day at command; with the difficulties and restrictions then to be encountered, it is astonishing.

Chapter IV.
"*There Lived a Man.*"

ON one occasion I spent a few hours in a new railroad town West of the Rocky Mountains. On leaving the train I saw a citizen standing in front of one of the board and canvas buildings on the principal street. He seemed to be the only man in the place who was standing still, so I approached him and made some inquiries concerning the young metropolis. He listened with good-natured courtesy and regretfully replied: "I'm sorry, stranger, but *I'm* a stranger here and can't tell ye much about it. But"—and here his face brightened benevolently, and his voice took a hopeful tone—"'here comes a man 't can tell ye all you want to know, fur he's one o' the first settlers in the place. He's been here a week."

The man was not joking. That town was just seven days old. It had a population of about 4,000 souls; long streets of shanties and tents stretched in all directions, and the business of the place, although not always of a type to be commended, was booming with a prosperous rush that was exhilerating.

To find out all that was to be found out concerning such a place as that would not be a hard matter, provided the investigator was prepared to accept the accompanying risks.

But it is difficult to trace the steps of a community that has traveled over a couple of centuries of history. The dust of the past has drifted deep and has packed down hard along the road, and in some places no efforts at excavation will avail. Under these circumstances there is comfort in the old saying that it is a happy people that has no annals. There is comfort, also, in the recollection that only fossils leave their exact imprint in the hardened mud of the past; and our old town is proving most conclusively that it is not a fossil. Still it could be wished that the record of old times was a little more complete.

In a certain way, and to a limited extent, Moorestown professes to be the monument of Thomas Moore; but the monument bears only his name. The epitaph has been almost wholly obliterated. Moore left his name to the town of his adoption, but with that gift his bequests ended; and even the name would probably have been forgotten had it not been transferred from the individual to the town. Many other names that have come down to us from times still earlier than the time of Thomas Moore have brought with them a strong flavor of personality; but there is only the faintest suggestion of such a flavor about the name of Moore. Of some who helped in laying the foundations of

Moorestown we know all the leading facts of their lives; the man who was important enough to give his name to the place is but little more than a myth. We know not whence he came, how long he staid or whither he went. Other men of the olden times have left descendants who still bear the historic name among us; we do not even know whether any child ever blessed the home of Thomas Moore. The original homesteads of some of the old settlers are still known and occupied; we do not know, with any degree of accuracy, whereabouts Thomas Moore lived; and his root-tree, wherever it was, has long since disappeared.

What manner of man was he? Was he big or little? fair or dark? jolly or morose? It would be interesting to know, but there is nothing to tell us even whether he was good or bad. It is not known where he came from; whether he came here as a young man, to grow up with the country; whether he remained until his death, or where and when he went if he moved away.

Thomas Moore appears to have settled here in 1722. In 1732 he bought thirty-three acres of land on the north side of the King's Highway. This purchase would indicate that he had a good head for business, for this was an exceedingly well selected tract. It extended from the west side of the Friend's grave yard on the East, to Locust street on the West; and from the north side of Main street on the South to the middle of Second street on the North. Somewhere in the western portion of this tract—just where is not known—Moore set up a hotel. What name the hotel had is a matter of ignorance; but whether it bore a taking title or not it seems, according to tradition, to have been a quite popular place of resort; perhaps because the tipple supplied there was good, perhaps because the landlord was a genial fellow with a taking way. At all events the place seems to have been one of importance, as importance was reckoned in those days.

Thomas Moore himself appears to have become recognized as an important personage in the community. He was apparently a keen and enterprising business man, and the records show that he did a great deal in the way of buying and selling town lots. He must have been a man of some strong traits, or he would not have been able to impress his individuality upon his neighbors so deeply that they chose his name as the one to be given to their village. He had a wife, and her name was Elizabeth, but even that much would not be known were it not that her name appears with his in the conveyances of some of his real estate. Beyond that one fact nothing seems to be known of the private and personal life of Thomas Moore. His biography might almost be summed up in the one line: "There lived a man."

Chapter V.

Revolutionary Days.

WHEN the Revolutionary war began, the dove of Peace was sore dismayed to find how many young eagles she had nurtured in her Quaker nest. Young blood is hot, and in war times it is apt to tingle as sharply under a drab coat as under a knight's armor; the restraining influences of faith and discipline are not always strong enough to hold in check its wayward impulses, and sometimes the man of peace becomes the man of war. Therefore it is that the Meetings had a good deal to do in those stormy days, calling to account those members who were guilty of bearing military arms in a military manner, and dealing with those who refused to return to the ways of peace.

It is to be supposed that Chester Meeting had its share of trouble with recalcitrant members in and about Moorestown; for unquestionably Moorestown had her spoon in the hot dish that was cooking by the heat of battle flames. The tradition is that the town furnished its quota of minute men under the act of August 15, 1775, and that they duly furnished themselves "with a good musket or firelock, and bayonet, sword or tomahawk; a steel ramrod, worm, priming wire, and brush fitted thereto; a cartouche box to contain thirty-two rounds of cartridges; twelve flints and a knapsack." At that time, although Moorestown remained, as it still remains, very largely a community of Friends, other elements had mingled in its population; and from these elements the minute men and the recruits to the Continental Army were principally drawn. Still the Society of Friends had among its members some who felt that, in such a time the ways of war were the ways of peace, and whose convictions drew them to handle the sword and shoulder the musket. No state gave a warmer or more cheerful support to the cause of the struggling Union than New Jersey; and Moorestown and the country around it was no with behind the rest of the State in the encouragement—peaceful or warlike—that it gave.

The terrors as well as the fervor of war were experienced here to the full. The British soldiery were here more than once or twice, and each visit added to the apprehensive terrors of the next. For a time the enemy had complete possession of New Jersey and during that time scouting parties and bodies of stragglers went to a good many places where they were not wanted, Moorestown among the rest. So, also, when Gen. Howe held Philadelphia, New Jersey was invaded by parties of raiders and all this section of the State was kept in a perpetual condition of worry and apprehension. The coming of the British was the haunting nightmare of the people here and hereabouts; and so extreme did this panicky condition become, not only here but throughout the State, that we are told "in 1779 there was a total cessation of public worship in the province."

The state of affairs which prevailed had its drawbacks, most certainly, but monotony and dulness were not among them. Everybody was on the alert, and the wits of the community became keen and sharp-set. It was known, from both direct and circumstantial evidence, that when King George's troopers were about, the best place for cattle and silver was a hiding place. An affinity existed between the soldiers and other people's property, and it was detrimental to the property. There was no use in attempting to break the bond of connection when it had once been formed; the only thing to do was to keep it from forming. To effect this it was necessary to know when the British were coming, and to get everything they would most desire out of reach before-hand. To accomplish these purposes kept people exceedingly wide-awake and active. Danger signals were established; warnings were quickly given and promptly heeded when cause for alarm appeared. Sometimes the hiding was accomplished unnecessarily; sometimes, alas!

it was not accomplished soon enough, and the consequences were disastrous.

On the farm of Mr. Hooten, on the Marlton road is an old bell which is said to be a relic of those stormy times. During the Revolution it was mounted on one of the farm buildings, and did service as an alarm signal, being rung for the warning of the neighbors and the calling of the men from their distant occupations when there were signs of British approach. At the sound of its note cattle and horses were hurriedly driven to safe places of retreat, and household and personal valuables were put out of reach as effectively as possible. In these days of humdrum peacefulness the bell has a more prosaic mission—that of calling the farm hands to dinner. Other signals were established elsewhere; and between here and the Penisauken self-appointed pickets did duty in times of special apprehension. At the warning they gave all the live stock was quickly driven off into the Deer Park Swamp. The times would seem to have been full of interest for the cattle as well as for their owners.

An instance is related which well illustrates the excited state of mind in which people lived at that time. It was a very successful scare, wrought up—most probably with malicious intent—by an eccentric and rather cranky individual who lived in Moorestown then. The incident occurred on a

Thursday morning, when the Friends were assembled in their meeting house for Fifth-day meeting. Suddenly the mischievous fellow rushed into the building and disturbed the solemn quiet of the assembly by shouting: " Here you are, all sitting with your hats on and the British just down by Neddy French's!" The British were not down by Neddy French's, but the announcement broke up the meeting all the same, and the result of the prank was everything that the pestilent fellow could have desired. The horses of the worshippers were driven out of the meeting house yard at a pace that astonished them and startled the neighbors; and it is safe to assume that after it was all over, some of those Friends inwardly wished that the discipline of their body had been a little less rigid concerning personal violence.

Not all the inhabitants were so grieviously disturbed at the imminence of a British visitation. There were some tories among the residents here as well as elsewhere throughout the country, and to them the prospective or actual presence of their red-coated friends, was not a cause for lamentations, but for rejoicing, rather. They made the soldiers welcome, and in return for this sympathy enjoyed freedom from the harassments and annoyances of their " rebellious" neighbors. They sold what they had to part with and received in return therefor good hard money of the realm, the virtue of loyalty not being, in those days, of the kind that is its own reward. But there were not many of the tories here, the community being for the most part warmly patriotic; and here as elsewhere the cause of independence had no more cordial supporters than the Friends, despite their deprecation of the appeal to arms.

There was at least one man who did not live here, and had no possessions or business interests here, but who nevertheless had reason to wish most devoutly that the British soldiers had 'staid away from Moorestown, and minded their own business. Kendall Coles was an active and widely known patriot, living a short distance south of Moorestown, on the road to Haddonfield. His principles and prominence brought him and his family into acquaintance with very many of the leaders of the Revolutionary cause, in the army and out of it, and among the rest with Lafayette. Lafayette had in in his train a number of gay young French officers, and Mr. Coles had in his household a number of young and attractive daughters. Now since the world began, properly constituted young men, whether French lieutenants or not, have sought the society of bright and winsome young women, and have overcome obstacles and braved dangers that they might enjoy the pleasures of such companionship. Therefore it is that on various occasions one and another of Lafayette's young friends were guests at the Coles mansion. One day a young Frenchman was enjoying the hospitality of the mansion when a scouting party of British soldiers rode up. There was consternation in the house, but quick wits were equal to the occasion. The imperilled guest was hustled into the cellar and effectually hidden, but in such close and straightened quarters as made him devoutly hope that the other fellows would not stay long. The British soldiers entered the door almost in time to see the hurried exit of their predecessor, and were in no haste to resume their ride. They did go at last but not until after what the Frenchman considered an extravagantly long stay; and the imprisoned guest resumed his visit where it had been interrupted.'

The evacuation of Philadelphia by the British under Gen. Clinton, and the retreat of the army across New Jersey towards New York brought sore tribulations to the people here and hereabouts. The evacuation took place in the morning of June 18, 1778, and the army crossed the Delaware into New Jersey. Three columns took up the march though the State by different roads, and one of the columns took the road through Moorestown. On the night of the 18th this body of troops encamped at Haddonfield, and on the morning of the 19th resumed the march in this direction. One of the daughters of Mr. Coles, then a young girl and afterwards the wife of Reuben Matlack, remembered vividly to the day of her death, the march of that June day, and in later years entertained her children and her grand-children with the recital of incidents that came under her observation. Happy were those patriots along the line of march who had received and heeded timely warning of what was coming; who had hidden their valuables and driven away their live-stock, and who kept themselves and their families in seclusion. And miserably unlucky were those whose action had been differently taken.

Mrs. Matlack, like the other members of her father's family, had had abundant opportunities of forming acquaintanceship, either personally or by description, with the prominent men of both sides of the great contest, and her belief was that Gen. Howe was in command of the column of the retreating army that passed over this road. However that may be, tradition has it that Gen. Howe was at one time personally in Moorestown and staid here over night. Whenever it was, the General seems to have had no scruple about giving trouble to his involuntary hostess on the occasion of his visit. The butter already on hand in the family spring house did not answer his purpose, and a special batch of "gilt-edged" was prepared. In a family now living in Marlton there is said to be still kept as an heir-loom, the churn in which the butter was made for Gen. Howe on the occasion of his visit to Moorestown.

The army reached Moorestown on the afternoon of the 19th, and encamped on ground not far from the Friends' meeting houses. Probably a more unwelcome body of men never made themselves at home where they were not wanted. Their popularity had not been great along the road; and they made life a burden to the peaceful folk here. They pillaged right and left, wantonly destroyed property they had no desire to possess, "confiscated" all the livestock they could lay hands on, and in various ways made themselves a grand nuisance.

Here as elsewhere the citizens who had timely tidings of the coming irruption made such provisions as they could in the way of getting their livestock out of reach and hiding their portable property. But there was no telegraph then to give news of the event before it had fairly happened; only mounted couriers could be depended upon to give the needed warning, and the men between here and Camden were too much occupied in looking after their own interests and those of their immediate neighbors to admit of a very early warning to their Moorestown friends. However, the warning came here in advance of the British, although not so far in advance that much margin of time was allowed for precautionary measures. Some of the people here had wonderfully narrow escapes from failure in their efforts to hide valuables. One of these was a farmer named Middleton who lived on what was more recently known as the Stiles Farm, on what is now Central avenue, north of the railroad and west of Chester avenue. When he heard of the approaching visitation he dug a hole in the ground near his house, and hurriedly deposited therein his silver and such other belongings as he wished particularly to save. He had just finished filling up the hole when the red coats appeared in sight down the road. Fearing that the fresh appearance of the earth would arouse suspicion he, with with a quick command of resources born of the time, scattered some shelled corn over his buried treasure and called the pigs and chickens to the spot. They soon obliterated the traces of the spade and his property was saved.

At that time one of the most prominent families here was that of Richard Smith; and his mansion, on the King's Highway was perhaps the largest and most pretentious in the place. At this house distinguished visitors to the town were received and entertained as guests; and on the 19th of June, 1778, distinguished visitors who were disposed to entertain themselves were received, under the pressure of circumstances over which the Smith family had no control. Their visit was of a distinctly different character to that of the visits the family had been accustomed to receive, and seems to have been an absolute reign of terror. The household at the time included a number of ladies, but there would seem to have been no men about the house except the servants. The chief of these menservants got notice in advance of the coming of the British, and he was prompt in running off all the horses belonging to the place, and shrewd in hiding them before the arrival of the unwelcome visitors. He took them through the woods at the back of the house into a swamp some distance away to the south, and secreted them there so successfully that none were captured; but they were the only livestock on the place that escaped the clutches of the soldiers.

It would have been well if the faithful servant had foreseen what was to take place, and had driven every other living thing on the estate into the same swamp; for the commanding officer of the British made the Smith mansion his headquarters, and that meant a great deal in the way of uncomfortable experience to the members of the household. He was accompanied by the members of his staff, as well as by a number of common soldiers detailed for headquarters duty, and his military family comprised a number of Hessians. The policy adopted of "living off the country" was freely carried out in this instance, and such resources as the house and farm afforded were taken advantage of to the utmost. They were bountiful and the resulting feast was in the nature of a carousal. Every fowl on the place was sacrificed, and to make the banquet complete a calf was killed, dressed and cooked. The roystering was loud and long continued, and the ladies of the house wished many a time before morning that either they or their guests were somewhere else.

On arriving, the commanding officer informed Mrs. Smith that she and the members of her family must remain secluded in their rooms, as otherwise he could not undertake to protect them from insult at the hands of his officers and men, particularly the Hessians. The ladies accordingly went into close retirement; but they did not all stay there, and a commotion was the result.

Visiting at the house was Miss Elizabeth Murrell, a niece of Mr. Smith. She was a bright and lively young girl of about fourteen years, whose home was in Burlington. Years afterwards she became the wife of Reuben Stiles; and when she was an elderly woman Reuben Stiles the younger—at the time of his recent death one of the best known and most respected citizens of Moorestown—was born to them, the youngest of their family of ten children. Mrs. Stiles retained to the time of her death a vivid recollection of the visit of the British at her uncle's house, as well as other memorable events of those troubled times, and frequently related the details to her son and other members of her family.

Elizabeth Murrell it was who went out of her room contrary to orders. During the evening she wished to go from one apartment to another—it is hard for young people to stay shut up on compulsion—so she peeped out of her door and thought the coast sufficiently clear to warrant the risk. She ventured out and very shortly was convinced that she had made a mistake. She had hardly got fairly into the hall before a Hessian caught her and tried to kiss her. She struggled and screamed, and her screams brought the commanding officer to the spot. At sight of him the Hessian released his indignant captive, giving her an impatient push and exclaiming, with a contemptuous wave of the hand: "Footy, footy, footy!" After this adventure the ladies remained closely shut up in one room with the door locked until their too demonstrative guests had taken their departure. The British commander placed a guard at their door, and they were secure from further molestation; but we can well fancy that they passed the night in a more or less hysterical condition.

In the morning the soldiers marched away; but not alone; for they drove off all the cattle on the place. However, the imprisoned ladies were once more at liberty; and that was a joyful fact until they had seen the condition of the house and premises, and then all joy was killed for the day. Such a condition of things as confronted them cannot be described. The chickens for the banquet had been killed, plucked and cleaned in the parlor; and blood, feathers and filth were on the carpet, the walls and every article of furniture. The other rooms of the house were in keeping with this; and a scene of ravage and desolation presented itself everywhere.

The horses were brought back from the swamp; and later in the day a vociferous cow ran bawling into the yard. She was the mother of the calf that had been slain to make the soldiers' feast, and she had been driven off with the rest of the stock in the morning; but her anxiety to get back to where she had last seen her offspring was more than a match for the vigilance of her captors. She made her escape in some way from the drove and ran noisily all the way home. She was the only member of the herd the family ever saw again.

Another old house in Moorestown associated in tradition with British visitations here is that belonging to the estate of the late Asa Schooley, at the corner of Main and Schooley streets. It seems tolerably certain that the British had possession of the building at one time, but tradition grows vague and weak when it comes to telling when, for how long, in what force or under what circumstances. It seems most probable that the occupation of the premises was, like the other occupation just described, on the 19th of June, 1778, and that the house was used as headquarters by some of the lower officers of the command. There is no certainty, however, in the minds of any regarding the facts.

The mansion of Richard Smith was the scene of another reception, very different in character to that of the men who killed the chickens and drove off the cattle. Lafayette was the visitor, and his visit preceded that of the British. Elizabeth Murrell was a guest at her uncle's house on this occasion also, and she is the authority for such details of the visit as are now known. This was an honored guest who came with a gallant party of young aids to the hospitable mansion, and he was made welcome with all the stately and elaborate courtesy of the time. He was on his way through New Jersey to join Washington, and spent a night at the house of his entertainer. It is related that he had been ill for some time, and still showed the effects of his sickness. Mrs. Stiles' memory was strongly impressed by the pale face and delicate, refined appearance of Lafayette. Another of her abiding recollections was of the remarkably fine horse he rode. It was a sorrel, and was extraordinarily handsome. The animal had hurt its foot in some manner, and one of the General's aids, with a servant to hold the torch, went out in the evening to examine the injury. Elizabeth Murrell watched the investigation from the porch, and admired the horse at her leisure.

The tradition is general and persistent that Washington not only passed through Moorestown, but that he passed a night here. No well regulated old place considers itself quite happy without the existence of some such link connecting it with Washington, and that hero-statesman would have needed a longer and more slumberous life than the one he lived to have slept under all the roofs assigned to him throughout the country. He was pretty enterprising, and a good deal of a traveller, but even he was not equal to all the claims made upon him by tradition in behalf of sacredly historic feather-beds and guest-chambers.

One of our local stories is that he passed a night at the old Smith mansion previously referred to. This, however, is contradicted by those most likely to know, and the explanation is given that the tradition arose from the visit of Lafayette to the house in question. Another and more positive statement is to the effect that Washington made his halt for the night at an old house on Main street below Church Road, which was torn down only a few years ago. One or two other old houses are mentioned as having had the honor of sheltering the Father of his country on the vague night in question; among them being the ancient building at what is now known as Fair Ground avenue, in which Mrs. Mary Lippincott's boarding school was kept. The claim in all these cases is prefaced by "they say," and is unsupported by anything like incident or definite statement of any kind.

A very positive statement has been made that Washington did pass the night on one occasion at the old Matlack homestead, between the Haddonfield and Camden roads, a couple of miles below Moorestown. This visit was said to have been a matter of history supported by positive evidence, and not dependent upon tradition at all. Trees were said to be still standing on the place which were marked in a peculiar manner on the memorable occasion—whether by the historic hatchet of immortal visitor was not stated. Inquiry of Mr. Mordecai Matlack elicited the information that if such a visit were ever made he never heard of it; a statement rather discouraging to further investigation in that direction.

It is pretty certain that if Washington passed a night on the Matlack farm, he did not pass a night in Moorestown—on that march at least. For the Commander-in-Chief of the Continental Army was not travelling for pleasure; and the distance from the Matlack homestead to Moorestown would not constitute a day's march, even in more leisurely times than the Revolutionary period. Pleasant as Moorestown is and always has been, he would hardly have tarried here for the mere sake of enjoying the beauties of the place.

The discrepancy between the different traditions is reconciled in some minds by the supplementary theory that two visits were made. Indeed the tradition exists, independent of any effort to reconcile conflicting statements, that Washington traversed the highway through Moorestown on two different occasions—going from Philadelphia at one time, and again going towards that city. The confirmation of this belief would verify the claims of two of the houses that sheltered Washington over night; but the others would still have to be content with the lesser glory of a possible daylight visit.

It will be seen that the record of Washington's visits here would make a long and interesting chapter; but after all it would be in the nature of that famous chapter which was headed "The Snakes in Ireland," and which consisted of the one line, "There are no snakes in Ireland." We greatly fear the conviction must be accepted that the great Commander never was in Moorestown at all.

But if Washington never saw Moorestown, at least one person intimately associated with Moorestown saw Washington. It was the same Elizabeth Murrell who had the memorable adventure with the too gallant Hessian, and who seems to have had the luck of seeing notable people and witnessing notable events. She had returned to her father's house in Burlington, and there, as the French say, "assisted" at a grand review of the army by the Commander-in-Chief. Mrs. Washington—or "Lady Washington" as she was then called—accompanied her husband; and the General's scrupulous and deferential attention to his wife struck this girlish observer as something remarkable even for those ceremonious days. She used to relate that the General, in order that his wife might enjoy a better view of the proceedings, procured a thick and heavy book for her to stand upon. This he laid upon the ground as a pedestal upon which her feet were to rest; but before he permitted her to stand upon it he took out his handkerchief and carefully *dusted off* the cover of the book, in order that it might be clean enough to fittingly support the feet just lifted from the muddy earth. Truly either George was a model husband, or Martha well knew the value of discipline!

The father of this same young military reporter, and the grandfather of our townsman, Reuben Stiles, was an officer in the Continental army; and his exceptionally intimate knowledge of the country led to his being selected as a cavalry scout, his duty being to obtain and impart such information as was possible of the enemy's whereabouts, doings and purposes. When the British held Burlington Captain Murrell made frequent night entries to the own, in one disguise or another, and besides visiting his family, managed to take away with him considerable useful knowledge.

On one of these occasions he learned that a council of war was being held in a certain house, and mounting the steps of the building he proceded to investigate through the key-hole. There had been a recent fall of sleet and the steps were slippery. As a consequence the uninvited member of the council took a tumble off the steps to the pavement. The noise of his fall was heard within the house, and the assembled officers rushed to the door just in time to see him rise to his feet and make off. In his haste the coat he wore as a disguise was disarranged, revealing his Continental uniform beneath. He was recognized and the British officers made straight for his house, supposing that he would go there for concealment. By the time they reached the house, however, Captain Murrel's fleet horse had borne him to a safe distance in another direction, and as the officers afterward stated, they "found the nest, but the bird had flown."

Chapter VI.

Rapid Transit.

IT is a very curious twist in human nature—the human nature of these days at least—that causes men to be always in a hurry when they go from one place to another. They may have an abundance of leisure and more time than they know what to do with; but they don't like to spend any more of it than they are compelled to on the road. The highest priced horse is the one that can save a few seconds in taking to a given point a man who has nothing whatever to do when he gets there, unless it be to turn around and come back at still greater speed, if possible. The train that lowers the schedule time between New York and Chicago is the train that commands the greatest patronage from the moneyed people of leisure. I have seen men elbow their way to the bow of a ferry-boat as it entered the slip, jump ashore before the boat was made fast, and then stand by idly, with their hands in their pockets and watch the last man and woman file off from the boat. And yet we talk of the luxury of leisure.

This same luxury of leisure, looking at things from our stand-point, was enjoyed to the full by those who preceded us here. They did not fly at top speed from one place to another; they did not tear about the country and about the world, spending the Fourth of July in Canada and Christmas in Florida; the month of March in Santa Barbara and the month of November in Rome. They had all the time there was and they used it in a very deliberate fashion. Most of it they used in one place; for when they got anywhere they were very apt to stay there, and to take the weather and the other conditions of life as they came along. It is a recent idea, this one of rushing away to a hot country in cold weather, and to a cold country in hot weather. It has a good deal to recommend it, but it did not enter into the plans of the old-time folk. Indeed if they had tried to carry out such an idea the weather would have had plenty of time to change before they had got to the place they set out to reach; for when they did go from one point to another they took plenty of time for it.

But it was only because they had to. They would have been just as migratory as the rest of us, and just as speedy in their migrations if they had known how. Their blood would have been fevered by the ferment of unrest to just the same extent that ours is; and their nerves would have been stretched and racked to the same degree as ours by the demon of hurry, if there had been a chance for hurry to accomplish anything. Indeed I imagine they did hurry as much as we do, only in slower fashion. They got over the ground as fast as they could, and wished they could go faster; and that is all we do. The difference is merely one of standards. It is quite possible that bye and bye, when men go flying through the air in balloons sped by electricity, they will regard the crawling pace of our present railroad trains much as we regard the cumbrous wagon travel of the men who lived before us.

There were all sorts of difficulties in the way of rapid transit for them; but they accomplished it according to their ideas and opportunities, and were tolerably well pleased with the results—until they could see the way to something better, and then they tried for that. The great drawback in the way of free and easy going about was the character and general condition of the thoroughfares that had to be traversed. We can form only the faintest and most incomplete idea of what the roads were then, or of what tribulations beset the tourist between here and Philadelphia. That bit of travel does not afford an experience of delight even now if it be undertaken in a springless wagon in an "open winter" or in the early spring; but it is as the flight of the swallow compared with what it used to be. The experiences of long ago are probably being repeated now, in modified form, in remote wooded regions that are newly settled; but we can form no conception of them, and therefore can have no adequate sympathy with either our predecessors or our contemporaries.

The earliest roads were scarcely roads at all, although dignified by that name. They were little more than bridle paths, and were not constructed with the view to accommodating vehicles. To be sure there were not many vehicles to be accommodated; but neither were there any modern appliances for the removal of stumps, and any wagon or cart which had attempted the passage of a public road, even where it was broad enough, would have had a rough and stormy voyage and would most probably have been wrecked on some stumpy reef before the passage had been completed. Indeed many of the less important of the old roads were only foot-paths.

As time passed on there was improvement, of course; but even so late as 1716, in the rates allowed by the assembly for the New Brunswick Ferry, provision was made only for "horse and man," and for the "single person," no account being taken of vehicles. So the improvement could not have been very rapid. If wheeled vehicles had had been in use to any extent they would certainly have been considered and that they were not more generally in use argues a most undesirable condition of even the most important public roads.

Even such use as was made of wheeled conveyances serves, rather than otherwise to emphasize the difficulties that beset the traveller. There was no public means of conveying passengers; but private individuals had obtained privileges, amounting to monopoly, in the way of transporting persons and goods between New York and Philadelphia. A man named Delaman seems to have had things all his own way in this respect. He had in some way attained special privileges; and although he had no set time or regular prices for his trips, he held his right against any proposed competition until after Governor Hamilton's recall in 1710. Then his monopoly ceased and there was competition. A new era of travel began, and "stage-wagons" were run between the two great cities. We smile as we read the proviso that invariably accompanied their announcement: "Wind and weather permitting." The restriction must have been an elastic one, or travel must have been frequently interrupted; for during a considerable portion of the year the weather in this section of the country is apt to be not of a permissive character.

In 1750, such had been the progress of improvement, a line of transportation was established, the owner of which informed the public that a stage-boat would leave New York every Wednesday, for the Amboy Ferry on Thursday, where on Friday a stage-wagon would immediately convey the patrons to Bordentown; whence another stage-boat would convey them to Philadelphia. In 1752 such advancement was made that the stage-boat left New York twice a week instead of once; and the increase of speed had been so great that the trip to Philadelphia was sometimes accomplished in five days, although it more commonly occupied seven. Later still stage-wagons "with seats on springs" (mark the luxurious ease the travelling public in indulged in) made the summer trip in two days; the winter trip occupied a day more, but the spring seats still made glad the passenger. The wagons that achieved this phenomenal speed were justly called " flying machines."

That was all very well and compels the belief that very great improvement had been made; but we are led with many misgivings, to inquire what must have been the unimproved condition of affairs, when we read what Governor Franklin said so late as 1768. In a speech delivered in that year, urging upon the assembly the necessity for an improvement of the roads in the province, the Governor stated that "even those roads which lie between the two principal trading cities of North America are seldom passable without danger or difficulty." The Governor may not have been so good an authority as his father on many subjects, but when it came to the condition of the roads he undoubtedly knew what he was talking about.

With such a rate of progress as we have described, and with such a condition of roads as Governor

Franklin described, between the great centres of population, it may readily be imagined what kind of travelling facilities existed between Moorestown and the outside world. The trip to Philadelphia was a more or less adventurous journey, by forest path and winding stream; and it was not always free from the added excitement of Indian dangers and annoyances. True the aborigines here were for the most part friendly, and did not go regularly upon the war-path, but still they sometimes caused the settlers' souls to be more or less tumbled up and down within them.

But with or without aboriginal accessories the journey was a rather momentous one. And it was a journey that had to be undertaken from time to time. The commerce of the place was not large, and the demands of the Philadelphia markets were not excessive in the early times. Still there were things to be sold, and things to be bought; and there were no "drummers" then to come out from the city, show samples, take orders and send the goods delivered by express or mail; and there were no dealers or dealers' agents to go through the country districts, gather up the spare produce and pay the market price for it. Those things had to be attended to by the parties interested; and therefore Moorestown had to go to Philadelphia sometimes.

The first part of the journey was made on horseback; and if the female members of the family wanted to do any shopping — and what female member of any family does not want to do shopping sometimes?—they went along, also on horseback, but not always on separate horses. More frequently the lady rider sat on a pillion behind her male escort, and secured herself in her seat by clasping him around the waist. To make things even, the front end of the conveyance was balanced by a bag of grain laid across its shoulders, a quantity of fresh meat sewed up in a cloth, a basket of eggs, or a basket of garden produce—for the "truck business" was very early entered into hereabouts. Considering what can be achieved even now in the way of mud, it is natural to suppose that in those days horse and man and woman would sometimes conclude by the time they got back home, that living in the country had its disadvantages as well as its pleasures.

But a change of conveyance was necessary before the journey was completed. There were streams in the way that had not been bridged and were inconvenient to ford. And in any case the trip by boat was easier and more expeditious than by horse. So when Penisauken was reached the horse was unloaded, and the passengers and merchandise stowed into a skiff or flat-boat, and the remaining distance was accomplished by water. The water highway to Philadelphia was not a very formidable or turbulent one, but it involved its share of adventure, difficulty and discomfort, especially when "wind and weather" were not of the favoring sort. The boating part of the expedition had one thing to recommend it. Penisauken was the port for the farmers in all parts of the section; so the Moorestown travellers had for fellow passengers in the boat men and women from other neighborhoods, and thus contact with the outside world was established to some extent, and the marketing party came home richer in social experience as well as in more material ways.

If the thoroughfare between here and Philadelphia were of a character to impose such difficulties, what must the roads connecting Moorestown with the other out-lying places have been like? We read that roads were open in this direction and in that, and that the region all about gradually filled up with settlers. They must have been a self-reliant and self-contained sort of people, inured to solitude, and content to invite their own souls; for it would have been difficult for any other souls to respond to an invitation given Family life ought to have been very sweet and satisfying in those days, for it had to suffice in very great measure for the needs of every member of the family.

The social instinct must have been subjected to a severe strain, and the visiting between distant friends was, we can readily believe, something like the proverbial visitations of angels, as to frequency of occurrence and shortness of intervals between them. Still visitations did occur from time to time. Solitary imprisonment is a thing not to be endured, either in the wilderness or the penitentiary, if there is any way of avoiding it; and in the wilderness even greater obstacles than the old roads offered would not have sufficed to keep people wholly apart. So neighbors did visit from time to time. And I doubt if any people ever did succeed yet in constructing a road bad enough to keep the young men wholly apart from the young maidens that attracted them, no matter how great the distance between them. Happily the roads here were not bad enough to accomplish such a result, and courtship and marriage went on almost as if the roads had been good.

The obstacles in the way of intercourse grew less with time, and in the progress of events wheeled vehicles could be used with more or less difficulty. But not yet had the time of the gently swinging phaeton and the luxurious family carriage arrived. Heavy wagons, frequently of the Conestoga pattern, were the village carts of the olden time here. Such as they were, however, they made sociability more attainable, as well as the transportation of market commodities more easy. There yet linger traditions of wagon journeys to and fro "for fun" which bore something of the character of the "straw rides" of to-day.

From the first the difficulties in the way of going about were not sufficient to keep the sturdy worshippers of old from gathering themselves together in the places appointed for the religious services they loved. The first settlers here were of the sort that gave first care and thought to the matter of regular and authorized worship. They believed most heartily in going to church or meeting; and they went, be the weather what it would or the condition of the roads bad as it might be. As the obstacles grew less, the lessening made the attendance at worship easier, but it may be doubted if it made it more general.

At first thought we would suppose that the postal service would have illustrated the high water mark of rapid transit, in the old times as in the new; but in its beginning it did not; people were not yet accustomed to having the news sent to them, and had not acquired the habit of being in a hurry for it. The element of speed seems not to have been considered in the inception of the enterprise. The scheme which finally resulted in the establishment of the post office was devised and patented about 1694 by Col. John Hamilton, son of Governor Andrew Hamilton. The patentee sold his right to the crown, but the enterprise does not seem to have been pushed forward very rapidly in the line of improvement. Some attempt was made at regularity, but the main idea was that the mail should go through sometime; how long it took was a minor consideration. But after a time speed came to be thought of, and in the course of events the boast was made that the mail achieved even better time than the flying machines; which is accounted for by the fact that it was carried on horseback. It was subject to the weather, however, then as now; and in May 1704 a New York paper complained that "the last storm has put our Pennsylvania post a week behind, and it has not yet com'd in." In 1754 under the superintendency of Benjamin Franklin, the service was so far improved that the mails left Philadelphia and New York three times a week. But notice was given that after Christmas they would leave only twice a week, "being frequently delayed in crossing New York Bay."

All this notable improvement was of value to the dwellers here, although only indirectly. No mail came here. Indeed in 1791 there were only six post-offices in New Jersey, and none of the six was in Burlington county. Moorestown had to wait until after the Nineteenth Century had begun for its postoffice. But as has been said it derived indirect benefit from the general progress that had been made. Philadelphia had postal communication with the world at large, and Moorestown had communication, more or less interrupted, with Philadelphia. The man who rode to market in Philadelphia came back home with a morsel of outside news to impart to his neighbors; and so the community came to feel on more intimate terms with the world. It seems a curious state of affairs to us who are taken aback if telegraphic communication is interrupted for even a day, and who would feel a sense of personal loss if anything were to happen to the Atlantic cable; but they were as happy under their conditions as we are under ours.

One of the results of the difficult communication was that doctors and patients saw far less of each other in the old times than now. A call for the doctor and the doctor's response to the call constituted an enterprise having time and difficulty for its chief elements; and only a case of exceptional importance was held to justify it. When the regular physician adjusted his saddle-bags and rode off through the woods it betokened something more serious on the part of the patient than an "attack of malaria," or "an inactive liver," or "a functional derangement of the diaphragm," or "a run-down condition of the general system." Every family had within itself sufficient medical knowledge and skill to cope with any of the every-day ailments that afflict humanity; and the neighborhood held more than one kindly old woman whose special knowledge of the healing virtues of "roots and 'arbs" constituted her a practicing physician in the homes of her neighbors. The medical profession had its firm footing, however, and the physician, in those days, as in these, was the friend as well as the protector of those among whom he lived. More than one honored name has its place in the early medical records of Moorestown and vicinity; and more than one of these names illustrates anew to-day the honor that its early possessor bestowed upon it.

Of course we look back with a sigh of wondering sympathy to the early experience of our ancestors. That is the proper thing to do; and not one of us would change places and times with them. But after all they may have got a kind of enjoyment out of life that we can know nothing of. It may not have been a *better* kind of enjoyment—it certainly was not—but it was a *different* kind. There was a bloom on the peach for them, as they rode their horses through the woodland paths, that the swift rush of life has brushed off for us.

Chapter VII.

Coaching Times.

"AND now, Sammy," said the elder Mr. Weller, "it's time I was up at the office to get my way bill and see the coach loaded; for coaches, Sammy, is like guns—they requires to be loaded with very great care, afore they goes off."

Mr. Weller liked his little joke on occasion, but even his jokes had the core of a serious philosophy in them; and the weight of his business was never wholly lifted from even his sportive thoughts. He was a thorough expert in coaching, with an expertness to make ashamed the millionaire revivalist of stage-coaching in our days; and when he had loaded his coach we may be very sure that it went off in a proper manner, in spite of the little accident on the canal bank the night before election, as described by his son Sam.

But the art Tony Weller possessed was expended on such stage-coaching as England knew in the good old times—the coaching that Irving and Dickens have delighted to celebrate, It was all very charming and picturesque, with its summer beauties and its winter cheer; with its robust heartiness and its inspiring speed; with the gay music of the guard's horn, the quaint humor of the driver's talk and the odd characters among the "insides" and the "outsides." But it is interesting to speculate how long the heartiness and the inspiration and the gayety would have lasted, and what relations would have been developed between guard and driver and passengers if the whole party of them had been set going in a Jersey coach, on a Jersey road a hundred years ago.

What must by courtesy be called a stage-line was established between Mount Holly and Philadelphia at a very early period; but it did not move to the gay tra-la-la music of a guard's key-bugle, and Dickens or Irving would have had hard work to adjust his enthusiastic paragraphs to its description. It afforded plenty of opportunity for picturesque writing, but its picturesqueness was of a totally different kind to that dwelt upon by the authors mentioned, and was made up of elements that they were not familiar with, or at all events chose not to say anything about.

The coach of that ancient stage-line was a Conestoga wagon; and when we take into account the fact that it had no springs, and the further fact that the roads in its day were not Telford pavements, we may conclude that a reasonable amount of discomfort could be got out of the ride to Philadelphia. Such measures as could be taken to lessen the discomfort were brought into use. Wooden bows spanned the top of the conveyance, and over these bows canvas was stretched, so that the passengers were shielded from the sun and the rain, and measurably from the wind also. Their view of the landscape was somewhat curtailed, but there is no pleasure without its compensating disadvantage, and they could not expect to have everything.

The stage-wagon ran at uncertain intervals, and the journey was of uncertain duration. Whether the modern livery practice of charging by the hour for the ride was adopted we are not informed, but probably not. At all events, such as it was, the line was run for the convenience of the public, and the people were enabled to make the trip in rather less time—occasionally, perhaps, with rather less comfort—than on foot. When there was mail to be carried the stage-wagon carried it; and from that day until the railroad came into operation there was always a stage line running from Mount Holly to Philadelphia, and it always carried the mail.

The Conestoga, we are told, held its position as the public conveyance until about the year 1826, when it was superseded by a modification of the Concord stage-coach. When that made its appearance the travelling public felt that the acme of luxury had been reached, and that frame of mind was enjoyed to the full until the railroad put new notions into the public head, and bred discontent.

In the meantime Moorestown enjoyed the **advantage** of the best that was to be had in the travelling way; for the road from Mount Holly to Camden runs through Moorestown, and the stages took up and set down such passengers as might so desire. In process of time these passengers became so numerous that the advantages of an independent stage line from Moorestown to Camden suggested themselves. Just when the idea began to take shape, and when it was practically carried into effect are points that nobody seems to have definite information about. Neither is it positively known to whom the honor belongs of starting the first stage-line from Moorestown. Whoever he was he had a goodly share of energy and enterprise, qualities that were by no means lacking in the community generally.

One of the earliest stage proprietors of whom we have mention here was Peter Venable, and it is probable that he ran his line of coaches about 1820. He was succeeded in the business by John Keen. How long either of them maintained the business is not known; but David McCoy, who succeeded John Keen as proprietor, is thought to have taken the business before 1825. Under his administration two coaches were run, and McCoy and Charles Wilcher were the drivers thereof. McCoy seems not to have held the proprietorship of the line for any very long time, but sold out in his turn to

John West, and became once more a driver in the service of the new proprietor.

The business of the line in the meantime continued to increase as Moorestown and the region around it gained more and more in population. The two stages of the line went and came loaded with passengers, for the people of the place kept up a brisk communication with Philadelphia. There were good inducements for them to do so, aside from the fact that Philadelphia is a desirable place to be in communication with. In the first place the fare was cheap—only thirty-seven cents; and in the second place the stages were "accommodation wagons" in the literal sense, and went out into the country round about, within reasonable limits, to take up outgoing passengers and leave incoming passengers at their homes. The vehicles used, too, were now comfortable spring wagons, with curtained covers.

The condition of affairs was such as to invite competition, and competition came, as it is very sure to do in any promising line of business. About the year 1831 William Doughten, a resident business man here, established an opposition line of stages, and from that time for a term of years Moorestown enjoyed the experiences of a lively business contest in that particular industry. The old line had its headquarters at the William Penn Hotel; the new line established itself at the Washington Hotel, and so the people of both sections of the town were given the right to feel a proprietary interest in the two enterprises.

The proprietor of the opposition stages offered his patrons the inducement of improved vehicles to ride in. His coaches are said to have been handsomer and more comfortable than those previously in use. What additional advantages were offered by the old line we are not informed, but we may be sure that the new line was not permitted to have things all its own way. The great advantage, however, was offered by both lines to the general travelling public; and it came in such shape as is now offered to competing railroads that take position outside the pool—"cut rates." It is not recorded that the cutting in fares reached such an extreme as they once did on the Hudson River, when one line of steamers advertised to take passengers from Albany to New York and back for nothing, and the rival line promptly offered to pay every passenger a silver quarter for taking the trip on its boat; but still the reduction in rates was appreciable and appreciated.

Which party began it we are not informed, or how deep the first cut extended; but the fares were finally reduced by both parties from thirty-seven cents to twenty-five cents for the trip. Moreover, the extent of territory outside the village to which the accommodation was offered grew wider and wider. In the days before the opposition the stage was accustomed to go a mile or so outside the town to accommodate a passenger; but under the new order of things the opposing lines beat up the country within a circuit of five miles, and passengers as far away as Borton's Landing took a breezy stage-ride to Philadelphia for the sum of twenty-five cents.

In the meantime two lines of stages were running from Mount Holly, the through fare from that place being fifty cents. Truly those were lively times for Moorestown, and we can fancy the brisk state of affairs on Main street at "stage time," and the excitement at the opposition hotels when the local stages were arriving and departing, and the Mount Holly stages made their stops in going and coming. Their stops, by the way, were a mere matter of form except for the changing of the mail bag, for there were no Moorestown passengers for them at that time. Home patronage of home institutions was the motto then, we can believe.

The earnest competition of the two lines was shared to the full by the local population, and the community ranged itself, on strictly party lines, in two bodies, according as sympathy lay with one proprietor or the other. Party feeling ran high at times, and an unpleasant state of affairs existed in the neighborhood. The contention took a range outside of strict business limits and became in a manner a public issue. It became more and more desirable that the business difference should be adjusted and the resulting irritation allayed. Whatever efforts at compromise were made were ineffectual, and it became evident that the only practicable way was the consolidation of the two lines.

About the year 1831 William Doughten's son, George F. Doughten, had come to Moorestown to establish a mercantile enterprise. He formed a partnership with John Courtland Haines, and they began keeping a store in the old frame building that occupied the site where George F. Doughten's store now stands, at the corner of Main street and Chester avenue. It was through the action of these two partners that the competition in the stage business, and the unpleasantness resulting from it were ended together. This desirable end was was accomplished in the most direct manner possible, by the purchase of the two opposing interests, and the consolidation of them into one enterprise.

It was about the year 1835 that Haines & Doughten bought and consolidated the two lines, and the competition had existed then, with varying degrees of acrimony, for about four years. The term of the new ownership was of a duration not to be compared with that, and was probably the shortest period of proprietorship in the history of stage-coaching here. In fact the new owners did not harness a team, start a coach or crack a whip while they held control of the consolidated lines. They made their purchase on Saturday evening, after the week's travel had ended, and sold out early the following Monday morning, before the week's travel had begun. The last trip of one week was made under the old conditions of sharp competition, and the first trip of the next week was made under a single ownership without rivalry; and the business had changed hands twice in the interval.

David McCoy, the man who had succeeded John Keen as proprietor of the single line, who had sold out to John West, and subsequently acted as his driver, purchased the consolidated line from Haines & Doughten, and again became proprietor of a single line, composed of the two strands that had wrought such a tangle in the intervening years. He established the headquarters of his coaches, not at the William Penn or Washington Hotels but at Cox's Tavern, the building now occupied as a double dwelling house just above the residence of Mr. George F. Doughten, on the Main street. He built a barn on the premises, which is still standing there, and had a shed put up which would hold six stage wagons. The shed occupied the ground on which Mr. Doughten's residence now stands. In 1842, after occupying the tavern for several years as a renter, McCoy purchased the Cox property. Previously he had endeavored to buy the lot on which the wagon sheds stood, with a view to building there, but Mr. Doughten had already negotiated for the purchase of that as a residence lot, and McCoy concluded to stay where he was.

After exercising the rights of ownership for a number of years David McCoy sold the stage line to Abel Small. McCoy's proprietorship had been without competition; but the administration of Abel Small was marked by a revival of opposition, accompanied by some degree of the old neighborhood feeling. Elihu Sheppard Low—or "Shep" Low, as he was generally called—established an opposition line, and for a time Moorestown experienced a revival of the old lively scenes. This state of affairs seems not to have lasted very long, however, and the conflict was settled by the purchase of Small's interest, and the consolidation of the two enterprises under the partnership of Low & Westcott. After a time the firm was changed by the sale of Westcott's interests to Nathan H. Stokes, by which substitution the firm name became Low & Stokes.

Stokes was at that time proprietor of the Washington hotel, which was the headquarters for the coaches. Low represented his own interest on the coach box by driving for himself; but Stokes had to employ a substitute in that capacity, as his time was fully occupied by his hotel interests. On Dec. 1, 1850, E. B. Brown came to Moorestown to drive stage for Stokes. Two stages ran each way every day; one down in the morning and up in the afternoon, and the other down in the afternoon and up in the morning; and Low drove on one of these round trips and Brown on the other, occasionally "changing off" with each other as mutual accommodation made it desirable.

After an experience of four years as driver, E. B. Brown bought the interest of Nathan Stokes in the line, and the style of the line became Low & Brown. Under the new administration Moorestown invaded Mount Holly and absorbed its stage coach interests. Low & Brown maintained two lines of coaches, one running from Mount Holly to Camden and back, and the other running from Moorestown to Camden and back. The Mount Holly coach carried the mail and as it passed through Moorestown on every trip this place enjoyed the full advantage of both lines. Low drove the Mount Holly coach and Brown the Moorestown vehicle.

The coach headquarters in Mount Holly was the Arcade Hotel, and after a time Low purchased the hotel and employed a driver to represent him in the stage coach business. He retained his partnership interest for some years after his purchase of the Arcade, but finally the firm of Low & Brown was dissolved and the Mount Holly and Moorestown stage lines became distinct, Low retaining the proprietorship of the Mount Holly business, and Brown becoming sole owner of the Moorestown line. The old firm had held the contract for carrying the mail; and when the new contract was let after the dissolution of the partnership, it was found that Brown's bid was the bid which had won, and to him was given the job of carrying the mail between Mount Holly and Philadelphia. The mail bag went back and forth on his former partner's coach, the only difference being that Low got his pay for carrying it from Brown instead of the Government.

In the summer of 1860, Mr. Brown decided to dispose of his stage coach interests and go into other business. So he sold the stage line to Chalkley Justice, and went into mercantile business where the store of E. B. Brown and Brother now is. Justice, after his purchase from Brown, entered into partnership with Low, and once more the Mount Holly and Moorestown stage lines came under one management. The new partnership was not of long continuance. Some time the next year Low and Justice sold the two lines to John Coles; and he, after a rather short term of ownership, sold them to William A. Nestor, of Philadelphia. Nestor kept the business but a few months, and then in 1863, sold out to C. C. Coles and Benjamin Coles, brothers of John Coles, former proprietor. The style of the firm was C. C. Coles and Brother. They ran the two lines for four years and during those years did a splendid business. Population had increased, the road had been improved, and travel to and from the city was exceedingly brisk.

But on October 20, 1867 their enterprise came to a sudden stop, and the stage-coach business between here and Philadelphia received its death blow. The railroad had been completed, trains had begun to run, travellers went by rail instead of by coach, and the Coles Brothers found themselves in possession of several coaches and a number of good horses that they had no earthly use for. The horses were disposed of from time to time as opportunity offered, and the coaches were sold at public sale, at more or less of a sacrifice. The brothers had become proprietors of the William Penn Hotel, and devoted themselves to the business of hotel keeping. Their mail contract continued in force till the following spring, and with its expiration the last link that connected them with their former business disappeared, and the old coaching days became a tradition, so far as Moorestown is concerned.

One can sympathize with the sigh of regret with which the former proprietors speak of those old stage-coach times. Even the enthusiastic admirer of English coaching might have had some inspiration from the later years of stage coach experience here. This was a splendid line—probably the best in New Jersey; and after the turnpike was made the road between here and Philadelphia was a fine one. The horses were of good stock and the coaches were comfortable and easy vehicles. Travel was very active, and it is said that during the height of the competition a good many people went to Philadelphia who had no other reason for going than to patronize the line they favored and show on which side their sympathies lay.

Saturday nights and Monday mornings were the times of especially heavy travel. At that time Mrs. Mary Lippincott's boarding school was in the full tide of its prosperity, and pupils living in Philadelphia, or between here and there, crowded the Saturday night stages going home and the Monday morning stages coming back. Moreover, Moorestown was a favorite place for rural sojourning, and city people came out here in numbers on Saturday nights and returned Monday mornings; and so the tide of travel swept heavily in both directions at these times. Six horses to the coach was the rule for those trips, and we are told by some of the proprietors of single coach loads composed of fifty-three passengers. It would seem that the art of high pressure packing did not originate with the street cars! But even this does not fully indicate the extent of travel over this line, for the regular coach had to be supplemented on extra occasions by another, and it was no extraordinary thing for the Saturday night trip to be made by four or five coaches and a hack beside.

In the competition days there was hot haste in making the trips, we may be sure; the drivers entering into the spirit of the contest as ardently as the proprietors. The drivers of each line made every effort to make better time than their rivals; and if one of them could achieve the feat of overtaking and passing an oppsition coach on the road it was a thing to remember and boast of in after years. But the highest glory for a driver lay in securing for his own coach a passenger that the other line regarded as already secured for itself. It is related of one driver that he not only overtook the opposition coach on the road; but that recognizing a lady acquaintance in the other vehicle, he invited her to finish her ride with him, and actually transferred her to his own conveyance and drove off with her, while his discomfitted rival exhausted the English language in expressing his emotions. Verily, fine stirring times were those old Coaching Days.

Chapter VIII.

Coming of the Railroad.

HUMAN life adjusts itself pretty readily to circumstances, and in that way becomes measurably independent of them. It is an easy thing to do when the adjustment is in a forward direction, and the change is from bad circumstances to good, or from good to better; but it is more difficult in going backward. Horseback riding and skiff navigation were all well enough so long as there were no more expeditious ways of accomplishing the desired journey; but when the old stage-wagon and the stage-boat came to the fore the people were ready for them and the new methods readily became the accustomed methods. These in their turn were all right until the Concord stage and the more commodious passenger boat made their appearance; then these quickly took their place in the established system of things and were most satisfactory institutions. The stage in turn gave place to the railroad car, and people adjusted themselves with wonderful facility to the new mode of progress.

But how would it be about going back from the railroad car to the stage-wagon, or even the newer Concord? It could and would be done, of course, if the necessity arose; but it would not be done with the same readiness as in the other cases, for it is harder to walk backward than forward. A railroad is a very hard thing to do without when you have once got used to it; and we have become thoroughly accustomed to it. Our system of life is adjusted on that basis, and it would be hard indeed to re-arrange our way of living so as to have no reference to the iron rails.

Stage-coaching ended abruptly when railroading began. They did not overlap; and they did not go on in parallel lines. The stage-coach was exchanged for a railroad-car, and that was the end of it. The time was not so very long ago that the exchange was made, but even now the event seems to belong to a remote historical epoch, and the old stage-coach is nothing to us but a picturesque tradition. Some of the men who owned and drove the old coaches are still among us, in the prime of life; but when they tell of their coaching experiences they seem to refer to a very far away time, instead of to a time that ended less than twenty years ago.

It was not by wishing for it that Moorestown got the railroad, nor yet by striving for it. The attitude of the community toward the projected enterprise was rather that of expectant waiting than that of active effort for or against. How it might have been if this had been a terminal point of the proposed line cannot be said. Then there might have been active hostility and ardent advocacy and a sharp drawing of lines on one side and the other. But Moorestown would be an intermediate point if the road were built, and therefore had less at stake upon the decision for or against than it otherwise would have had, and so waited on the issue of the contest waged by others, herself taking no very active part one way or the other.

The community waited with a divided mind, however. The prevailing sentiment was in favor of the proposed railroad, and the majority of residents welcomed the prospect with gladness. The new mode of transit would be an added convenience, they argued; it would bring Philadelphia on the one hand and Mount Holly on the other nearer to Moorestown, and the result could not be otherwise than good. New people would come here, the town would be built up and its prosperity advanced, while life would have new pleasures and opportunities added to it. That was the feeling of the majority; but there seems to have been a strong minority entertaining a very different feeling. With this class the very arguments advanced in favor of the railroad were arguments against it.

Philadelphia would be brought closer to Moorestown, but to Moorestown's disadvantage, they thought. The business of the local storekeepers would be injured by the easier access to the city.

New people might come, but there was the fear that the good and desirable new-comers might be outnumbered by a class not at all desirable. Property might be advanced in value, but taxes would be correspondingly increased. And after all, said some of these objectors, things were very well as they were. There was no need of a railroad. The drive to Philadelphia was a very pleasant one, and people could go there very comfortably whenever they needed to go Many of the residents owned their carriages, and for those who did not the stages were always available.

These were the grounds the two opposing parties occupied on the railroad issue. The difference of sentiment did not advance to the point of controversy, and if there was no very ardent and enthusiastic support given to the enterprise here, on the other hand there was no active and organized hostility to it. In the end those who had favored the building of the road were made glad, and those who had not favored it made the best of what had to be, for the railroad came and staid.

It was by a somewhat complicated series of links that this place became finally bound to the railroad system of the State. If Mount Holly had desired such a connection less strongly and pertinaciously than she did, Moorestown might have been without it for an unknown period. In 1836 a company was incorporated under the title of the Mount Holly and Camden Railroad Company. The charter was granted for a railroad to extend from Mount Holly to Camden. A large amount of stock was subscribed for the enterprise, but not enough to insure its success. It is said that the Camden and Amboy Company discouraged the project and brought their forces to bear against it. At all events the road was not completed within the specified time and the charter became void. So Moorestown did not become a railroad town then.

Another charter was granted in February, 1848, which specified that the proposed railroad was to run from Mount Holly to Camden, passing through or near the village of Moorestown. The bed of the road was to be not more than sixty-six feet wide, with as many sets of rails as might be necessary, and the road was to be completed within five years from the next ensuing Fourth of July. But the specified time passed, and Moorestown did not celebrate its Fourth of July with the aid of a railroad train; neither were there any rails for the train to run upon.

In 1848, which seems to have been a very good year for paper railroads, the Burlington and Mount Holly Railroad and Transportation Company was incorporated by act of the Legislature. The enterprise, it is stated, was fostered by the Camden and Amboy Company, to enable the people of Mount Holly and vicinity to go to Philadelphia by way of its railroad. The road was to run from Mount Holly to Burlington, and was to be completed and in use within five years from the next Fourth of July. The road was promptly built and put into service. In 1857, by a supplementary act, the name of this company was changed to the Burlington County Railroad Company, and the company was authorized to build an extension of its road from Mount Holly to Pemberton in this county, and to New Egypt, in Ocean county.

The Mount Holly people were not yet satisfied with their railroad facilities; and notwithstanding the failure of their previous experiments they besieged the Legislature industriously for another charter, and finally, notwithstanding the opposition of other railroad interests, they got what they were after. In March, 1859, the Camden, Moorestown, Hainesport and Mount Holly Horse-Car Railroad Company had been incorporated. The road was to run from Camden to Mount Holly, passing through the villages of Moorestown and Hainesport, and was to be completed within five years from the same patriotic date specified for the other roads. The idea of a horse-railroad, derived from the successful experiments in that line in England and in some parts of this country, seems to have been entertained in good faith, and the line was located with a view to horse-power rather than steam-power.

The horse railroad was not put through; but the

promoters of the railroad project succeeded in using the old charter indirectly. On the 6th of February, 1866, the Legislature passed an act consolidating the Burlington County and the Camden, Moorestown, Hainesport and Mount Holly Horse-Car Railroad Companies, under the name of the Camden and Burlington County Railroad Company. This change of name was of the utmost benefit to railroad literature; for few things can be imagined more appalling than having to write or to read the string of initials that would have been necessary had the old name been retained. People would have been justifiably afraid to ride on a train run by the C., M., H. & Mt. H. H. C. R. R. Co.

The capital stock of the consolidated company was $300,000, with the privilege of increasing the stock to $500,000, divided into shares of $25 each. The consolidated company was authorized to connect with the Camden and Amboy Railroad before reaching Camden, and to run their cars and trains upon the same on such terms as might be agreed upon by the two companies. The road was required to pay to the State a tax of one half of one per cent. on the cost of the road annually.

Full right and authority was given in the charter to use steam on the road; and when work began it was not work such as would be required for a horse car railroad, but for a regularly equipped steam road, and the horse-car fiction dropped finally out of sight. Work was pushed forward and the opposition which had existed ceased. It was changed to active support, and the opposing force turned its efforts towards securing a controlling interest in the new road. In October, 1867 trains, began running between Mount Holly and Camden, and Moorestown became at once a railroad town, connected with Philadelphia on the one hand; and, by a very convenient railroad system, with numerous desirable points on the other.

In 1861 the Vincentown branch of the Burlington County Railroad was incorporated, and afterward consolidated with the latter road. In 1864 the Pemberton and Hightstown Railroad was incorporated, to run from Pemberton, in this county, to Hightstown in Mercer county; connecting at Pemberton with the Burlington Country road, and at Hightstown with the Camden and Amboy road; and passing the villages of Wrightstown, Cookstown, New Egypt, Harmertown, Filmore and Imlaystown. The Mount Holly, Lumberton and Medford road was chartered in 1866. It runs from Mount Holly to Medford, passing through Lumberton. In 1866 the Columbus, Kinkora and Springfield Railroad Company was also incorporated, the road to be laid on the old bed of the Delaware and Atlantic Railroad Company. The Long Branch and Seashore Railroad Company was incorporated in 1863, the road to run from " a point on

Sandy Hook in the county of Monmouth, at or near the Horseshoe, running through Long Branch; thence through or near Squan village to a point on Tom's River, at or near Tom's River village in the county of Ocean; thence to Tuckerton in the county of Burlington." In 1870 this company and the New Jersey Southern Railroad Company were authorized to consolidate, the roads to be united at or near Long Branch. This road ran to Pemberton, and in 1878 the mortgage on it was foreclosed, and Isaac S. Buckalew was appointed receiver. He sold it May, 1879, and afterwards it was reorganized as the Pemberton and Seashore Railroad. With all these, and more, railroad connections it would seem that Moorestown has a very fair opportunity to do business errands or go pleasuring by rail.

At present these roads all form parts of a compact system under the control of the Pennsylvania Railroad Company. First the Pemberton and Hightstown road; the Columbus, Kinkora and Springfield road; the Camden and Burlington County; and the Mount Holly, Lumberton and Medford roads, and the Vincentown branch were leased to the United New Jersey Railroad and Canal Company; and then the United New Jersey Railroad and Canal Company was leased by the Pennsylvania Railroad Company, at an annual rental of ten per cent. upon the capital stock and interest on its bonds free of all taxes. All the roads mentioned above are operated by the Pennsylvania Railroad Company as lessees of the United New Jersey Railroad and Canal Company.

This lease was effected June 30, 1871, and on March 27, 1873, an act was approved by which the lease and contract "between the Delaware and Raritan Canal Company, the Camden and Amboy Railroad and Transportation Company now merged into and known as 'The United New Jersey Railroad and Canal Company,' which companies, together with the Philadelphia and Trenton Railroad Company, are the lessors; and the Pennsylvania Railroad Company, which is the lessee, be and the same is validated, ratified and confirmed," &c.

The first passenger train from Camden to Mount Holly passed through Moorestown on the opening day of the Mount Holly Fair, in October, 1867. It stopped here, and the people of Moorestown enjoyed their first opportunity of going to the Fair by rail. That was a special train, however, and not the first of the regular running. It was but a short time afterwards that the road was fully opened to business, and trains were set going on regular schedule in both directions. There was no formal demonstration at the opening of the road. Several friends of the directors took a ride to Mount Holly as invited guests, had supper there and came back home, and that was all.

At the beginning of its railroad experience

Moorestown had but one station, and that was the one at present called East Moorestown. It was not so designated then, but was simply the Moorestown station. The location of the stopping place was the subject of a good deal of discussion, and the occasion of some feeling between the two sections of the town. When the present site of the station was suggested, the people in the western portion of the town entered a protest against the location as one that would render the railroad almost impracticable for them, being so far away from their homes. With such a journey to accomplish they would never be able to catch a train, and as they were unaccustomed to the work of catching trains, it would be hard enough under any circumstances. Residents in the eastern part of the town argued that it was just as far from East to West as it was from West to East, and therefore they did not favor a station in West Moorestown. A location at the foot of Mill street was urged as one that would accommodate the people of both sections. This was opposed on the ground that it would not accommodate either, but would be inconvenient for both.

Those who favored East Moorestown were convinced that in the course of time another station would be built in the western part of the town and that in the end the people of both sections would be better served by having the first station put near one end of the town, even if the other end did have to wait a little while for the fulfillment of its desires. Their efforts were successful, and the first station, as has been said, was established at East Moorestown. Some public spirited property owners gave the ground on which the station stands, and when the trains began running that was their stopping place. For a time a platform was the waiting room and a switch-house the ticket office; but that was only for so long as it took to build the station. The station was built and ready for occupancy when the winter of 1867 began. It is a neat and comfortable frame building with a waiting room at each end, one for ladies and the other for gentlemen, the ticket office being between. Some time after its erection it, like all other stations on the road was lowered, together with its platform, to conform to the newly adopted style of steps on the cars. The first ticket agent at East Moorestown was Allen Haines, son of Barclay Haines, one of the directors of the road. He was succeeded by Robert Stimus, who remained in charge there until his transfer to West Moorestown. His successor was William Carney, whose term of service extended through several years and ended with his transfer to Camden. After Mr. Carney came Mr. Lamb, then Mr. Evans, then Mr. Wright, and last Mr. Lippincott, the present agent.

The people in the Western end of the town did

not forbear to agitate the subject of a station that would be more convenient for them, and eventually they succeeded in their efforts. The present station on Church Road was erected in the latter part of 1870, and was opened for business January 1st, 1871. On that date Mr. Stimus was transferred from East Moorestown to be the West Moorestown agent, a position he has filled uninterruptedly ever since. This station was the freight and express station for the town from its first establishment, and was provided with a freight house and platform, and with the necessary switches and sidings. It was after the erection of this station that the distinction was introduced of East Moorestown and West Moorestown.

Over a dozen trains going East and as many going West stop at each of these stations every day and Moorestown very reasonably prides herself on being a well served railroad town. Even those who regarded its advent with more or less of foreboding have long since been brought to rejoice in the coming of the railroad.

Chapter IX.

New Elements.

IN this country all the elements of population are comparatively new elements. England goes back to the time of William the Conqueror for the standard of family antiquity; in China the Emperor is brother to the sun, and all the nobility have claims to some sort of celestial relationship which imply a considerable degree of remoteness in the time of the starting; India dates back very successfully, and in Ireland it is well understood that Adam came to that country for his second wife. But here we are all new comers.

The first white residents in Moorestown constituted an entirely new element; and there is small reason to doubt that the original—or aboriginal—first families regarded them somewhat in the light of intruders, and were to some extent inclined to receive them in war-paint and feathers. The red aristocrats, however, making a virtue of necessity and accepting the inevitable, as we all must do, decided to forego their exclusive preferences, and at least make the best of their interloping neighbors, since they could not get rid of them. It was the wisest thing they could do. The right to come and go is inalienable, and no community can forbid its exercise. New elements will appear, and the thing to do is to attract the best, and then accept the fact that the resulting compound cannot be quite the same as the old one. In the long run it will generally be found that the difference has its advantages. The intrusion brings its own compensation, if only in the way of varied interests and added life; for even in a small stream a moderate current is far better than the quietest stagnation. So the Indians did well to accept the situation.

For a time after the white settlers began to make their homes here there was a continual mingling of elements going on. The community grew by accretion, and the additions were as diverse as they were active. Those who were already here were glad to welcome the next new-comer because his coming added to the resources of the growing place; and the new-comer was glad to find the others here before him, because they gave him the more to do. It was a time of growth; the place assimilated all the new food it could get, and was continually hungry for more.

This went on for years; then at length there was a pause in that phase of the community's growth. The diversity in the character of the additions became less. The place continued to grow, but more by the increase of elements already introduced, and less by the introduction of new elements. It had shaped itself into a more or less homogeneous body and its growth was the growth of proportions already established. It was very far from settling into inactivity; its activity became more and more vigorous. Enterprises which, considering the resources at command and the difficulties to be overcome, were remarkable in their inception and results were undertaken and successfully carried through. But the activity was on lines already laid down in harmony with the tendencies of an established community, not so much in experimental directions as in the earlier period.

Later still another stage was reached in the process of development. As a man of energetic nature but of moderate and disciplined desires, after acquiring by hard toil and vigorous struggle, a sufficient fortune to maintain him in reasonable comfort, will sometimes relinquish the effort for more and settle down to the peaceful enjoyment of what he has; so now and then a community, looking at the position it has conquered for itself and seeing that it is very good, rests for a time in the pleasant enjoyment of what it has earned. It is a rare enough thing for either a man or a community to do, and in this time of feverish and never-satisfied hurry we could wish the example were more frequently set; for it is a good example if not carried too far—if the man does not rust and the community does not stagnate.

Some such point of quiet, restful content Moorestown reached in the process of time. It had achieved, now it would enjoy. It had quiet tastes, and its pleasures it took quietly. But though quiet it was as far as possible from lethargic. From the first a goodly degree of culture and refinement had characterized the place, and these became more and more characteristic of it. A circle large enough at least to give tone to the little community took pride and pleasure in keeping up with the best that was achieved in literature and science. Public spirit found its mission in ministering to this predilection, and men of wealth, scholarship and energy organized to promote the best enjoyment of the community in the most thorough manner. Educational and literary facilities were systematically increased, and season after season courses of lectures on literary, scientific and historical subjects, by the best lecturers obtainable, were furnished the public. And the public responded most cordially. People came from every part of the town and from the surrounding country to listen to the speakers who came, and every lecture night the hall was crowded.

In the meantime the population of the town was increasing, but by the addition of people quite in harmony with the general community. Prosperous farmers who felt that they had earned rest for the remainder of their years, sold their farms or made them over to their children, bought houses in the village and with their wives and some portion of their family circles, entered into the quiet pleasures of life as they were to be found here. The people were acquainted, every man with his neighbor, and social life of a serene and undemonstrative, but not the less pleasant sort prevailed

But Moorestown was young yet, in spite of its generous measure of years, and had the vigor of a wholesome prime within it. In youth and middle age the greatest of pleasures is the pleasure of new achievement. A resting spell is highly enjoyable, but it adds a new zest to the work that comes after it. The community as a whole was ready to welcome new elements and such changes as a wholesome admixture of them might produce.

The new elements came, and the ferment of new influences began to be felt in the life of the place. The people came, not from the neighboring farms this time, but from the busy streets of the city. Before the advent of the railroad the advantages of Moorestown as a good place for city people who wished a home in a rural quarter had begun to be recognized, and now and then a city family had taken up its abode here. But these had not been numerous. Visitors had come from time to time, taking pleasant recollections away with them; occasional leisurely sojourners spent a summer here, and enjoyed their quiet experiences; pupils at the boarding school, and friends who had visited them, remembered what a goodly place Moorestown was. But all these impressions and recollections referred to a place apart; a place that was good to visit but would be inconvenient to live in. So people from the city were slow in coming to make their homes here.

The railroad came, making the pleasant old rural town practically a suburb of Philadelphia. Then the gathered recollections of the people who had been here began to suggest practical possibilities. The railroad had made available what before had been out of reach. Here was a beautiful old village set amid delightful country surroundings; its location was most encouragingly healthy; it was the home of an orderly and well-settled community, with solidly established social life and institutions; there was nothing new and raw about the place; here pure country air could be enjoyed, and the wholesome quiet of village life realized; the expenses of living would be lessened and the advantages of living—some of them at least—would be increased; and the railroad placed this desirable opportunity for a change of home within reach of the city clerk and the city business man by enabling him to pass quickly and conveniently between his country home and his city working place, and so enjoy the pleasures of country living and the profits of city working. Is it any wonder that Philadelphia families began to invade Moorestown in increasing numbers?

The desire of the man who lives in the city to get into the country is only equalled by the desire of the man who lives in the country to get into the city. Here was a good place for both classes to compromise on; a place where they could have the advantages of the country and still be within easy reach of the city when they should want the city. So those who were already here staid, and those who were not already here came—a good many of them at all events. Men from the city bought houses and established their families here; other men from the city bought lots here and built houses to suit themselves; while still others, who could not afford to build, or who wished to try the experiment of a temporary residence first, became tenants and rented such houses as were for rent. And so the population grew and the old town enlarged its borders.

These new-comers brought with them their own ideas and predilections, and a new force was introduced into the life of Moorestown. A big stone had been thrown into the placid pool and the surface thereof was broken into restless ripples. The spirit of change had begun its ceaseless work, not violently but none the less effectually. New impulses rubbed against old methods and the result was agitation in a greater or less degree. The movements of life became modified in one way and another by the action and reaction of the new elements and the old, and changes gradually came to pass. The old social life maintained itself, but another type was established beside it. Facilities for education had to be increased to answer the purposes of so many additional children brought from the city by the new residents. Business, which had dreaded the influence of the railroad to some extent as a depressing force, was increased by the demands of the added population. The churches felt the force of the change and had a larger and different membership. In every direction a difference was felt.

The community as a whole welcomed the difference and accepted the changed conditions. But for a time there were exceptions. Not all the old residents could see and feel that this state of affairs was any improvement over the old. Some of these new-comers, they said, were very outspoken about demanding improvements and very reticent about paying for them. Others insisted on changes which were not to the taste of the old community. Others were here merely for their own temporary advantage, with no corresponding advantage to the place. Burdens were being put upon the whole community for the sake of benefitting the new-comers solely. Altogether the change was not unqualifiedly for the better, they thought.

But this state of mind—at no time the general state of mind—gave place to other convictions in the course of time. The changed condition of affairs was accepted, and now everybody's clock is set according to the new standard of time. Moorestown is what it is and not what it was; that fact is acquiesced in by all. The two populations, the old and the new, have become one population, and a well ordered progress in the line of desirable improvements is the common purpose of all. Business and social life have been adjusted to the new order of things. Enterprises have been projected and carried forward, with the aim of making a residence here still more attractive and advantageous to new-comers; and the general tone of feeling in the community is that every addition to the right kind of new elements here is a thing to be greatly desired.

Chapter X.

Streets and Roads.

THE Main street of Moorestown extends from Mount Holly to Camden, and thus affords ample scope for the growth of the town, in either direction. The old Burlington and Salem road—"The King's Highway"—laid out in 1682, occupied in its course through Moorestown nearly the same ground that the Main street now covers. In 1794 the present turnpike from Mount Holly to Camden was laid out; and from the toll gate on the East to the same distance below Moorestown on the West it extends over much the same course as the old highway, and comprises the Main street as one of its parts.

As the region filled up with settlers other roads were constructed from time to time, connecting the newly settled portions with the established centers of population; and with the river on the one hand and the ocean on the other, these roads have a double usefulness to-day, when the regions they connect are no longer new. They form the channels though which flows a rich and never-ceasing tide of traffic, and they offer a series of the most delightful rural drives to those who seek the opportunity to enjoy one of the prime pleasures of life.

As its name implies, Main street is the principal thoroughfare of the place. It is a section of the turnpike road, and is broad and well kept. It practically forms the Southern border of the town, and as a street may be said to extend from Mr. Arthur Miller's residence on the East to the "Forks of the Road"—where the Mount Holly turnpike and the Haddonfield road separate—on the West, over-looking the southern valley through all its length. On this street are located all the churches save one; both the Friends' meeting houses; nearly all the stores and shops; both the hotels; the Academy, the Bank, the Postoffice, the Town Hall and the various lodge and society rooms.

But it is not merely—or chiefly—a business street; it is also one of the principal residence streets of the town, and, ranged on either side of it throughout its extent, are many beautiful homes. In no part of its course is the street entirely given over to traffic; and business houses are neighbored by private residences with their well-shaded door-yards, and in some cases their long stretches of lawn and shrubbery. Along the South side particularly, there is an almost continuous line of residences through the distinctly business portion of the street; and each of them is set well back from the highway and fronted by green lawn, shaded by noble trees and made more attractive by flowers and ornamental shrubbery; while in some instances the houses are old mansions with historic associations gathering about them. Below Church Road and above Chester avenue the street is almost entirely given up to homes.

As has been said, many of the dwelling houses on this street are old homesteads and venerable structures, as that term goes in this country; and these afford fine examples of the plain and solid merits of old-time architecture. Many more are modern buildings; and some of these are handsome specimens of the more elaborate and ornamental styles of building that now prevail. The two types combine well to make Moorestown the very beautiful and interesting place it is.

Many a rural town has pretty streets. Indeed a village street with anything like a fair opportunity is very sure to make itself pretty and picturesque. But one must journey long and far to see a village thoroughfare more beautiful than our Main street, with its long lines of noble old shade trees, its ranks of handsome and comfortable looking residences and its charming glimpses of the lovely southern valley and the heights beyond. Even in winter its picturesque beauty does not depart from it, and in spring, summer and autumn it is lovely indeed. Perhaps the same degree of exciting activity does not characterize it now as in the old stage-coach days, when the Mount Holly and Moorestown coaches rattled along its length, and the throngs of incoming and outgoing passengers hurried to and from the stage offices; but there are animation and variety now—as much as comports with the pleasantness of a rural home-town, and enough to suggest the prosperous activity of the resident and surrounding community.

It is the highway of the farmers and "truckers" between their homes and the city markets; and in the recurring seasons processions of farm-wagons or "shelvings" pass along the street, drawn by teams of the fine horses that the people here pride themselves upon, and loaded high with hay or straw, or with baskets of glowing fruit and other farm products. Phaetons, buggies, family carriages, and not unfrequently the more conspicuous village cart, and the more elegant private turn-out add liveliness to the movement. People in the city have learned that Moorestown is a very pleasant place, and that the road leading to it offers a goodly drive; and in addition to those who make prolonged summer sojourns here, pleasurers drive out on occasions. The bicycler has discovered Moorestown also, and besides our own numerous wheelmen, many picturesquely costumed riders from Philadelphia make tours to this place and beyond. So there is no lack of variety to meet the demands of any reasonably moderate taste.

On the north of Main street, and also running lengthwise of the town, Second street extends from Chester avenue on the East to join the turnpike on the West, after it has turned off in a northwesterly direction at the Forks. The two streets are not strictly parallel, being considerably closer together at the western portion of their course than at Chester avenue. On this street are the Friends' High School building, the Public School building, the Friends' Greenlawn Cemetery, the churchyards of the Baptist and Episcopal churches, and two or three business places; but for the most part the thoroughfare is devoted to residences. A large proportion of these are small in size and modest in appearance; although among them are some of larger proportions and more elaborate modern construction. Nearly all give the idea of a quiet, cosy comfort; and almost without exception they are set a little back from the street, and are surrounded by moderately proportioned grounds, set with fruit trees, shrubbery and flowers, while at the porch of nearly every house are climbing vines of one sort or another.

Second street was laid out about forty years ago— at least that portion of it extending from Chester avenue to Church Road. It was not until several years later that the street was opened through the remainder of its present course. It seems a curious thing to us present dwellers here, but way had to be made for the new thoroughfare through the woods by chopping down trees and grubbing up stumps. Where the pretty homes of Second street now stand a thick forest then existed, which stretched far away to the northward. Men who are not now past middle-age tell stories of getting lost in the woods when they were school boys, and wandering for hours unable to find their way out. Of course it is an easy thing for a school boy— still more easy for two school boys together—to get lost in the woods on a pleasant autumn day, when they utilize the noon intermission for a little scout after nuts. But for those same school boys to go wandering about the woods for a considerable space after supper time, and then emerge on an obscure road half a mile to the north, with a necessary walk of a couple of miles still between them and supper, argues a degree of earnestness about the getting lost that is not quite consistent with "hookey"; so we may accept the fact that the woods were dense and wide.

North of Second street, and parallel to it, is Third street extending from East Moorestown station to a considerable distance below the station at West Moorestown. Along a portion of this street is the railroad, but the railroad was an after-thought, and the street was a village thoroughfare many years before the iron horse adopted it as a race course. Third street was laid out about the same time as

Second street, and encountered just about the same difficulties in getting a start. The woods have receded far enough from it now, but then the retreat had not been effected.

The two railroad stations are on Third street; and at the southwestern corner of this street and Chester avenue stands the *Chronicle* Building, the new and substantial brick structure in which Moorestown's one newspaper is published. Warehouses and coal yards have place near the eastern and western stations on the street, and near the eastern end is a small building erected for manufacturing purposes; but with these exceptions the thoroughfare has only dwelling houses upon it. They are principally upon the southern side, and there is a considerable portion of the street not yet built upon. Third street and the railroad form the Northern boundary of the older portion of the town.

These three streets, Main, Second and Third, running in a general way east and west, form what might be called the warp of the older section of the Moorestown web. The transverse streets form the woof, and the resulting meshes are rather open, for the cross streets are a considerable distance apart. In the eastern portion of the town, just beyond the residence of Mr. Isaac Collins, the Mount Laurel Road leaves Main street at right angles, runs down into the southern valley and up the opposite hill, as straight as a crow's flight. The road is an old one, having been laid out as a public highway in 1761. It originally formed part of a road running from the Delaware river to the ocean. It cannot be called a street, however, and is to be reckoned a part of Moorestown only as it forms a link of communication between here and somewhere else. Its value in that way is great, for it penetrates a rich and populous country.

A little west of this a street starts beside the residence of Dr. Newlin Stokes and runs northward across the railroad to Oak avenue in the northern part of the town. This is Chestnut street, and it is a broad and well located avenue. It was opened about 1870, at the urgent instance of some of the dwellers north of the railroad, who desired a connection with Main street in that vicinity. They carried their point, and now the street is about to be carried still further north to join Maple avenue, a new thoroughfare to be opened in the northern part of the town. For some distance after leaving Main street Chestnut street is bordered on the West by the grounds belonging to the residence of Dr. Stokes, and on the East by a portion of an old farm. The northern part of the street is occupied by a goodly number of residences.

A little farther west Schooley street, a short and narrow way, leaves Main street for the North, running down beside the residence of the late Asa Schooley, and extending past the canning factory to the railroad. It makes but slight pretense to beauty, but boasts a historic landmark as its starting point, the old Schooley house at its southeast corner dating back beyond the Revolution, and having associated with it memories of that perturbed time.

One of the most important of the cross-streets is Chester avenue, upon which the East Moorestown station is located. At a considerable distance west of the Mount Laurel road this broad avenue leaves the Main street at right angles, and stretches away northward. At the head of the avenue, and facing it on the south side of Main street, are situated the two Meeting Houses of the Friends, the Academy and Library and the spacious and beautiful grounds surrounding them. On the north side of Main street and extending along the western side of Chester avenue, from Main street to Second street, lies the Greenlawn Cemetery, more generally known as the Friends' Burying Ground. Its entrance is on Chester avenue about midway between the two streets. At the northwestern corner of Chester avenue and Second street stands the handsome building of the Friends' High School, already referred to. The grounds belonging to this extend for some distance along Second street, and originally stretched along Chester Avenue to the railroad. Recently lots facing on Third street have been sold off the lower portion of the school grounds, and their northern limit now falls that far south of the railroad. The *Chronicle* building, at the corner of Third street and Chester avenue, stands on one of these lots.

The arrangement of these grounds results in the noticeable peculiarity that for two squares along the western side of this important street there are only two buildings, and neither of those is a residence. The eastern side of the street, however, is fully built up, from George F. Doughten's store on the Main street corner, to the East Moorestown station on the railroad; and in this unbroken line of dwelling houses there are some residences of noticeable beauty, while there is not one that does not suggest a home of pleasant comfort. The only interruption of the line is caused by a pleasant little street known as Cherry street, which leaves the avenue at the side of Dr. Jayne's residence and runs a little way eastward, stopping when it gets to Schooley street.

Like Main street Chester avenue is part of an old road. So long as it stays in town it is a street, with its claims in that character fully recognized; as soon as it gets out of town it is a country road, leaving its town characteristics behind it like a man who has forsaken the cares of business for a holiday jaunt among the farms and all the pleasant distractions of rural experience. In both its characters it is a thoroughly agreeable and desirable acquaintance. It was laid out as a road in 1720, and when it is not Chester avenue is known as the Riverton Road, a finger board at the Main street corner giving to the wayfarer necessary information as to the points reached by it and the distances thereto.

The next cross-street west of Chester avenue—and a goodly distance from it—is Mill street. It leaves Main street by the residence of Mr. William Buzby, runs north and has been extended some distance beyond the railroad. It takes its name from Hopkins' (formerly Buzby's) steam grist mill, which stands on the western side of it between Main and Second streets. With the exception of the mill and a small shop the buildings on this street are all dwelling houses.

Between Chester avenue and Mill street two alleys extend from Main street to Second. One is Haines' alley, which leaves Main street by Brown's store; and the other an alley running down by the Skating Rink. A short street passes from Second to Third by the residence of Mr. William Thomas, and is known as French's avenue. These three narrow ways are the only means of passage north and south between the widely separated Chester avenue and Mill street. Efforts have been made in the past to have an adequate thoroughfare opened, but they have come to naught.

Another section of road forms the next cross-street west of Mill street. This is "Church Road," a highway running from Marlton on the south to Palmyra on the north. It takes its name as a street from the fact that the Episcopal Church stands on the northwestern corner of the intersection with Main street. Along the western side of the street the Episcopal church-yard extends from the church to Second street. At the northeastern corner of Second street the Public School building is located, its grounds extending some distance toward the railroad. On the southeastern corner stands a store, and the remainder of the street is occupied by dwellings, except at the railroad, where the West Moorestown station is placed west of the street, its grounds, side track, freight building and platforms occupying space on both sides of the street. Lumber and coal yards and a warehouse also occupy grounds on this street near the station. Shortly after crossing the railroad on the north, and shortly after beginning the descent into the valley at the south, the street becomes a country road, and is known as the Marlton road and the Palmyra road, according to the direction spoken of. In either direction it affords a pleasant drive—pleasant in itself, and pleasant for what it leads to.

The remaining cross streets below Church Road are Union street and Locust street. These both start at Main street and end not far below Third. Union street leaves Main with a decided northeastern inclination, and at Third street there is only a short interval—the length of the station platform—between it and Church Road. Both Union and Locust are exclusively residence streets, and both are decidedly pleasant streets to live upon, or to pass through.

North, south, east and west, almost without exception the roads leading out of Moorestown lead into pleasant country regions which afford delightful driving opportunities. The road between here and Camden furnishes a drive which is heartily appreciated by very many who are not residents of Moorestown. The same is true of the Haddonfield Road which leaves the Camden turnpike at the Forks of the Road, just west of the village. Going toward Mount Holly the greater part of the way is through a pleasant country, with village interruptions to vary the experience; and in travelling either north or south one is sure, whatever road he chooses, of coming back the richer by an added enjoyment.

Chapter XI.

North of the Railroad.

NEW elements promote new growth. If the added materials are of a good sort and the soil is favorable the new growth will be strong and vigorous and will shape out the old tree to a better form of comeliness than before. When the stock is strong and thrifty and well rooted in a generous soil, and the new scions engrafted upon it are of good variety, then all the conditions of the best growth prevail and the fruit of that tree will be something very desirable. After the railroad had taken its way through here the old Moorestown tree was budded with many new grafts, and the most conservative social horticulturist, viewing the growth they have made, would readily pronounce that they were all good.

The greater proportion of the dwellers here owned their homes in the pre-railroad times. Superfluous houses were few and the demand for them as temporary abodes not great. When a man did want a house, as a general thing he built it; unless he had the good fortune to inherit it, which mode of acquiring property has been considerably in vogue here from very early times. Renters were not numerous, and the 25th of March was not nearly so much of a "movable" feast—or fast—as it has since become. Therefore the tenant class came in but slowly at first, not for want of desire, but for want of 'opportunity. Later, as property owners—always conservative—saw their way more clearly, more houses became available for those who wished to rent, and the demand always at least equalled the supply.

But here and there one of the old houses was offered for sale from time to time, and an outside purchaser learned of the chance and availed himself of it. Again a would-be purchaser coveted a home that was not offered for sale, made his bid and either got the place or bided his time until he could get it. Others who had made up their minds that they wanted to live here bought lots and built houses for themselves. So the new-comers increased in number and the old town increased its dimensions. It grew to the East and it grew to the West, and it filled up more compactly in the middle. Still there were more people who desired to come than the older portion of the place had accommodations for. There must be more space or fewer people. Main street seemed to be the fixed boundary on the South, and the population has not at any time broken over that bound and flowed down into the valley to any extent. The North must be the direction of the new expansion, and so it came about that the region north of the railroad became a very important, populous and beautiful part of Moorestown.

Beyond Third street and the railroad was the country. Farms spread their acres close along the edge of the track, and were neighbored by other farms at the north. On both sides of Chester avenue they lay, and some of them were among the best to be found in this section. Some of the farm houses were venerable structures, possessing all the solid comfort and stability of old time architecture, and with plenty of historic associations clinging about them, while the land belonging to them gave generous return for the labor expended in its cultivation.

The willingness of outside people to come to Moorestown was manifest, and it occurred to some of the practical business men here that it would be a good thing to meet that willingness half way; to provide good accommodations and then cordially invite people to come and dwell here. Some of the farming land north of the railroad could be made available for charming village homes, and a careful consideration of the matter convinced some of these men that a good many of the acres over there would yield a better return as building lots than they did in the production of market vegetables.

If the opportunity were offered purchasers would undoubtedly come forward promptly, and be ready to pay such prices as would afford a good return for the money invested. This course of reasoning commended itself not only to some of the moneyed men here, but also to some in Philadelphia who knew a good thing when they saw it. As a consequence the desired opportunity was offered to home-seekers; and the extent to which it was accepted may be seen north of the railroad to-day.

In 1864 a company was formed with a view to purchasing farm land north of the railroad opposite East Moorestown, and disposing of the same under proper restrictions in lots of suitable size for building upon. The company consisted of ten men. Half of them were Moorestown men, one was from Rancocas, and the others were Philadelphians. The company they constituted was simply a partnership which expired with the completion of the particular enterprise for which it was formed. This enterprise was distinctly understood and defined from the beginning. The parties knew just what they wanted to do, and proceeded at once to do it.

One of the very choice farms in the vicinity was the one at that time owned by Charles Collins. It was a property associated with the early history of the neighborhood and had always been rated as a most desirable possession. At the time now spoken of it was devoted to the culture of berries and market produce. It lay east of Chester avenue and extended from the southern boundary of Dr. John H. Stokes' farm—where Oak avenue now is—to the railroad, comprising within its boundaries forty-eight and a half acres. It was this farm that the newly formed company contemplated purchasing and laying out into building lots.

Immediately upon its organization the company appointed Dr. John H. Stokes, one of the ten partners, trustee with authority to buy and sell in accordance with the agreement entered into. The trustee at once purchased for the company, from Charles Collins, the farm just mentioned, paying for it the sum of $20,000. The purchase effected, the work of apportionment was at once begun. The ground was laid out in lots and two streets—Central and Oak avenues—were opened east and west through the property. Then each member of the company selected and purchased a lot, under an agreement to build or cause to be built within a reasonable time upon the grounds he had purchased, a dwelling house to cost not less than $5,000. This part of the agreement was not rigidly enforced, as some of the houses erected cost rather less than the specified sum. The purchaser of the old homestead—at present the residence of Mr. O. B. Morris—was exempted from this provision, of course. There were other restrictions and conditions by which each purchaser was bound. Nothing objectionable was to be placed or permitted on the ground purchased; and the term "objectionable" was so construed as to cover slaughter houses, liquor saloons, stores, shops, etc. A specially emphatic injunction was placed upon pig styes.

After these selections and purchases had been made the remainder of the ground was divided among the members of the company, each member becoming an individual proprietor, holding in his own name the title to his share of building lots to be disposed of according to his own desire or opportunity. With this final division the company completed the purpose for which it was formed and the partnership was dissolved. Sales of lots by the individual owners were effected more or less rapidly, the same conditions attaching to the sales as in the first instances; except perhaps as to the cost of the house to be erected.

Such was the genesis of the "Company Grounds" —the wholly undescriptive name by which this portion of Moorestown is known to this day. The enterprise has been dealt with somewhat in detail because it was the first premeditated and comprehensive invitation to outsiders to make Moorestown their abiding place. The manner in which the invitation was responded to has led to others being extended in later years. Some time since a portion of the farm of the late Dr. John H. Stokes, also east of Chester avenue, and adjoining the original "Company Ground" on the north was placed in the market. Oak avenue borders the new extension on the south, and a new street called Maple avenue, running eastward from Chester avenue, has also been laid out through the property, north of Oak. The Stiles farm, on the west of Chester avenue, has also been purchased, laid off in lots and offered for sale. This is the old Middleton farm, whereon Nathan Middleton buried his valuables when he saw the British troops coming in Revolutionary days. The property passed from the Middleton family to Amos Stiles and from the Stiles family to its present owners.

On both of these properties lots are being disposed of quite rapidly, and new homes are being created. The greater portion of the original "Company Ground" was long since disposed of, and the vacancies that still exist there are now fast disappearing. At the time this is written a building epidemic is prevalent in force north of the railroad. New houses are going up, and others are in contemplation; the indications all point to the increase of this constructive disposition rather than its abatement. Truly the invitations extended have been heartily accepted; and there is manifestly no danger that any future proffers of hospitality will be rejected.

What has been accomplished in the past has made North Moorestown a very important and notable factor in the present experience and future progress of the village. A wholly modern addition to the old town has been developed there. The only old houses in the section are the old farm homesteads that still remain as mementoes of the historic past; and even in the case of these the results of modern taste have been combined with the picturesque effects of the olden time so that old and new are blended in a thoroughly pleasing manner. Moreover the district is devoted exclusively to dwellings and their appurtances. No stores, shops or business places of any kind exist in North Moorestown. Inconvenient? The people there do not find it so; for the store-keepers send their order-and delivery-wagons everywhere; the butcher and the baker call at every house, and so would the candle-stick maker if there were any desire for his services. Furthermore many of the residents there have their own horses and carriages and find a drive into the old part of the town no inconvenience; and at the worst a walk to the Main street is by no means a formidable undertaking.

A large quarter devoted exclusively to modern residences is something of an innovation for a rural town with a couple of centuries behind it. That it is an innovation that gives an added charm to an already charming place only a walk through North Moorestown is needed to demonstrate. There are two streets running north and south through this section. One is Chester avenue, which crosses the railroad by the East Moorestown station and remains Chester avenue for a goodly distance before it becomes the rural Riverton Road. Some distance east of this is Chestnut street, which leaves Main street by the residence of Dr. N. N. Stokes and extends through the original "Company Ground," and the newly opened tract north of it. Intersecting these Central avenue takes its way east and west some distance north of the railroad. Still further north Oak avenue runs parallel with Central, and marks the boundary of the original purchase. Beyond this Maple avenue is laid out through the Stokes' tract, and runs to an intersection with Chestnut street.

On these various thoroughfares are ranged beautiful homes in the utmost variety of modern design and construction. Many of them are elaborate and costly structures, in the building of which the resources of recent architecture have been freely drawn upon. Within they are supplied with all the conveniences and luxuries available for rural homes, and without they are fittingly surrounded by lawns and shrubbery. Others are small and simple homes, and between these two types are very many of differing grades of architectural importance; but all share one characteristic in common—they are set back in their own grounds, large or small, and are surrounded by greensward and various sorts of ornamental growth. And nearly everywhere there are trees. They border the streets and beautify the private grounds. About some of the newer homes the trees are small as yet, but they are there and give good promise of future shade. Even in the case of these same newer homes in many instances there are fine old trees that antedate by long years the survey of the lots on which the homes are built; and in the older places there is a plentiful supply of the shade and the beauty that only large trees can give. Take it all in all, it is a very important and a rapidly increasing part of Moorestown that lies north of the railroad.

Chapter XII.

Religious Bodies.

IT is accepted as an axiom that the community which freely supports churches gives but scant custom to jails and penitentiaries. Gauged by this standard Moorestown takes an enviable rank; for not many places of its size have within their borders a greater number of buildings dedicated to religious worship. There are five religious denominations represented here—the Friends, Episcopalians, Baptists, Methodists and Roman Catholics. Of the Friends both branches are largely represented; and of the Methodists there are three bodies—the Methodist Episcopal, the Methodist Protestant and the African Methodist. Each of these eight religious bodies has its own house of worship, and each of them numbers a goodly membership.

THE FRIENDS.—Philadelphia, in the beginning of its history, was not more pre-eminently a Friends' settlement than was Moorestown. The first title-holders were Friends, and it is probable that even before the title-holders made their first purchases those who came less formally to possess the land were largely of that denomination. Very early in the history of the place property was taken up and applied to the use and benefit of the Friends as a body for religious purposes.

But before that was done the Friends of the vicinity had their stated worship, making the best of circumstances as they existed. The Meeting at Burlington authorized those Friends living in the Penisauken neighborhood to hold meetings in the houses of members until such time as a regular place of meeting could be secured. Therefore the members of the body met and worshipped at each other's houses according to appointment. So also of the Friends in the Rancocas settlement—the various dwelling houses were meeting houses in turn. Of course it was desirable that this condition of affairs should be changed as soon as it could be accomplished, and a settled place of worship substituted for the various and incommodious meeting places then in use. Moorestown possessed the most advantages for such a permanent location as was desired. It was convenient for the worshippers in both the settlements, and was a growing settlement itself. In Moorestown, accordingly, (it was not Moorestown then, however,) the Meeting House was established.

In the Secretary's office at Burlington is recorded a deed of conveyance by James and Hester Adams to John Hollinshead, Thomas Hutton and ten other Friends, of whom Sarah, widow of John Roberts, was one—the only instance of a woman acting as trustee for real estate in the Friends' Society—"for one acre of ground on which the Quakers' Meeting House was then standing, for the sum of fourteen shillings current lawful money of the Province of West New Jersey; dated 9 day of 2 month, commonly called April, 1700." Land was cheap in those days, and one can hardly help thinking regretfully of the time when one acre of ground in what is now the heart of Moorestown was sold for fourteen shillings.

In the Secretary's office at Trenton is recorded another deed of conveyance by Joseph Heritage (grandson of Joseph Heritage who survived all the other grantees named in the deed of 1700) to John Warrington, Joshua Hunt, Hugh Cowperthwaite, Robert French, Edmund Hollinshead and William Roberts, Trustees appointed by Chester Preparative Meeting as successors of the original grantees, "in order to continue the good uses for and to which the said acre of ground was and is appropriated, as well as for and in consideration of five shilling hard money to him in hand paid. Dated 15 day of 5 month, 1782."

This acre of ground lies at the corner of Main street and Chester avenue, adjoining the William Penn Hotel, and forms a part of the Greenlawn Cemetery, or Friends' burying ground. The meeting house that was "then standing" on it was a log structure, small, but large enough for the requirements of the time. An old citizen who lives near Moorerestown, in looking over some ancient deeds and records some time since discovered a roughly executed draft of this ground as it was then arranged. This draft showed the meeting house standing in the southeastern corner of the lot, next Chester avenue and facing Main street. Extending westward from the meeting house, toward the hotel, was a wagon shed under which the vehicles of the worshippers were ranged on meeting days; and at the end of this, still nearer the hotel, a smaller shed for the saddle horses on which some of the young men—and young women too—rode to meeting.

In this old meeting house worship was conducted for a number of years, the Friends of the Penisauken and Rancocas regions mingling there with the Friends resident in Moorestown. For those who had to ride long distances the fervor of devotion was tried sharply sometimes, for the journey then meant far different things to what it would mean now. But the test showed strength, not weakness. The hearts of the settlers were in their worship, and they felt they paid but lightly for their privileges of conscience.

In the year 1720 the old log meeting house was burned down in some unexplained manner, and the calamity was sorely felt by the society. For a time they were again without a suitable meeting place, and had to hold meetings once more in dwelling houses. However this was only for a little interval. They had their ground now to build upon, and plenty of energy to repair the loss they had sustained. They at once began the work of rebuilding, and the new meeting house, when completed, was a good deal more substantial and commodious than the old. A portion of it was of stone, and the building altogether was held to be a credit to the society and to the place. It answered the purpose of the worshippers for over eighty years. Population in the meantime increased, and the building which had afforded accommodation in 1720 had been outgrown by the end of the century.

On the 27th day of 12th month 1781, Ephraim and Hannah Haines, for the sum of ninety-six pounds, five shillings and seven pence, gold and silver, conveyed to Joshua Roberts, Jacob Hollinshead, Jonas Cattle and John Collins, Elders and Overseers of the Society or Congregation of Friends belonging to Chester Meeting in the township of Chester, two acres, three roods and twenty-three perches of land, lying southeast of a line beginning at a stone near Isaac Lippincott's—formerly Gilbert Page's and running north, 79° 45' east, 5 chains and 26 links to a stone corner of Joseph Lippincott's lot; "to be applied to such use or uses as the body of Friends belonging to the above named meeting shall think proper."

This purchase was on the south side of Main street, opposite the head of Chester avenue, and hither in the course of time the Friends removed, there to remain until the present time. In looking over the ground selected one cannot but admire the taste and judgment that guided the men who decided on the location, for no lovelier spot can be found in the entire region than that whereon the Friends' Meeting Houses are situated. A broad lawn, beautifully shaded by noble trees, slopes southward into the valley, and from almost any point commands a view of surpassing loveliness. True the first choice was theirs, but it required discrimination to make such a choice as they made.

In 1802 the large brick meeting house which now stands in the eastern portion of this enclosure was completed and the Friends occupied it as a place of worship, forsaking the little building across the way which had served them so long. The new building was of was of proportions beyond the needs of the society as it existed then; but the future was wisely kept in view, and time vindicated the good judgment exercised. In after years it proved none too large. The old building they had heretofore occupied was torn down and the stone from it used in the construction of a school house in the meeting house enclosure across the street. After its removal the lot in which it had stood was devoted exclusively to the purpose of a burying ground, which use it still serves.

The ground purchased from Ephraim and Hannah Haines affords space for two Friends' meeting houses. The frame building on the western side of the lot was erected in 1829, soon after the division in the society. It was built by the members of the original society as their meeting place, and is still occupied by them. The separatists took the brick building as their meeting house, and it is still their place of worship. It is larger than the newer building, and the other branch of the society freely use it for their meetings on all extra occasios. A good state of feeling exists between the members of the two branches, and they are very harmonious neighbors.

In addition to the ground devoted to the burial of their own dead it is recorded that, on the 10th day of 2d month, in the year 1770, Ephraim Haines sold and conveyed to Joshua Roberts and Edmund Hollinshead, for the Chester Meeting, one rood or one quarter of an acre of land, and in 1784 Joshua Roberts, who survived Edmund Hollinshead, did, "in consideration of the sum of five shillings hard money to him in hand paid, and in order to continue the good uses for and to which the said rood of ground is appropriated—viz. for the purpose of a burying place for strangers and other Christian people who do not belong to the

Society of Friends (otherwise called Quakers), and for no other use whatever"—convey the same to John Warrington and other Friends, agreeable to a declaration of trust to be executed by them. This lot was located where the southeastern corner of Chester and Oak avenues now is. It served the Christian purpose for which the society purchased it for many years; and at length, in 1821, the trustees of Chester Meeting conveyed the lot to the inhabitants of Chester. The township in turn conveyed it to Dr. John H. Stokes in 1870.

EPISCOPALIANS.—As has been said, the Friends were the principal and controlling religious element, here as in all other parts of West New Jersey, when settlements began to be made, far outnumbering the members of all other religious denominations. But they did not constitute the whole of the new population. The first Friends who arrived were accompanied by other adventurous souls who did not belong to the society of Friends. Some of these came as servants in company with their employers, and others came independently, for the betterment of their own fortunes, for the love of change and adventure, or from regard to the ties of friendship and affection which differences of religious faith had not weakened. Here as well as elsewhere in the new land the greater proportion of these were members of the Church of England. So, in the new home as in the old, the two forms of faith were established side by side, only here their relative positions were reversed.

From the very first the population of Moorestown numbered Episcopalians among its elements. They were not numerous enough, however, to organize a parish of their own, and for a time they, like the Friends and the members of other denominations, were without a stated place of authorized worship. With them as with the Friends, this was a serious deprivation, and as early as might be the condition of affairs was remedied. This was not effected so early as with the Friends; and when it was effected the result was not so satisfactory as in their case. The members of the Episcopal Church were widely scattered in the little settlement and the surrounding country, and the concentration of the sparse membership at any one point was a difficult matter.

At a very early date, however, the difficulty was overcome in a measure. St. Mary's Episcopal Church was established at Colestown. Just when this was effected cannot now be ascertained, but it is known that St. Mary's is a very venerable church. In fact there are only two churches in New Jersey that are older, and I believe only one church building that is older than that now standing in Colestown. Services can be traced back with certainty in this old church to 1753, and although the record stops there, it is certain that services had been held in the church for some time previous to that date.

It was important enough to win favor with Queen Anne, and she presented to the parish a communion service which is still in use.

Of this old church Episcopalians in Moorestown and the vicinity became members, and there they used to gather from all directions for worship. It was a long ride for many of them, but weather and distance and bad roads did not daunt them any more than their Quaker neighbors. Through fair weather and foul, through mud and through dust, the Episcopalians of Moorestown drove to Colestown to church every Sunday, year after year. The whole family went, including the grand parent and the little child, and not forgetting the servant or the apprentice. Those who had no conveyance of their own were carried to church in the vehicles of their more fortunate neighbors; or if the more fortunate neighbor did not come along in time, walking was a resource always at command. Whatever the method of transit they got there; and many are those who new recall their participation in one or the other of the two regular processions—one going from Moorestown to Church in Colestown, and the other coming from the intermediate region to Meeting in Moorestown.

As time passed on St. Mary's became more and more of a Moorestown parish. The membership here attained greater and greater proportions as compared with the membership within the limits of the parish itself, until at length the procession which drove along the Haddonfield road comprised the greater share of the worshippers in the old church. This state of affairs became more and more unsatisfactory. The distance between Moorestown and Colestown had not increased, but the aggregate of the inconvenience of having to travel that distance every Sunday was greater, because there were more people who suffered it, and to each one it seemed worse than when there were few. The journey always had been a trouble, endured because there had been no help for it. Now, people began to feel that there was help for it, and bestirred themselves to bring matters to a more satisfactory adjustment. The obvious thing to do was to establish a separate parish here.

This, in the course of time, was accomplished, and Trinity Parish was formed in Moorestown. A lot of ground, situated on the north side of Main street and the west side of Church road, and extending north to Second street, was given to the parish by Mr. Elwood Harris, on which to erect a church building and parsonage. Mr. Harris also contributed $500 towards building the church. The corner stone of the new church was laid on October 2d, 1837, and the Rev. Samuel Starr, in an address made at that time, said: " For several of the last years past, as you will all testify from your experience of inconvenience, the congregation has not only been in scattered locations, but all whose interest and influence can at all be depended upon are at a very inconvenient distance from the church. So remote, too, are the children of the congregation that they cannot be gathered with any success for their profit in Sunday school, or even for the recita- of their catechism. Besides, the Church of Christ is aggressive in its character, and if the members are faithful will everywhere be aggressive in its results." His address concluded as follows: "When your course on earth is about to terminate, and your day of worship here below is fading into the light of eternity, you will rejoice in the reflection, as you take a final farewell of the walls here to be reared and consecrated to the service of the Lord, that you have provided on this spot one of the choicest legacies that you can leave to your posterity."

The building erected was of stone, and is a very satisfactory specimen of church architecture. It fronts toward the Main street, with a side porch on Church Road. As it stands to-day with its walls hung thick with ivy it forms one of the beautiful features of the village picture. The church was rapidly completed, and was consecrated by Bishop Doane on March 2d, 1838. The building of the church as it first stood cost $4,020.26. From the minutes, which have been very exactly kept from the first, it would seem that the church paid off the debt of the building, and then got into debt again for a parsonage; afterwards again for improving and enlarging the church. Never, until the first of April, 1878 was the church without its task of raising something of the interest and principal of the debt thus incurred. Now there is no burden of debt upon it, and the church property has a value of over $15,000. The parsonage is a good sized frame residence just west of the church and like it fronting on Main street. Back of the church the church yard—always kept in the most scrupulous order—stretches to Second street.

The first Rector of the new church was Rev. Francis Lee, whose term of Rectorship included the years 1837 and 1838. His successor was Rev. Henry Burroughs, who remained through 1839 and 1840. From 1840 to the close of 1845 Rev. Andrew Bell Patterson was Rector, and during his term here the rectory was built. During the years 1846 and 1847 Rev. Thomas L. Franklin was Rector, and for the two years succeeding there seems to have been no Rector. From 1850 to the end of 1853 Rev. Samuel Randall held the office, and during a part of 1854 there was a vacancy again. In July 1854 Rev. H. Hastings Weld took charge and continued here until Jan 1st, 1870. During his Rectorship the church was thoroughly renovated, new pews and new windows put in, robing and organ room built and the organ removed from the gallery to the side of the chancel, and thirteen feet added to the church, all at a cost of $600. Rev. Samuel Ralph Asbury took charge in the latter part of 1871, and continued until the summer of 1873. On December 1st, 1873, Rev. De Witt C. Loup took charge and remained until the 1st of April, 1878, when the present Rector, Rev. J. H. Lamb, took charge of the parish.

During the eight years that the present incumbent has been here about $23,000 have been raised for various church purposes, and in 1885 the church was enlarged and materially improved, sixty-four new sittings were added, and the accommodations are now adequate. The cost of the last improvement was about $2,000.

For two years and six months after the formation of this parish it was connected with St. Paul's, Camden; but in March, 1840, it was agreed to dissolve this connection and let each church stand alone. The parish still retains a connection with the Colestown parish, and the Rector holds a service there once every month. The first Wardens of Trinity parish were Dr. J. J. Spencer and Samuel Rudderow; and among the first Vestrymen were George F. Doughten, the late John C. Haines and the late Samuel Jones.

BAPTISTS.—Members of the Baptist denomination were not among the earliest settlers here, or if they were they were very few in number. That church seems not to have had many adherents in the community until after the present century was well advanced, and for a time the growth were slow and the results of labor bestowed were far from encouraging. That labor was earnest and persistent, however, and eventually the seed that had been so hopefully planted and so patiently and diligently nurtured grew, flourished and bore fruit.

It appears that the earliest Baptist preaching in Moorestown was in the year 1810. In that year and the two years subsequent to it there was preaching here at intervals by a number of young ministers who were under the instruction of Rev. William Slaughter, D. D., then pastor of the Sansom street Baptist Church of Philadelphia. During those years these young men went out from time to time into the villages in the vicinity of Philadelphia to preach, and several of them preached here on different occasions. Among those early preachers were some who afterwards attained distinction. Of the names recalled are those of Rev Daniel Sharp, D. D., for many years pastor of the Charles street Baptist Church, Boston; and Rev. G. Summers, pastor of the South Baptist Church in New York city for a long term of years.

There was no place of public worship here controlled by the Baptists at that time, and when the ministers of that denomination visited the place they preached at the house of Mr. Edward Harris—

the old Smith mansion of Revolutionary times. Mr. Harris, an Englishman by birth, was a member of the Church of England, but his liberal hospitality led him to open wide his doors to the members of all religious denominations, and he perhaps extended a more cordial welcome to members of the Baptist Church than to any other outside of his own denomination, for his wife was a Baptist and a member of a prominent Baptist family. Mrs. Harris was a daughter of the Rev. Thomas Ustick, A. M., for many years pastor of the first Baptist Church in Philadelphia. She was an invalid for a number of years and died in 1810; and it is not probable that any public services were held in her husband's house until after that time.

The connection of Mr. Harris with this distinguished Baptist family, together with the pleasant welcome always to be found at his house, rendered the visits of Baptist ministers to Moorestown more frequent than they otherwise would have been. The young men under Dr. Slaughter's instruction were not by any means the only ministers who preached in the Harris mansion. Among those who held services there were Rev. Mr. Barton, of the Welsh Tract Church, Delaware; Rev. Mr. Cox, of Ohio; Rev. James McLaughlin, of Burlington; Rev. Luther Rice, one of the first missionaries from America to the heathen; Jonathan D. Price, M. D., also a missionary; and Rev. Mr. Lawson and wife,

English missionaries, on their was to the East Indies. In 1813, '14 and '15, during the second war with Great Britain, Rev. John Sisty, then residing in Mount Holly, visited Moorestown at intervals and preached at largely attended meetings.

After the death of Mr. Harris, which took place in 1822, the visits of Baptist ministers here were less frequent than before, and there was preaching only at long intervals. In the meantime a church building had been erected by the Methodists on grounds given to the society by Mr. Harris. The donation had been accompanied by the condition that the house should be free for the use of all evangelical ministers, and in this church such Baptist ministers as occasionally visited the place preached their sermons. At this time there were probably not more than one or two persons in the place who belonged to the Baptist denomination, and these were members of the Haddonfield church.

In November, 1835, upon invitation of Miss Miriam Shinn, one of the Baptists resident here, Rev. Peter Powell, of Burlington, visited Moorestown and preached in the town hall. Afterwards he continued to visit the place at intervals for a time; but in February, 1836, he lost a valuable horse in the snow and his visits ceased. In the year 1835, during the Christmas holidays, Daniel Kelsey and John L. Clinger, two young ministers studying at Burlington, came here on a missionary visit. They preached two sermons in the town hall, and as a result of their labors four persons were converted who afterward became constituent members of the church here. These were Thomas Venable, William Smith, Samuel Wisham and his wife. After this preaching became more frequent and several conversions took place. The town hall could not be had for night meetings after a few times, and services were held at private houses.

The ordinance of baptism was first administered in this vicinity on the 8th of May, 1836, the candidate being Amanda Mayland. After this baptisms became quite numerous; preaching services were held with more or less regularity; prayer meetings were held at various houses, and conference meetings took place. Those who were baptized became members of the Haddonfield church; but in 1837 the membership here had so largely increased that it was determined to establish an independent Baptist Church in Moorestown. The separation from the Haddonfield church took place and on the 7th of May, 1837, a council met at the town hall here for the purpose of recognizing the newly formed body as an independent church. A large congregation assembled on the occasion, the sermon being preached by Rev. Samuel Aaron.

The constituent members of the new church were Benjamin Jones, Martha Jones, Moses Hammel,

Jerusha Hammel, S. Wisham, Elizabeth Wisham, William Smith, Hannah Smith, Thomas Venable, Sarah Venable, Isaac Shinn, Amy Shinn, Charles Kain, Jr., John F. English, Charles Clements, John Middleton, Charles T. Peacock, Samuel Foster, Margaret D. Vanderveer, Hannah Walker, Ann Creely, Ann Gill, Elizabeth Wright, Ruth Davis, Hope Pippett, Mary A. Barnett, Maria Cannon, Rebecca Ann Gifford, Amand Maylan, Lydia Ann Wooley and Margaret Wells, from the Haddonfield church; and Miriam Shinn and Ann Perkins from the Evesham church. Arrangements had been made with J. M. Courtney, a student at Burlington, by which preaching was had regularly every Sunday from January 1st, 1837, the salary at first, after the constitution of the church, being $300. This was subsequently increased to $350, by the addition of $50 appropriated by the State Convention.

The new church was received into the New Jersey Baptist Association September 26th, 1837. The same year it was decided to erect a house of worship in Moorestown, and soon after the decision was made the contracts for the work were entered into. The material selected was stone, and the size of the building was to be 40 feet by 45 feet. A building lot had been purchased of William Doughten for $500. It is on the Main street below Mill street, nearly opposite the old Harris mansion in which the first Baptist services in Moorestown had been held, and extends back to Second street. The building fronts directly upon Main street, with no intervening yard, and the ground back of it constitutes the grave yard belonging to the church.

In the spring, after the beginning of the work a fire destroyed the carpenter shop in which the lumber for the church was being prepared, and the church thereby suffered a loss of some $250. The work was soon resumed, however, and the building was completed in due time at a total cost, for ground and building, of about $4,000. Those who directed the building, being inexperienced in such matters, felt that although a basement could not be afforded, a cellar must be constructed. So on moonlight nights the brethren assembled and dug the cellar themselves. A few years later a portion of the cellar was finished as a basement, which has been in use ever since for Sunday school and prayer meeting purposes.

The house was dedicated on Friday, August 10th, 1838, the sermon being preached by Rev. Samuel Cornelius. On Thursday, November 15th, 1838, Rev. John M. Courtney was ordained pastor of the Church to receive a salary of $300. In 1840 he became joint pastor of the Moorestown and Marlton churches, receiving from each church a salary of $225. The succession of pastors in the church since its beginning has been as follows: Rev. J. M. Courtney, 1837—1841; Rev. J. W. Wigg, 1842; Rev.

E. Sexton, 1843—1844; Rev. J. M. Challis, 1845—1851; Rev. E. D. Fendall, 1852—1864; Rev. Miller Jones, 1864—1867; Rev. J. E. Bradley, 1869—1872; Rev. J. H. Brittain, 1873—1882; Rev. E. McMinn, from January 1st, 1883 to the present time.

During Mr. Fendall's pastorate a baptistery was built in the rear of the meeting house, and some other improvements were made. The church debt was entirely extinguished also, but in after years a new indebtedness was incurred, and a debt of about $2,000 now rests upon the church. A very memorable historical sermon was preached by Mr. Fendall during his stay here, and from it most of the facts here given relating to the early history of the church have been obtained. Under the ministrations of the present pastor the membership of the church has been increased, a new organ has been procured, various improvements added to the building and about $500 of the debt paid off.

The present membership of the church is about two hundred and fifty. There are, besides the home school, three mission schools, one at Fellowship, one at Mount Laurel and another at Hartford. The average attendance at all the schools is about two hundred and fifty. Evan B. Brown is superintendent of the Sunday school, and William Mortland is clerk of the society. E. B. Brown, William Mortland and George W. Heaton are the deacons of the church. The value of the church property is about $15,000. This does not include a parsonage as there is none belonging to the church. The present pastor owns the house he lives in, as did his immediate predecessor.

M. E. CHURCH.—The Methodists, like the Baptists, did not have many, if any representatives among the original white population, and the denomination does not appear to have obtained a foothold in the place until about the beginning of the present century. At that time the Itinerants were diligently at work in this section of the country, and some of their work was done here with appreciable results. An interest was awakened in the minds of some, and eventually the interest became more and more wide-spread. There are no records and therefore the knowledge of the beginnings and the progress of the denominational work here is very meagre. Who were the early workers here; who were among the first to feel the effects of their preaching; what progress was made in the work; what discouragements were encountered—all those points in the process of the development of Methodism here are things that are not known and cannot be known.

According to the most authentic traditions the first class in Moorestown was formed some little time previous to 1818. Probably it was a few years before that date, but how long is not known. We

only know that in 1818 Deacon Brock was class
leader here, and the supposition is that the class
had been established some time before. It is
known, also, that Micajah Dobbins was an exhorter
in the Methodist Church here in 1820, and that in
1825 James Moore was one of the leaders. Among
the early members of the church were James Moore,
Esther Moore, Rhoda Conover, Micajah Dobbins,
Caleb Fennimore, Lydia Fennimore, William D.
Brock, Mrs. Brock, Hannah Garwood and William
Crispin.

When the original Methodist meeting house was
erected here is not definitely known. It was sometime before 1820, and was after the formation of the
class. As nearly as can be ascertained it was about
1815. This appears to have been the first house of
worship built in the place after the Friends' Meeting house was erected, and the interval between
them was a long one. The Methodist house stood
on the south side of Main street by the large white
oak tree still growing in the sidewalk on the line
between the grounds of Dr. Thornton's residence
and that of the Misses Matlack. The ground for
the church was given to the society by Mr. Edward
Harris on the condition that the church be free for
the use of all evangelical ministers, of whatever
denomination. The condition was accepted, and
on the ground was erected a plain brick building of
moderate size, without bell-tower or spire. It is

recollected that while the church was building a great storm visited this region and the gable end of the unfinished structure was blown down. The work was at once resumed, however, and the structure completed. Under the condition mentioned ministers of different denominations preached in the church from time to time, but it was distinctly the Methodist Church.

Eventually the question of building a new church was agitated, and was the occasion of a good deal of discussion and pronounced difference of opinion, some of the members maintaining that the old building was ample for the needs of the congregation, and others as strongly urging that a more commodious house of worship was needed. These latter carried the day, and the new church was built. In the meantime Mr. Harris had sold to Mr. William Buzby the property in front of which the old church stood. The old meeting house was torn down about 1867, and the lot on which it had stood was also sold to Mr. Buzby. He subsequently sold a portion of his purchase, including the church lot to the Matlack heirs, and a house, now occupied by the Misses Matlack, was built upon the place.

The building now occupied as a house of worship was erected by the Methodist society in 1861. It is a brick structure, standing on the north side of Main street, about midway between Chester avenue and Mill street. A parsonage was also built back of the church. It is a frame building, fronting on Second street, and is a very pleasantly located residence. At present it is not occupied as a parsonage, but is rented; and the pastor, Rev. Andrew Cather, has rooms in another house, his family remaining at their own home in Virginia.

A full list of the preachers who have served here during all the years since the establishment of the church it would be impossible to obtain. Among the names recalled are those of the Revs. Street, White, Maddock, Sunderlin, Bartram, Chattain, Whitecar, Dugan and Lavelle. It was in the early part of the present decade that the differences which had for some time existed in the congregation resulted in a permanent division of the society. The trouble culminated in 1883, but it had its origin at an earlier period than that. For a considerable time there had been a want of harmony among the members. The first causes of the difference are obscure, and seem to have been unimportant in themselves. As is the wont in such cases, however, the little matter became a considerable fire, and slight differences grew into a serious disagreement In 1882 the breach between the two church parties widened materially. The pastor recognized one party as being more nearly right in his estimation than the other, and thereby alienated the sympathies of the opposing party from himself.

Thus he was fully identified with one side of the quarrel, and was looked upon by those on the other side as the representative of their opponents. At the end of his term two opposing influences were brought to bear from the Moorestown church upon the Conference—one urging the return of the same pastor for another term and the other urging just as strongly that another pastor be sent. The first influence prevailed and and the pastor was returned. The party he represented in the church was ardent in his support and the opposition was equally strenuous. The opposing party claimed to constitute the society proper, and asserted the right to control the property of the church, including the church building. The doors of the church were locked against the pastor and his adherents, and an appeal was made to the courts, with the result that the doors were ordered to be opened. This was done; but the outcome of the unhappy difference was a permanent disruption of the congregation, the disaffected members withdrawing in a body in the spring of 1883.

The present value of the M. E. Church property here is about $12,000. The membership at present is about 45. Wilson chapel, at Wilson Station is a preaching station for the pastor connected with this church. The Sunday School here numbers about 75 scholars at present, a considerable increase within the past year. The Wilson Station school, connected with this, is also well attended.

M. P. CHURCH. — The Methodist Protestant Church here came into existence as the result of the trouble in the Methodist Episcopal body. After the action of the Conference in March, 1883, became known the protesting members of the old body, about fifty in number, gave formal notice of withdrawal. Their intention was fully carried out a little later, and they declared themselves outside of the old church. Some time was spent in deciding what subsequent course to pursue. Some were in favor of distributing themselves among the other churches in the place, according to individual preference. This idea did not meet with much favor, however, the general feeling being that they should form a distinct body of worshippers, and not sacrifice their identity. Frequent meetings were held for consultation, and at length the suggestion was made to attach themselves to the Methodist Protestant Church. The suggestion was favorably considered and a committee of inquiry was appointed. The committee proceeded without delay to make the necessary investigations. The President of the M. P. Conference was consulted with, and the explanations inclined the inquirers still more strongly toward the proposed connection. The President urged a fuller and more prolonged consideration of the matter, however, and himself visited Moorestown several times and participated in the the meetings held to consider the question.

Finally it was fully decided that the seceding members of the M. E. Church here should unite with the Methodist Protestant organization, and on May 24, 1883, the M. P. Church of Moorestown was formed, twenty-three constituent members signing the register. The newly formed church was recognized by the Conference, and Rev. J. H. Algor, from the Mount Pleasant Circuit, Atlantic county, N. J., was assigned to the charge. A unanimous request from the Mt. Pleasant church that Mr. Algor be sent back there was over-ruled by the Conference, and the new pastor took up his residence and assumed his duties here on the 24th of October, 1883. Here he has remained ever since, at the unanimous request of his congregation.

No time was lost in making necessary arrangements for a house of worship, and in the mean time the town hall was made to serve as a temporary meeting house. Regular services were held there twice every Sunday, and the children of the congregation as regularly gathered into the Sunday school there. The lot selected for the church building was situated on the north side of Main street, a little east of Union street. It belonged to the estate of David Heaton, and was occupied by an old blacksmith and wheelwright shop. This was purchased for $2,000, and the erection of the building was begun October 29th, 1883. A neat brick building 37x58 feet in size was constructed, with audience room, lecture room and capacious storage cellar. The lecture room was finished and opened for service March 12th, 1884, and in it, since that date, the services of the church have been held. The audience room proper is not yet quite completed. The spire of the new church building bears the only "town clock" in the place.

At the time of its formation, in the spring of 1883, the church, as has been stated, numbered twenty-three members. Each year has shown a marked increase in the membership, and now there are seventy-four names on the roll. The present Board of Trustees consists of B. J. Sutton, Michael Dubel, George Knell, Jr., A. M. Risdon, George Maines, W. E. Jones, F. M. Johnson. The Sunday school was organized June 22d, 1883, with a membership of twenty-three, including both teachers and scholars. At present the scholars alone number one hundred and sixty-five, and with the officers and teachers the number belonging to the school amounts to one hundred and eighty-three. The pastor is the Superintendent, with J. Edwin Baker as Assistant Superintendent. The library of the school is well selected, and numbers three hundred and thirty-seven volumes, to which a considerable number are about to be added. The present value of the church property is estimated at $8,000 on which there is still some debt resting.

A. M. E. Church.—The colored Methodists of Moorestown and vicinity have not long been in possession of a house of worship. Formerly they were members of the Mount Laurel Church, and attended service there. The walk to Mount Laurel and back every Sunday was a tax on the strength and fervor of the worshippers that they felt severely; and at length they decided that the inconvenience of going so far from home to attend service was too great. The result of this decision was the formation of the A. M. E. Church of Moorestown. The organization of the church was effected several years ago, and measures were taken soon afterward to secure a church building. Such progress was made in the raising of funds that they were enabled to buy the necessary ground, and a lot was purchased on the west side of Church Road, a short distance north of the railroad.

In process of time such additional funds were raised as seemed to warrant the beginning of building operations, and accordingly a plan for the church building was decided upon, and the foundation of the structure was completed. But there the work stopped, and it seemed as though it had stopped permanently. For a long time the foundation was the only part of the projected building that had come into existence, and efforts to accomplish more seemed all in vain. In the meantime the members held services in each other's houses and hoped against hope for the time when they would have a special building devoted to that purpose.

After a considerable time of fruitless endeavor it became manifest that to succeed some new method must be adopted, and it was urged that some white men be added to the Board of Trustees. This suggestion was acted upon, and Mr. Gilbert Aitken and Dr. Joseph Stokes were invited to become members of the Board. They both accepted the invitation and entered cordially upon the work before them. Under the united efforts of the new and the old members of the Board matters speedily took an encouraging turn, and in a short time such progress had been made that building operations could be resumed.

The first meeting of the Board as a joint committee on the building of the church, after the addition of the white members, was held at the house of Daniel Fountain, on July 7, 1883. At that time Rev. Geo. M. Witten was pastor, and remained in charge until the church was built. The enterprise was pushed forward with vigor; contributions came in more and more liberally, and a good degree of enthusiasm was awakened where a short time before there had been only discouragement.

The corner stone was laid May 1st, 1884, and the church was completed and opened for worship the same year. The building is a small but very neat frame structure, surmounted by a cupola. The seating capacity of the church is about two hundred. The value of the church property at present is about $1,000. The present pastor is Rev. Isaac Accoe, who also has charge of the churches at Mount Holly and Mount Laurel. The Board of Trustees as at present organized consists of Gilbert Aitken and Dr. Joseph Stokes (white) and George Ambrose, James H. Bowers and Daniel Fountain (colored). The present membership is about fifty, although the attendance at Sunday services is much greater than that. The Sunday School is quite largely attended, and much interest is taken in its progress and welfare.

ROMAN CATHOLIC CHURCH.—The Catholics of Moorestown, as of New Jersey generally, originally belonged in the Diocese of Philadelphia. Eventually New Jersey was created a Diocese by itself, known as the Diocese of Newark, of which Bishop Daley, afterwards Archbishop of Baltimore, was the first Bishop. At that time the Catholic Church at Fellowship was the nearest church to Moorestown, and the Catholics of this town and vicinity went there to worship. It was a formidable journey, and the inconvenience of it was seriously felt by the worshippers here. The Fellowship church was a missioner, attached to a church in Camden, and ministered to by a priest from that city.

In the spring of 1867 the church at Fellowship was destroyed by an accidental fire, and the necessity for supplying another house of worship led to the consideration of a more convenient location for it. By this time Moorestown and its neighborhood supplied the majority of the members; moreover Moorestown was a much larger place than Fellowship, was directly on the railroad and was altogether a more suitable place for the church than the old location. It was determined, therefore, that the new building be erected in Moorestown, and that it should be a church fully suited to the needs of the worshippers.

At the time the Fellowship church was destroyed it was under the charge of Rev. Father Burns, of the Church of the Immaculate Conception, Camden, and it is to his zeal and energy that the Catholics of Moorestown owe the beautiful building in which they now worship. A lot on the south side of Main street, a short distance above Church Road, was purchased from William H. Haines, and on it in the summer of 1867, the present building was erected. It is a handsome building of brick, set well back from the road, and surrounded by well shaded grounds. It has a seating capacity of about 350.

The Moorestown church continued as a mission attached to a Camden parish for several years. About the year 1874 it was detached from Camden, and became attached to Mount Holly. Rev. Father Hugh McManus, of Mount Holly, took charge and held services here twice a month. In March, 1880, this was made a separate parish, and the present pastor, Rev. Father James McKernan took charge of it. The present membership of the church is between 500 and 600. The parish is of considerable extent, and the members are scattered over quite a wide region. Owing to this fact the attendance at Sunday School is a matter of difficulty to many, and of impossibility to some, and therefore the school is not so large as it would otherwise be. The attendance of children at the school is about sixty.

Since Father McKernan's residence here he has added considerably to the property of the parish. He has purchased the present parochial residence adjoining the church, and added another lot to the property. The present value of the property is about $14,000, on which there is some debt still remaining. The debt is being rapidly reduced, however.

Chapter XIII.

The Schools.

FROM its earliest days Moorestown has been a good place for schools. Whether a school master was among the first squatters on the ridge I do not know; but if not he made his appearance here very soon afterwards, and has staid here ever since. About the first thing those old pioneers wanted, after they had secured a shelter for their families and a place to hold religious services, was a school house for their children. They seem always to have had a teacher at hand to occupy the school house as soon as it was ready; and the teacher, from that day to this, has never lacked for full employment, for the earnest attention bestowed on educational interests in the beginning has never been relaxed.

The first schools, like the first places of worship, were provided by the Friends. Among the members of that society who were the first comers here were people of higher education and larger attainments than ordinary, and they were sufficient in number and influence to give a flavor of culture to even the rude elements of a pioneer settlement. Their successors have always had among them a sufficient representation of their class to retain in the community that flavor in its full strength, and a large element of the population here has, from the first, been characterized by a goodly degree of literary cultivation and taste, and of scholarly attainments. So, although quiet and undemonstrative about it, Moorestown has taken a just pride in the educational position it has always occupied. That kind of pride is a very good thing, and the state of affairs that inspires it is a still better thing.

A community dominated by such an influence must have schools, and they must be good ones, and good schools Moorestown has always had, and has to-day. But in the matter of the early schools, as in other of their early enterprises, our old time predecessors did not take much pains to let us know what they did, which of them did it, or when, where and how it was done. They were as far as possible from sharing the sentiments of the traditional statesman who protested: "I don't believe in doing so much for posterity. What has posterity ever done for us?" They did much for posterity, and did it bravely and lovingly; but they didn't tell posterity anything about it. Consequently we know almost nothing as to where the first schools were established, or the names of those identified with them.

THE SCHOOLS.

The schools were the result of private effort, undoubtedly, and were little neighborhood enterprises, established in the houses of those who taught them. The first of which we have any account—but that does not imply that it was the earliest school—was kept in a log house near the forks of the Penisauken Creek. Emanuel Beagary lived in the house and taught the school for several years, and afterwards became Assessor of the township. If the children of Moorestown had to attend Friend Beagary's school they undoubtedly found the hill of learning a toilsome and oftentimes a muddy one to climb. But they had schools nearer home very soon, if not at first; for there are a number of old houses now standing here in which schools are reported to have been kept in very early days. One of the old schools was kept in the house now occupied by the Roberts sisters on the south side of Main street, nearly opposite the site of the old tan-yard where Moore's hotel is supposed to have been located. A store had been kept in the building, and when it was moved to other quarters the house was occupied for school purposes. Ezra Roberts and Darling Lippincott kept a boarding and day school there for a number of years. A building not now standing but only recently removed is said to have been used for school purposes, possibly at a still earlier period than the Roberts-Lippincott school just mentioned

This was the old frame house formerly owned by James Sankey and used by him as a cabinet shop until it was torn down to make room for the present Bank building.

Besides these and other schools kept in dwelling houses in early times there were others, here and hereabouts, kept in buildings specially devoted to that purpose. A frame school house stood on the old Ferry road, near its junction with the Salem road, in which a neighborhood school was kept until 1784. There was also a frame school house at Fairview, at the junction of the present Haddonfield road with the old Salem road, in which a school was kept until 1781. It is known that a brick school house had long been standing on the ground purchased by the Friends from Job and Anna Cowperthwaite in 1784, near the residence of George Matlack. Coming down to later times, a frame school house was erected in 1829 on the lot north of Second street and west of Chester avenue, which was in use until 1880, when it was taken down. About 1835 a frame school house was built on the north side of Second street and the east side of Church Road. It was used as a neighborhood school until 1873, when it was removed.

The educational methods that prevailed of old differed in more than one material respect from those now in force. The course of study pursued was less comprehensive, "the three R's" constituting, in many cases, the bulk of the curriculum. As a consequence while the hours of school were about the same as now, the hours of study were materially less—whether to the advantage or disadvantage of the pupil is a question which still causes some discussion occasionally. Under the old method, too, the pupil came into closer contact with the personality of the teacher, and did not feel the system drawn so closely about him. If the teacher were of the right kind the system was pretty sure to be of the right kind, too; and if otherwise, otherwise. If the teacher was changed the system was very certain to be changed also; and so the pupils, by the time they stopped "going to school," had generally tested a variety of educational methods.

But in one particular every system of teaching closely resembled every other one. Different teachers might hold radically conflicting views as to the proper manner of holding the pen, of working out a "sum" or of the correct attitude in class; but they all had very much the same way of whipping a scholar who did not properly "toe the mark." There are plenty of people now among us who, when they recall some of the experiences incident to their close personal contact with the teachers of their childhood, and contrast them with the experiences of their grandchildren in schools from which the rod is banished, feel a shuddering conviction that they were born too soon and missed their full share of good luck. Some of them on the other hand, insist that a judicious admixture of good thick switches with the present educational diet would be a good thing for all concerned. It would emphasize and enforce the teacher's authority, they argue, and so would enable him more effectually to keep young feet from straying into vicious ways, and thereby benefit the community at large.

Whether right or wrong this used to be the generally accepted idea, and the old school discipline included the whip as naturally as the spelling book. Some of the incidents related of those old times would make the school boy of to-day think twice very carefully before deciding upon his course of conduct if he thought his teacher was likely to copy very closely after the old masters. It is related, for example, that a boy at one of the schools who had a bad habit of bullying the smaller boys was brought to book one day for bullying one little fellow in quite too serious a fashion. He threw a piece of wood at the small boy in play spell (they did not have any "recess" at that time), and the missile struck the child on the forehead, inflicting a wound from which the blood flowed in a stream. The master was informed of what had taken place and ordered the offender to stay after school for a little conversation. School was dismissed at the usual time and almost the first one outside of the room was the boy who had been told to stay inside. At the instant of dismissal he had jumped for the door and got safely out. But the master, whip in hand, jumped almost as quickly. He overtook the fugitive at the gate of the yard seized him by the collar and then and there administered such effective chastisement that the boy's shoes had blood in them when he finally started for home. Nor was it the boys alone who smarted under the hot infliction. No strained notions of chivalry were allowed to interfere with the welfare of the girls, and they received their whippings on occasion, as impartially as the boys.

The Friends, as has been said, were the leaders in educational enterprise here; and the schools were not left to depend on individual effort. The Society took organized action at an early day to secure good schools and place them on a permanent basis. It is recorded that on the 27th day of 12th month, 1781, Ephraim and Hannah Haines, for the sum of 96 pounds, 5 shillings and 7 pence, gold and silver, conveyed to Joshua Roberts, Jacob Hollinshead, Jonas Cattle and John Collins, elders and overseers of Chester Preparative Meeting, 2 acres, 3 roods and 23 perches of land, lying southeast of a line beginning at a stone near Isaac Lippincott's —formerly Gilbert Page's residence—and running north and east to a stone corner of Joseph Lippincott's lot; "to be applied to such use or uses as the body of Friends belonging to the above named meeting shall think proper." One of these uses was the establishment of a school which is still prospering there.

In 1784, 8th month, 31st, Friends of Chester Meeting bought of Job and Anna Cowperthwaite, "for one shilling hard money," one acre and one rood of ground near the residence of George Matlack. It is probable that the first school established hereabouts by the Friends as a Society was established on this ground. A brick school house had been placed on the premises, and in this a school was opened on the 6th day of 12th month, 1785. In the same year or the year following a stone school house was erected on the lot bought of Ephraim and Hannah Haines; and in 1786 the Friends of Chester Meeting appointed their first committee to have the oversight of the education of their children.

A committee was appointed by the Chester Meeting in 12th month, 1788 to visit and have the oversight of a school kept by Abraham Warrington in or near Westfield (as is supposed), and Joseph Warrington, Thomas Lippincott, Samuel Lippincott and Samuel Shute were requested to continue the care over this school for the next year. Thus far the work done had been determined by the occasion as it arose; but in 12th month 1790 the Monthly Meeting of the Friends of Evesham (of which Chester Preparative Meeting was a constituent) took into consideration the promoting and raising of funds for schools; also a uniform plan for the settlement of schools in proper places, and the appointment of Trustees to have supervision of the same.

The Friends of Chester Preparative Meeting in 7th month 1791 purchased of Samuel Shute, for 6 pounds, hard money, one acre and one perch of land where Westfield brick school house now stands. An ancient log house, brought from the neighborhood of Peter Stimms' and Henry Warrington's residences on Penisauken Creek, was standing on the place, and was located for a time a short distance southeast of the entrances to the premises of Nathaniel N. Stokes and William Parry. Shortly after the purchase this old log structure was removed, and for several years afterwards was used as a sheep cote by the father of William and Israel Lippincott. The log building was replaced on the recently purchased ground by a permanent stone school house, which for several years went under the name of Chester Lower School House. For some time, by permission, meetings for Divine worship were held in it, but from the first it was a school house and nothing else.

Six years later, in 3d month, 1797, the Friends of Chester Meeting bought of Thomas and Abigail Lippincott, for 122 pounds and 12 shillings, hard money, 15 acres of land lying west of the Burlington Road, not far from the school house lot just mentioned, "for the sole use of Friends in the compass of Chester Lower School; which is to be under the management of Friends, members of Chester Preparative Meeting, aforesaid." Coming back now to Moorestown proper the Friends of Chester Meeting, on the 17th of 2d month 1795 purchased of Nathan Heritage and wife, for 179 pounds, 6 shillings and 3 pence, "hard money," 5 acres, 3 roods and 39 perches of land; one acre and one rood of it to be "for the sole use of the society of people called Quakers for a grave yard to bury their dead; and for such other religious purposes as the said people in their said Preparative Meeting shall direct and appoint the same to. The balance of said lot, or other described lot therein contained, for the sole use of Friend's School at Moorestown, under the direction of the Trustees of said school, appointed by the Preparative Meeting at Chester aforesaid, for the purpose of building a dwelling house thereon for the residence of the teacher, or such other use or uses as the said people in their said Preparative Meeting House by their Trustees shall direct and appropriate the same to." It will be observed that real estate had advanced in price since the purchase from James and Hester Adams —which this last adjoined—was made for fourteen shillings in 1700. It would seem that the "dwelling house for the residence of the teacher" was not erected on this lot; but a school house was, and it staid there until replaced by a better one in recent years.

The organized work of the Friends' society in the cause of education, the early progress of which has just been briefly traced, has never been relaxed. On the contrary more active efforts have been put forth as the needs of the time seemed to demand them, and their educational work to-day touches the high water mark of progress in that direction. Their schools have been kept fully abreast of the advancing time, and are a source of just pride. While they have been making this progress as a society, and while the community at large has been watchfully working in behalf of public instruction, there have been private efforts put forth in behalf of a higher and broader education than was attainable in the smaller private and neighborhood schools mentioned earlier in this chapter.

For many years a boarding school for young ladies, was maintained by Mrs. Mary Lippincott, and was an institution of such recognized high character that it added not a little to the reputation and educational importance of the place. The school was established in 1843 in the Lippincott mansion, a very old building which stood at the eastern extremity of the town, where the Fair Ground Avenue improvement is now in progress. Mrs. Lippincott was a woman of high culture and great enterprise. She had had much experience in teaching young ladies, and when she decided to open a school in her own house she brought to the work a ripe ability and an established reputation. These, and her great executive talent insured for her enterprise a large degree of success. She had pupils from near and far, including many from Philadelphia; and a goodly proportion of the extra travel on the old stage coach lines Saturday nights and Monday mornings consisted of "Mrs. Lippincott's girls" going home and returning to school.

The proprietress and principal was assisted in her work by an able corps of teachers, and the course of study included all the branches essential to the higher standard of female education. Moreover the school was delightfully located, and the pupils, aside from their first-class educational advantages, enjoyed those of a remarkably pleasant and healthful country home. The regoin all about them was exceptionally beautiful; and in addition to that was historically interesting. One of the favorite walks of the pupils was to a spot known as the Indian Spring, some distance south of the school. This was a very abundant spring of clear water, which was said to have very pronounced mineral qualities, and was very interesting from the tradition that it had been a favorite Indian camping place. The spring itself had been very carefully attended to by its dusky proprietors, and was still in those days in the same condition as they had kept it. Then too, there was always the exciting chance of finding some specially choice Indian relic in the neighborhood; and many were the stone arrow heads the young ladies took back home with them as trophies of their visits to Indian Spring.

For a number of years after her husband's death Mrs. Lippincott continued her boarding school with eminent success; and when she finally relinquished it she was not quite ready yet to give up teaching altogether, and for some years longer she kept a day school for boys and girls in her house. In 1883, three years ago, after forty years of constant labor, she abandoned teaching entirely, and since that time to the present summer, the old homestead that was formerly so full of young life has stood unoccupied. Mrs. Lippincott herself is now living at a very advanced age in Camden.

Rev. H. Hastings Weld, who was Rector of the Protestant Episcopal Church here from 1854 to 1870, taught a school in the rectory during a part of that time. Both male and female pupils were received in this school, and were well instructed in higher and more numerous branches than were taught in the district school. Mr. Weld was a very successful teacher, and those now among us who were his pupils bear loving testimony to the happy manner in which he made school days pleasant as well as profitable. During a part of the time his daughter also had a private school for smaller scholars, conducted on the same principles and with the same aims as her father's.

We come now to the consideration of the Moorestown schools as they are to-day. These are three in number—the Public School and the two high grade schools under the control of the two branches of the Friends' Society, known as the Friends' Academy and the Friends' High School. All three of these institutions occupy ground that is more or less historic, and all are the outgrowth of very old schools. In each instance the advanced modern development had its beginnings in the early educational efforts of the community.

THE PUBLIC SCHOOL.—The public school house stands on the north-eastern corner of Second street and Church Road, the lot it occupies extending a considerable distance along both streets, and affording ample room for the children's play ground. The ground had been previously occupied for several years by a school house; and the school house which occupied it had, for many other years, occupied another lot in the immediate vicinity. This old school house was a frame structure, and in the beginning of its career stood on the opposite side of Second street, very near the spot now occupied by Gilbert Aitken's store and cabinet shop. There, with the woods all about it, it for many years served its purpose as a neighborhood school. Then it was moved across the street to the lot now occupied by the public school house, and staid there until it was removed to make way for its more modern successor.

The old frame school house was occupied, in the course of its history, by a goodly number of teachers whose names are well remembered by many of the citizens whose young ideas they taught how to shoot. A full list of these names cannot be given, but among the teachers were Edward Allen, Thomas Blackwood, Moses Hamill, and his daughter Miss Eliza Hamill, John Stiles, John Curry, Charles Vansciver, Jeremiah Haines, two sisters of Charles Vansciver, Miss Sallie Borton and Miss Flora Roberts.

Moses Hamill taught in the winter term, as did most of the other male teachers, and his daughter taught the summer school. Years ago in most country and village districts a winter school was held to be beyond the governing powers of a woman, on account of the number of "big boys" who came to school winters and had to work summers, and who, according to the theory of the time, could only be kept in order by a strong arm wielding an effective rod. The idea survived until quite recent years; so the summer schools were reserved, for the most part for female teachers.

Thomas Blackwood, one of the teachers mentioned, showed, in his career, the adaptability to circumstances and the command of resources which are recognized as American characteristics. He was a cabinet maker, employed by the late Samuel Jones. In the course of his shop-work he met with an accident which disabled one of his hands to such an extent as to interfere seriously with manual work. Therefore he turned to the employment which, half a generation ago, was the resource of a great proportion of men who wanted to bridge a chasm—school teaching. He took charge of the west Second street school; but not as a finality. In the intervals of leisure permitted by his new occupation he studied medicine, with the result that when he gave up teaching he entered upon practise as a physician. He is still in the practise of his profession in Camden.

The old school was in a manner the "district school" of the place. It was not a free school but was partly supported by taxation, with small sums paid by the parents for the tuition of their children. The school depended on the efforts of a single teacher, but on the other hand the course of study was less comprehensive and complicated than in the graded schools of to-day, so that one person was equal to all the demands upon his time and resources, and was quite equal to meet the requirements of the "A B C class" and the class in the "double rule of three" in the same half day, and through an indefinite number of half days.

In 1873, the lot on which the old school house

THE SCHOOLS. 175

stood having been purchased for a public school, the old frame structure took leave of its boys and girls, and the place which had known it knew it no more. It was not destroyed, but was re-established on old familiar ground. Mr. Andrew Aitken purchased it and moved it across Second street to very nearly the same site it had occupied in the first place, and to-day, disguised in paint and embellished with modern additions, it does duty as a part of the building in which Mr. Gilbert Aitken has his furniture store. The old teachers' desk before which, through a long, long term of years, trembling urchins stood to give an account of youthful misdeeds, is also on duty in Mr. Aitken's shop at the present time. The last teacher in the old frame building was Miss Hannah Garwood, who is still a teacher in this vicinity.

The idea of a graded public school did not, at first, meet with unqualified approval in Moorestown. Some of the older and more conservative residents here thought that the educational facilities afforded by the three schools then in existence here were ample for all the needs of the community, and that the proposition to replace one of them with such a school as was contemplated would only be to impose a burden of taxation without any sufficiently compensating advantages. The younger and newer elements carried the day, however, and the public school was finally decided upon. There are those who still secretly wish that things had been left as they were, and that the old frame school-house with its single teacher were still one of the institutions of the place as of old.

In 1873, the public school having been decided upon and the ground for it having been purchased, the present building was erected and occupied. It is a two story brick structure, fronting on Second street, and was constructed according to advanced ideas of public school architecture. It has five school rooms, arranged to meet the requirements of its five departments.

The staff of instructors consists of a Principal and four assistant teachers; and the course of study is a thorough one according to the present standard of public school education. The finishing term takes the pupil through all the studies of the Philadelphia High School except three, the exceptions, I believe, being Chemistry, Logic and Synonyms.

The seating capacity of the school is 250, with a total enrollment of 285, and an average attendance of 203 scholars. This district also includes the school at Wilson's Station, which has a seating capacity of 50, a total enrollment of 35, and an average attendance of 30. The number of children in the entire district between the ages of five and eighteen years is 564. The present value of the school property here is about $10,000. The school is supplied with a large and well selected library, and also with well chosen illustrative apparatus.

The first Principal of the public school was Miss Rebecca T. Garrigues who filled the position from the opening of the school in 1873 to the autumn of 1877, when she resigned the place. She was succeeded in September 1877, by Miss Anna Weld, who resigned the position in January, 1878 on account of her failing health. Miss Ella M. M. Carr assumed the duties of Principal on the 21st of January 1878, and continued to exercise them until December, 1885, when she resigned. Mr. Henry C. Herr was her successor. He assumed the position January 1, 1886, and still holds it. He is assisted by Miss Marion Brown, Miss Mattie Cook, Miss Jamieson and Miss Irene Benyaurd.

The present Trustees of the district are Elwood Hollinshead, Samuel Dager and Gilbert Aitken.

At the Centennial Exposition, in the Educational Department of New Jersey, there was exhibited a large photograph, giving views, side by side, of the Moorestown Public School Building and of the old frame school house which it supplanted, the purpose being to emphasize the contrast between the old and the new styles of school house as they existed in New Jersey. The old frame school was labeled "One Hundred Years Old."

THE ACADEMY.—The school from which the present Friends' Academy has developed was the first of the schools established in Moorestown by the Friends as a society. In 1781, as has already been stated, the Elders and Overseers of the Meeting purchased of Ephraim and Hannah Haines the ground on Main street at the head of Chester avenue, where the two meeting houses now stand. This was to be applied to such uses as the meeting should think proper, and the two uses that seemed eminently proper to the members were religious worship and education. Accordingly besides erecting a meeting house on the eastern part of the lot, they built a school-house a little west of the middle of the enclosure.

This school-house was a small, square structure, solidly built of stone. It was erected about the year 1785. and cost the society 253 pounds and 12 shillings. It is related that the greater portion of the stone used in the construction was quarried from the ground on which the building was placed. Not all of it, however; for it is also related that the stone which had formed the foundation of the old meeting house on the north side of Main street was taken across the street when the meeting house was torn down, and built into the walls of the new school house. It would have been difficult to find anywhere a pleasanter location for a school than the one selected for this. The building stood well back from the street—or the "King's Highway" as it then was—on the southward slope that overlooks the beautiful valley, and was well shaded, as it is now, by noble trees. The quiet and seclusion certainly favored uninterrupted study; but whether uninterrupted study prevailed I shall not undertake to say. Probably not, for I have heard that some of the teachers occasionally punctuated the quiet day with very unquiet whippings.

In this stone school house the Friends maintained a school for their children and the children of the neighborhood until very recent years. They employed good teachers, exercised a strict supervision through the representatives of their meeting, and in all ways kept the school up to a high standard. The result was that until very recently the school was held to meet very fully the needs of the community. A good, thorough common school education was obtainable here, and the school at Westtown, also under the control of Chester Meeting, furnished, as it does now, the opportunity for a well advanced education. The two together answered the purpose for which they were established very completely through a long term of years.

In the course of time, however, it became desirable to add to the resources of the Moorestown school. The advancing development of the community seemed to call for greater and higher facilities in the way of education than the old stone school house with its one teacher afforded. The thing to do was not to be decided upon lightly, and much careful thought was expended upon it, and much comparison of views took place before the final decision was reached. This was to the effect that the school should be changed from a simple neighborhood school to a high-grade institution; that its character should be modified and its scope largely increased, and the building should be so altered and added to as to meet the new requirements. In short a graded Academy was to be established in a suitable academy building.

So, after nearly a hundred years of usefulness to a number of rising generations, the little stone school house was deposed. It was not destroyed, but its identity was merged into that of a newcomer. It became, instead of an independent whole, merely a part of a much more elaborate building. In 1878 the present Academy building was completed, the venerable stone house forming the rear portion of the structure. The building, as it stands, is a plain one-story house, the front, or newer portion being of brick, and the back part of stone. At the left of the entrance hall is the room containing the library, and there are, in addition, three school-rooms, all well furnished with modern school appliances. The building has a seating capacity of about one hundred, and the attendance is very nearly up to that standard.

The change, of course, involved new aims and new methods, and the course of study, as now arranged, graduates the pupils after a thorough instruction in the higher branches of a solidly founded education. There are three departments in the school — the Primary, Intermediate and Academic. Pupils are admitted to the Primary department at the age of six to eight years, and the time occupied in this department is two or three years, according to the age and standing of the pupils at the time of entering. In the Intermediate department one year is consumed, and the Academict course takes four years; so that the entire course of study, from entering to graduation, occupies seven or eight years. The staff of teachers consists of the Principal and two regular assistant teachers, with an occasional extra assistant.

The course of study in the Primary department includes Arithmetic, Geography, Spelling, Reading, Writing, Object Lessons, Natural History and Drawing. The Intermediate department comprises two classes, C and B. In class C the studies are Arithmetic, Geography, Physiology, Popular Science, Language Lessons, Elementary Philosophy and Child's American History. The studies for class B are Arithmetic, Zoology, Physiology, Geography, Parley's History of the World, Study of Plants and Latin. The Academic department comprises four classes; they are class A, Second class, First class, and Senior class. In class A the studies are Arithmetic, Physiology, Latin, United States

History, Algebra, English Grammar, Natural History, and the Geography of the Old World. The studies in the Second class are Algebra, Physics, Latin, English History, German, Physical Geography, English Grammar and Higher Arithmetic. The studies in the first class are Geometry, Astronomy, Rhetoric, Constitution of the United States, Latin, German, American Literature, Botany and Studies in English Literature. The Senior class has Trigonometry, Geology, Latin, Chemistry, English Literature, German, Ancient History, Higher Algebra and Botany.

The pupils have the advantage of the free use of the excellent library in the building, and in addition there is a good collection of maps. There are also good physical and chemical apparatus, and students in physiology are assisted by the study of an articulated skeleton, and a good clastic model of the human system. The study of natural history is greatly aided by a cabinet containing mounted specimens of one hundred and fifty of our native birds.

The Academy was opened in the autumn of 1878, with Richard Cadberry as the first Principal. He served in that capacity for one year, when he was succeeded by Edward Forsythe. After two years of service he relinquished the position, and Wilmer P. Leeds became Principal. His term of service was also two years, and at the end of that time he was succeeded by Miss Ruth Anna Forsythe, who has held the position ever since. Miss Forsythe has for her assistant teachers, Walter Moore and Miss Emma P. Forsythe. The school is under the control of the Orthodox branch of the Friends, and a committee is appointed by the Meeting to have oversight of its conduct and affairs. The present committee is constituted as follows: William Evans, George Abbott, jr., Samuel L. Allen, David Roberts, Elisha Roberts, Henry Roberts, Alexander C. Wood, Mary Ann Haines, Sarah R. Allen, Rebecca Evans, Sarah Carter, Mary R. Matlack, Mary Anna Matlack, Sarah Ann Kaighn.

FRIENDS' HIGH SCHOOL.—The Friends' High School at the eastern end of Second street is also the outgrowth of a school which was established by the Friends as a Society, and which dated back to a time long past. In 1795, as has already been said, the Friends here purchased of Nathan Heritage and his wife, the tract of land lying on the western side of Chester avenue, and extending, originally, from Main street to where the railroad now is. In 1829 a frame school house was erected on this lot, about midway between the northern and southern boundaries, and fronting Chester avenue. Second street had no existence when the school house was built, and later, when the survey was made for that thoroughfare, it was found that either the street or the school house would have to turn out. The building was the one to yield. It was moved some distance toward the North, and thenceforth stood on the northwestern corner of Second street and Chester avenue.

It was a little, low, white frame building, with its entrance door toward Second street; and was a pleasant and picturesque feature of the locality, standing as it did in the shade of some large old trees. Like the stone school house, this was under the control of the Friends, but of the other branch; and while it gave their children the opportunity for being well taught, it was also open to the children of the neighborhood who were not identified with that society. For many years it served its purpose, and among the long list of teachers who gave instruction there, our townsman Judge Clayton Lippincott was one. As in the other schools, a solid common school education according to the old standards was the kind of education obtainable here. A good start up the hill of learning was given, but the climb to the upper part of the hill was not attempted. In the later years of its existence the school was chiefly devoted to small scholars; and more than one of the pupils now in attendance at the High School has happy recollections of the summer days spent in the "little white school house," under the loving ministrations of the kind young teacher who presided there.

It was this little school that expanded into the present High School. When the proposition was made to establish a high-grade school, offering ample facilities for acquiring an advanced education in accordance with the standard now accepted, and by the use of methods now in use, the suggestion was not favorably considered by the older and more conservative of those in authority. They were not hostile to the standard or the methods, but they doubted the success of their application here and now. The younger and more progressive ones, however, were sanguine and persistent, and their enthusiasm carried the day. The High School was decided upon; and when that decision had once been reached the determination was fully shared by all to make the new departure an unqualified success.

The little old frame school house which had been a landmark for so many years was torn down, and its successor, the present High school building, was completed in 1880. This is a handsome two story brick structure, standing on the west side of Chester avenue, and the north side of Second street. The front is toward Chester avenue, but there is an entrance, also, on the western side of the building, for the male pupils, the eastern door being for the girls. The building contains five good sized schoolrooms, thoroughly lighted by ample windows.

The internal arrangements are convenient, and the ground surrounding the school house affords abundant room for the sport and exercise the young folks need. The seating capacity of the building is a hundred and fifty and this can be somewhat increased if necessary by altering the present seating arrangements.

The school has three departments—the Primary, Intermediate and Advanced. A Kindergarten is also conducted in one of the rooms of the building at present; but although it is under the control of the school committee, it is not properly a department of the High School, being a distinct institution. It will be removed from the building the present year and established in separate quarters elsewhere. It is probable that in the course of a year or so a building especially designed for the Kindergarten will be erected in the present school grounds. In the meantime the room now occupied by it in the school building will henceforth be added to the school accommodations.

The corps of instructors in the school comprises a Principal and, at present, three assistant teachers. Hereafter there will be four assistant teachers instead of three. Besides these there is a special teacher of drawing and painting who gives instruction at stated times; and there is also a special lecturer who visits the school from time to time and lectures to the pupils on subjects connected with their regular studies. The efforts of these instructors are made more effective by a well furnished library of reference-books, by maps and globes, philosophical and chemical apparatus, a cabinet of minerals, a skeleton, &c.

The pupils in the three departments of the school are arranged in eight classes, ranging from " G" class in the Primary department to the Senior class in which pupils leave the Advanced department and the school. The full course of study occupies eight years, and is arranged for the various classes as follows: G class; Number, Reading, Spelling, Object Lessons, Oral Geography, Writing, Drawing and Molding. F class; Arithmetic, Reading, Oral Geography, Spelling, Language Lessons, Writing, Drawing and Molding. E class; Arithmetic Reading, Geography, Language Lessons, Spelling, Writing, Drawing and Molding. D class; Arithmetic, Reading, Geography, Elements of Natural Philosophy, American History, Language Lessons, Spelling Writing, Drawing and Molding. C class; Arithmetic, Reading, Intermediate Geography, Physiology, American History, Spelling, Etymology, Grammar, Composition, Drawing and Writing. B class; Algebra, Arithmetic, American History, Physical Geography, Grammar, Reading, Etymology, Composition, Drawing and Writing. A class; Geometry, Algebra, Arithmetic, History of the World, Physics, Grammar, Latin or German, Elocution,

Composition, Literature, Drawing and Writing. Senior class; Geometry, Intellectual Philosophy, Higher Arithmetic, University Algebra, Literature, Geology, Astronomy, Latin or German, Painting or Perspective Drawing, and Elocution and Composition.

One of the purposes of the school, as set forth by its managers, is to prepare students intending to take a course in college; and arrangements have been made with the managers of Swarthmore College whereby pupils may enter the Freshman class without examination by presenting a certificate from the Principal of this school. Another purpose is to offer the best possible opportunities to those pupils who do not purpose pursuing the entire course of study. In fulfilment of this purpose a Special Department has been instituted, in which pupils are privileged to select studies in any of the classes, and pursue such separate branches as may seem desirable.

The school was opened October 8th, 1880, with Miss Annie Caley, now Mrs. Doran, as the first Principal. She served as Principal for two years, when she resigned the position and was succeeded by Mr. George E. Megarge, who has since been, and still is the Principal. The assistant teachers at the present time are Miss Mary Willets, A. B., Miss Emma S. Pyle and Miss Ida Bonner. Miss Rachel L. Rogers is the Kindergartner, with Miss Sarah H.

Wilson as assistant. Miss Virginia Kaler is the teacher of drawing and painting. The present attendance at the school, including the Kindergar- is one hundred and twenty-five.

The Academy is under the charge of the Orthodox Friends; the High School is under the direction of the other branch of the society. A committee appointed by the Chester Preparative Meeting has direct supervision of it. The committee is at present composed as follows: John M. Lippincott, William Dunn Rogers, John S. Collins, Samuel C. DeCou, Joshua R. Evans, Levi L. Lippincott, Thomas D. Holmes, Martha DeCou, Sarah L. Holmes, Lydia L. Rogers, Emily H. Atkinson, Rachel A. Collins, Sarah R. Sullivan, Hannah B. Lippincott.

The High School and the Academy are both largely patronized by those who are not members of either Friends' Meeeting, but who are glad to have for their children the very liberal educational advantages offered by those institutions.

Chapter XIV.

Societies and Institutions.

ASSOCIATION is the key-note of modern life. It had a good deal to do with ancient life too, for that matter, but it is pre-eminently characteristic of our affairs to-day. Whether or not it is the American idea of union carried out to its extreme result, there certainly seems to be a general acceptance of the doctrine enunciated by a certain statesman when the Declaration of Independence was under discussion: "We must all hang together—or else we will all hang separately." Pretty much everything is done in partnership. Organized labor confronts organized capital; organized tourists are "personally conducted" through Europe by the agents of organized excursion makers; and things have got to such a pass now that in some places the school boys have organized syndicates to resist the encroachments of organized learning.

Moorestown is not greatly under the influence of this particular spirit of the age. There is no all-controlling syndicate here; the Knights of Labor are not a power, and I have never heard of a strike or lockout in the place. Organization here is not aggressive, and it is not defensive. It is harmonious and has only peaceful intentions; but there is a good deal of it. The principle of association is fully recognized, and there are a goodly number of societies and institutions here in which the idea finds a variety of practical expressions. There are literary, financial, beneficial, class and reformatory organizations. Some of them take the form of secret societies, and some take the public fully into their confidence; all have a distinct purpose to accomplish and are in earnest about achieving it. A very notable example of what could be done in this direction in times past was afforded by

THE MOORESTOWN LITERARY ASSOCIATION.— This organization no longer exists; but a quarter of a century ago it was a power and a resource. In looking back at what it was and what it achieved we cannot but lament that it has gone and left no fitting successor. The regret is tempered by the hope that its successor will yet appear; and the success of the old society, continued through a term of years, is an assurance that the new one will not lack for encouragement. What was true then is undoubtedly true now: The community is ready to welcome and support the best that can be offered it.

About the year 1854 a number of the prominent and public spirited men of the place set about devising ways and means to supply a manifest and widely felt deficiency in the social and intellectual life of the community. This deficiency existed in the fact that there was here no adequate means of suitable recreation for the people of the village and vicinity. There was no railroad, and a visit to Philadelphia for an evening's entertainment or profit was out of the question. The people must have their pleasure brought to them or they must go without it. Realizing this necessity the group of men alluded to undertook to meet it in the best way, and with this purpose organized the Moorestown Literary Association, which had for its object the furnishing of winter courses of good lectures to the people of Moorestown.

The association was made up of good material. Such men as Dr. J. J. Spencer, Rev. H. H. Weld, rector of the Episcopal Church, Rev. Dr. Fendall, pastor of the Baptist Church, Mr. Edward Harris, Mr. Israel Heulings, Mr. John W. Buzby and Dr. N. N. Stokes, composed the membership. Mr. Heulings was President of the society; and Dr. Stokes, then quite a young man and but recently established in practice here, was the Secretary. The list of members comprised other names which I have not now at hand, but these fairly indicate the quality of the material which composed it. Rev. Dr. Fendall, Rev. Mr. Weld, Drs. Spencer and Stokes and Mr. Harris were chosen as the Lecture

Committee, and carried their work through with energy and enthusiasm.

Before inviting the public to attend a course of lectures it was necessary to provide a place in which lecturer and people might meet. There was no public hall constructed with reference to lectures, concerts and other popular entertainments. There was only the little township building, and that was neither large enough, nor adapted otherwise to the to the purpose in contemplation. In the emergency the hall in the third story of Burr's store building was rented and fitted up as a lecture-room. To this room the community was invited to listen to good lectures; and the invitation was accepted with an enthusiasm that fully vindicated the wisdom of those who had assumed that a demand always exists for what is good. Every week during the season a lecture was delivered in the extemporized hall, and every week during the season a crowded audience gathered there to listen to it. An audience of four hundred people would be considered a pretty fair-sized one for a place of Mooretown's present size, but that number of people frequently assembled in the lecture room here a quarter of a century ago.

So hearty was the appreciation of the opportunity offered for hearing good things that the people used to drive into the village every lecture night from homes that were several miles out in the country, and then drive back again when the lecture was over. Under the starlight or under the clouds the people came to the lectures. And they listened to many a good man who had something to say that was worth the saying. Bishop Stevens was one of the lecturers, and Judge Kelley was another. They came season after season; and so did Rev. A. A. Willetts, who was a favorite here as every where else. Dr. Isaac Hayes, of Arctic fame warmed the Moorestown winter by detailing experiences that were so much colder. Isaac Hazelhurst, Esq., J. Wheaton Smith and President Allen of Girard College were some among the many good lecturers to whom the people listened on these memorable evenings.

The tribulations of the lecture committee were by no means ended when their hall had been secured and their lecture engagements made. The winter is the lecture season, and committees with a full command of railroad facilities know that there is apt to be a slip 'twixt a winter engagement and the fulfilment of it. A snow-blockade makes even an express train on a trunk line uncertain in its connections. What then must have been the cares, labors and anxieties of our committee, under the necessity of getting their lecturers here over country roads, by stage, or by private conveyance. Sometimes, in spite of the utmost efforts, there was disappointment. This was not often the case, however, and altogether the enterprise flourished greatly.

For three winters the lectures were delivered in the room over the store, but the necessity for a more commodious and more accessible place was strongly felt by the association The township building on the Main street was in a capital location, but it was too small, and moreover was under the control of the Township Committee for exclusively township puposes. Negotiations were opened between the association and the township authorities with the result that the association became joint proprietors with the township of the little brick building. Then the association issued stock and effected an improvement that was notable in its day. An addition was made at the rear of the building by which the size of the Town Hall (as it had now become) was exactly doubled. A platform was constructed, seats were put in, and Moorestown Town Hall in its new elegance was considered a decided credit to the place. Pipes were laid from the residence of Mr. Harris, and for a time at least, the new building was lighted with gas from his private gas machine.

The arragement with the township authorities left them the use of the hall for all township purposes, and the new partners had it for lectures and other purposes as they might desire. The joint proprietorship still exists, and the stockholders meet semi-occasionally to look after the state of their investment and declare or pass a dividend, as the case may be. It was in 1856 or 1857 that the new hall was opened for lectures, and the success that had attended the efforts of the association in their third story room followed them to their new quarters, and continued unabated until the final extinguishment of the enterprise in other and more intensely absorbing interests. The last course of lectures was in the winter of 1860—'61. Before another came the war had begun its strenuous discourse, and people were too intent on that to listen to literary lectures.

The Moorestown Literary Association is dead, and from its ashes no successor has yet sprung up. It is to be hoped the succession will not be long delayed. The opportunity is as ripe now as then, waiting only for the right men to pluck it. When they appear they will surely find as great a success following their endeavors as their predecessors had. Good lectures, concerts and scientific entertainments would certainly be as heartily welcomed now as before the war.

THE FRIENDS' LIBRARY.—An institution based on the same idea as that which formed the foundation of the Literary Association, is the Friends' Public Library. Happily, unlike the other, it is still in existence, and is advancing year by year to a higher standard of prosperity. Perhaps one reason for the difference is that the Library is exclusively in the hands of women, and it requires something more upsetting than a war to overturn a woman's purpose. At all events the Library survived the war, and has continued to go on from good to better, until, from a feeble beginning it has attained a sturdy maturity.

It was in 1853 that the Library was instituted. The necessity for a collection of good books accessible to the public was as strongly felt as the necessity for public lectures. This was a reading community and good books were always in demand. But so many books worth the reading were put forth every year that no private collection could compass them all, or even the best of them. Moreover there were here, as in every community, a very large proportion of appreciative readers who ardently desired the best but were able to buy but very little of it. If the people could have the opportunity, by the payment of a small sum each year, of reading some of the best literature and then putting the volumes back on the shelves for somebody else to read, they would gladly avail themselves of it. That was the reasoning in the minds of those who suggested and planned the Library; and the wisdom of their reasoning has been shown by the result.

They were convinced that the experiment was worth trying, at all events, and on the 15th of March, 1853, they began to put their convictions into practise. On that day the first meeting to consider the founding of the library was held in the old stone school house which now forms a portion of the Academy building. An adjourned meeting was held on the 27th of the same month, and at this meeting the enterprise was fully decided upon. A constitution which had been drawn up in the meantime, was presented, and after due consideration was finally adopted. The association formed was named the "Moorestown Library Association of Friends," and the experiment was fairly under way.

Joseph W. Lippincott was the first Secretary; and if he had very much to do it was not because the library under his charge was a big one. When first opened to the public the library had on its shelves about one hundred and twenty volumes. Donations of books had been received from Dr. Joseph Warrington, James S. Lippincott and some others in Moorestown; and thirty-seven volumes of Friends works had been received from one of the Friends' Meetings in Philadelphia. These last have always been loaned free of charge to any who might apply for them. The use of all the other books, of course, had to be paid for by those enjoying the privileges; but the charge has been, and remains, so very moderate that it is not felt as a burden.

The Association was formed and it had the books to start with; but like the Literary Association with its lectures, it must have a place to put them. It had no library building, and the erection of one was an idea it could not entertain for a moment at that stage of its progress. A ready made place must be found, and arrangements were made for placing the volumes in an up-stairs room in the store building of Haines and Buzby, which stood on the ground now occupied by the Brown Bros.' store. There was the first abiding place of the Friends' Library; and Mr. John W. Buzby, one of proprietors of the store, who a little later became one of the active members of the Literary Association, was the first Librarian.

In the years that have passed since then the Library has been to some extent a migratory itstitution, but its migrations have always been to better and more accessible quarters. After a considerable time spent in its old home it was removed to Howard Leed's jewelry shop, the proprietor acting as Librarian. Here it tarried for a time, and then was removed the millinery shop of Angela Adams, that lady in her turn acting as Librarian. After an interval it was again removed, this time to the millinery shop of Sarah Davis, who became Librarian. In these four places the Library spent twenty-six years. Finally, in 1879, it made its last change of place up to the present time. The Academy Building had been constructed in the Meeting House enclosure, and in the front room on the left of the entrance hall of this building, the Library was placed at the time mentioned, and there it still remains.

Great advantages were secured by this last removal. A room more suitable in its location and arrangement than any heretofore occupied was obtained; the expense of paying rent was obviated, and the further expense of paying for a Librarian's services was avoided. Under the present arrangement, each of the six lady managers of the institution acts as Librarian during two months of the year; and as their services are given gratuitously, every cent of revenue can be, and is, applied to the purchase of new books. Favorable as the present location is, however, the promoters of the enterprise are not yet fully satisfied. Their ambition now is to have the Library placed in a building placed in a building of its own; a building especially constructed and arranged for its accommodation. This will no doubt be accomplished in the course of time. Meanwhile things are very well as they are now, even if the ambition mentioned should never accomplish its purpose.

During the years that have passed since the first books were placed on its shelves there has been a gradual and steady increase in the number of volumes, until now the Library contains about eight hundred and fifty books. Each year of late between fifty and sixty works have been added to the catalogue. Last year (1885) nine hundred and and nineteen volumes were taken out by subscribers and casual readers. A clause in the constitution adopted in 1853 provides that "no novels, romances, or any works of an immoral tendency, or which derogate from the principles of the Christian religion shall be placed in the Library." This condition has always been strictly observed, and no work of fiction—with the single exception, I believe, of "Uncle Tom's Cabin"—is to be obtained here. But then, as one of the managers explains, " fiction can be obtained anywhere; and it seems best to spend the little money we have on something else." Happily there is a vast amount of good reading that is not fiction, and a great variety of this may be found on the shelves of the Library. Standard works of poetry, travels, science, biography and history (the constitutional clause not having been construed to forbid the kind of fiction that is often pressed between the covers of an historical volume) are here, and year by year some of the best new books are added.

The Library is open two afternoons in the week, with one of the managers in attendance. Annual subscribers, by the payment of a very moderate fee each year, are entitled to the free use of the books, and those who are not subscribers can have the reading of any book for two weeks for the sum of five cents per volume. The present managers of this excellent institution are Esther Robers, Martha E. Stokes, Sally Ann Kaighn, Mary W. Stokes, Rebecca Matlack, Mary C. Roberts and Sarah S. Carter. The Secretary is Esther Roberts, and the Treasurer Mary W. Stokes.

MOORESTOWN NATIONAL BANK.—One of the most recent additions to the institutions of Moorestown is, in its way, one of the most important. It does not deal in literature, except to a very limited extent; but without the matter that it does deal in, libraries would be but places of emptiness, and lecture committees would strive in vain to entice the public. It deals in money, and is a bank.

One highly gratified old citizen exclaimed, when the bank was opened: "It took Moorestown two hundred years to build a bank, and I hope it will take longer than that to tumble it down." Moorestown was not trying, through all of her two hundred years, to establish such an institution; but the effort had certainly been repeatedly made, and made in vain, a good many years before the endeavor that succeeded. It was Rev. James H. Lamb, the Episcopal clergyman, who actively began and pushed forward this last movement, and he was met by the discouraging assurance, from one after another of the prominent citizens whom he approached: "It can't be done. We found that out thirty years ago." Gradually, however, he brought them to realize that this effort was being made now thirty years after the one that had discouraged them. Then they began to think that it might succeed, and soon they were convinced that success was possible. This conviction made success certain; for all that was needed was to overcome the inertia. This done, rapidly accelerated motion was soon attained. The rate of progress was a sore surprise to some of the old conservatives. When asked to take stock they laughed and said they would subscribe the next year. To the next invitation they responded that they would "see about it Christmas." Before Christmas they had concluded that it would be as well not to wait any longer, and were astonished to have their applications for shares met with the assurance that every dollar had been sold. They bought shares, but had to pay a premium.

The agitation of the bank enterprise was begun early in the summer of 1885, and at first, as I have said, the general response to the idea was not enthusiastic. Everybody recognized the desirability of such an institution as was proposed, but "the place would not support it," was the fear expressed. Persistent argument bore down this kind of opposition (the only kind that was encountered) and sufficient co-operation was secured to put the project in proper form to present to the public. A call was issued for a public meeting, and at the meeting a still further advance was made toward success.

In a very little while the establishment of the bank became a certainty, and there was no trouble in raising all the money that was needed. In fact, before the final allotment of stock was made it was was necessary to refuse the applications of many who wished to purchase shares, and as has already been said, some who decided, in their half-skepticism "to wait until Christmas," bought shares at a premium before the summer was ended. The Bank Charter was obtained July 23d, 1885.

On the 30th of July a meeting of the stockholders was called. By that time the tide had set strongly in the direction of success. There was enthusiasm in the public mind, and the people already spoke of "our bank" as an accomplished fact that everybody had a right to be proud of it. Those who were not stockholders wished they were; and those were stockholders congratulated themselves on their good fortune. At the stockholders' meeting a permanent organization was effected by the election of the following directors: Clayton Lippincott, William M. Paul, William Parry, Henry W. Doughten, N. Newlin Stokes, M. D., Alfred H. Burr, John C. Hopkins, David D. Griscom and Josiah Lippincott.

At a subsequent meeting of the directors Judge Clayton Lippincott was elected President of the Bank, William M. Paul, Vice President, and William W. Stokes, Cashier. It was also resolved to erect a suitable building for the bank as soon as it could be effected. To find a suitable location for the building was the next thing in order, and a number of available properties were inspected and their merits and demerits considered. Finally it was decided to purchase the ground on which the work-shop of Mr. James Sankey stood, between his residence and that of the Misses Slim on Main street. The purchase was made, the old building— one of the ancient landmarks of the place—removed and work on the bank building was commenced September 21st, 1885.

In the meantime a room was secured in the residence of Mrs. E. A. Jones, near the site of the Bank. This was appropriately fitted up with Bank appliances, and here the Moorestown National Bank established itself temporarily, until such time as it could take possession of its own proper quarters, having been authorized by the Comptroller of Currency to commence business Aug. 31. It opened for business September 14th 1885. From the first day the business it transacted showed that those who had insisted that Moorestown wanted a bank had reckoned wisely. It showed, too, that Moorestown, conservative though it may be, is quite ready to welcome an innovation of the right sort, if the innovators have the pluck and persistency to carry their point and take the chances. The first day's deposits amounted to $3,266.47. The second day's business was still larger. The first statement was called for by the Comptroller October 1st, two weeks after opening, and showed loans and discounts amounting to $30,172, and deposits amounting to $33,073.87. Statements since then have shown deposits of over $100,000.

The Bank building was to have been completed by January 1st, 1886; but there were various delays which prevented this, and it was not ready for occupation until March. On Saturday, March 6th, the new building was formally taken possession of. The place was open for the inspection of the public on that day, and the public freely availed itself of its privilege. All day visitors thronged the building and the officers and directors were kept busy pointing out and explaining the various features. The location is a very favorable one; on the South side of Main street, and in the heart of the business portion of the town, it is convenient of access to all having business to transact there. On the following Monday Mrs. Jones' room was vacated, and business began in the new place.

The building itself has a frontage of 27 feet, and is 49 feet 6 inches deep. It is built of red brick, with stone basement walls. It is a plain, solid looking structure, without architectural pretensions. The front part is occupied by the banking room, which occupies the full height of the building. The room is well lighted and admirably arranged. Back of this is the depositors' room, and back of this again, the Directors' room. This is a room so cosy in its comfortable appointments, and so charming in its outlook over the Southern valley that to have a Board meeting every day would be a very natural desire on the part of the Directors. The remainder of the first floor is occupied by the safe-deposit vault.

This is a construction that fully justifies its name, and combines the most recent and effective appliances for repelling the effects of fire and the attacks of burglars. The foundation of the vault is of solid brick work, and contains 20,000 bricks. It is commenced a foot below the cellar floor, and is seven feet high, thirteen feet eight inches long, and ten feet six inches deep. The top of this brick foundation is entirely covered with large six-inch flag-stones. It will readily be seen that the attempt to tunnel through all this masonry would be somewhat discouraging. On this is set the vault, weighing twenty-two tons. At the sides and back of this there are three feet of solid masonry, and on top there are flag-stones again, like those below. It would be a tolerably safe place of deposit even if there were no iron or steel about it.

But there are iron and steel. The vault, or safe proper, is made of the best chrome steel and iron, metal so densely hard that the ordinary tools for working iron have almost no effect upon it, and the most finely tempered tools can be made to drill through only about half an inch of it in eight hours. The outside door of the safe weighs 4,300 pounds. Beyond this are the vestibule doors, and all are fitted with such an array of time and combination locks, and obstinate bolts that even honest men cannot get into the safe except at the right time; if a burglar, skilled in his profession and armed with the best tools of his craft—and unhappily the burglars have about the most scientific and effective that are going—were to begin work there on Saturday night, by the time Monday morning came he would have come to the conclusion that honesty was the best policy, would have given up the job and gone somewhere to rest.

Within all these safe-guards are the safe for the bank's funds, and the safe-deposit boxes. These last are one hundred and seventy-two in number, and furnish an excellent resource for those who have papers and other valuables which they want kept absolutely out of harm's way. Each box requires two keys to unlock it—the renter's key, and the master key of the cashier. Moreover no key will unlock any lock but its own. This department of the bank has also been thoroughly appreciated by the community, and the deposit boxes were readily rented from the first.

The officers of the bank are three in number: William W. Stokes, cashier; Joseph Lippincott, teller; and Charles W. Stokes, son of the cashier, assistant teller. Mr. Stokes came here from Medford to accept the position of cashier, and has had experience which fits him thoroughly for the place. Mr. Lippincott represents a well known Moorestown family.

WOMEN'S CHRISTIAN TEMPERANCE UNION.—Every reformatory movement is in its nature distinctly aggressive. The Women's Christian Temperance Union is exclusively reformatory in its character. It has an active and powerful existence in Moorestown; and therefore necessitates a modification of the statement that the organizations existing here were neither aggressive nor defensive. For a time past few interests have challenged a larger share of public attention here than the quietly aggressive work of this association. The cabalistic letters "W. C. T. U." meet the eye in the columns of the newspaper, on the posted hand-bill, on the sign of a reading room, and even on the sides of fire-buckets hung up ready for use. The name strikes the ear as frequently as the eye, and the purposes and achievements of the Union are the topic of no small amount of conversation. Weekly meetings are held, lectures are delivered, pledges and petitions are circulated and personal visitations are made, and so the interest in the work in hand is kept constantly awake.

The W. C. T. U. did not begin the temperance agitation here. That ante-dates the organization of the Union by many years; but it may be doubted if the cause of temperance reform was ever before so actively and generally labored for in Moorestown, or with such strongly marked effect as during the past year. Ladies of all Christian denominations have taken a zealous and enthusiastic part in the work, and they have had the hearty co-operation of a large portion of the men. They have not by any means contented themselves with exhortation and the distribution of tracts. They have gone systematically to work to curtail the liquor traffic under the law, and also to lessen its allurements by providing a recreative resort where liquor is not an accompaniament; and also by providing accommodations for the traveling public where liquor is not to be found.

In the latter part of January, 1886, the young men forming a class in the Friends' First-Day school invited Major Scott to visit Moorestown and deliver four temperance lectures here. He came, accompanied by his wife, and delivered the four lectures to large and interested audiences. In the meantime Mrs. Scott was moving to organize here a branch of the Women's Christian Temperance Union. A meeting for the purpose was held in the Baptist Church, but without finishing the work adjourned to meet in the lecture room of the Episcopal Church on the following Monday evening, February 1st. This meeting was largely attended, and the branch Union was organized, with an energetic and enthusiastic membership, composed of women who were fully in earnest for the work they had undertaken, and prepared to prosecute it to the utmost.

The first meeting of the newly organized Union was held in the parlor of Mrs. Edward Sutton, on Second street, on the afternoon of Friday, February 5th. After that meetings were held every Tuesday afternoon in the Friends' High School building on Second street. The society rented the room the Bank had occupied in Mrs. Jones' residence on Main street, and began their occupation of it March 23d. For a time after this they continued to hold meetings in the High School building once a month, but now all their meetings are held in their own room. They meet there every Tuesday afternoon and transact such business as they have on hand.

The membership of the Union has steadily increased since its organization, and now numbers about one hundred. Mrs. Edward Sutton is the President, Miss Mary Wilson, Recording Secretary, Mrs. H. Hartranft, Corresponding Secretary, and Miss Katie Aitken Treasurer. There is a Vice-President from each religious body in the place. Indeed the organization justifies its name by being thoroughly a union of Christian women of all denominations.

The work and the enthusiasm for it are not by any means confined to the women. To them belongs the credit of organizing and systematizing the labor in which both men and women have a zealous interest; and in their efforts they have won, as is the wont of women everywhere and always, the hearty co-operation of earnest and capable men of all denominations and various walks of life. The children, also, have entered into the spirit of the thing. A Band of Hope has been organized which numbers now one hundred and forty-four members, and the roll of membership is lengthening.

A logical and legitimate part of the work undertaken by the members of the Union and their co-workers was to formally protest against the granting of licenses for the sale of intoxicating liquors in the place. They meant that their protest should be not only formal but effective if they could make it so. A remonstrance against the granting of licenses, addressed to the Common Pleas Court, was prepared and circulated among the voters of the town by the ladies of the Union. When the remonstrance was presented in court it bore over four hundred signatures.

Remonstrating was not all that was to be done, however. If taverns with bars were to be successfully protested against, an equivalent without a bar must be provided; for the court fully recognizes the necessity for a place of public entertainment in the town, and if there is no such place without a bar the court will accept the assurance that the place *with* a bar is necessary. Therefore a temperance house must be provided. Overtures were made for the purchase of each of the established hotels, with a view to making a temperance house of it, but in each case the negotiations were ineffectual. Efforts were then made in a new direction, and in a short time arrangements had been made by which not one, but three temperance houses for the accommodation of travellers or permanent boarders were assured. The applications, duly signed, for the license of these three houses were presented in court before the remonstrance against the liquor license, and the licenses were granted. The two old hotels were also licensed again, in spite of the remonstrance.

The temperance house question had been solved in a manner to meet the present emergency, but the solution was not yet satisfactory as a permanent settlement of the matter. Accordingly it was energetically pushed still further. It was decided that Moorestown should have a fully equipped Temperance Hotel—one that should compete on at least equal terms as to convenience of location and completeness of accommodations for guests, with the houses that kept bars. Accordingly the subscription that had already been started was continued. It was liberally responded to, and in a short time a sufficient sum had been subscribed to lead to the anticipation of a regular temperance hotel here before the time comes to send in the next application for license.

So much for one branch of the work done by the Women's Christian Temperance Union, with the aid of the equally earnest men who have co-operated. In addition the Union has established a Free Reading Room. This is the room temporarily occupied by the Bank in the house of Mrs. Edith Jones, on Main street. The apartment is comfortably fitted up so as to constitute a cosy and inviting resort. On the book shelves are a number of good, readable books, and the number is increasing through private donations. Magazines and illustrated papers are on the shelves and on the tables. The Philadelphia daily papers, both morning and evening, are placed on file as soon as received each day. Writing utensils are conveniently placed. Those who relish a game of chess, checkers or backgammon can gratify their desire by using the handsome boards placed at their disposal; and those who merely wish to sit and rest or talk, can have the fullest opportunity of doing so. The room is open all day and every evening, and a cordial invitation is extended to all to come and make use of its resources and opportunities. It is a good place for a quiet hour of reading or writing and it is a good place for a social chat.

THE PURSUING AND DETECTIVE COMPANY.—Another organization that is both aggressive and defensive in its character, but always in behalf of the public welfare, is the Moorestown Pursuing and Detective Company. It has for its object, as stated in its charter, "the detection, arrest and prosecution of burglars, horse-thieves and other depredators; and the recovery of stolen property." It is a kind of modified vigilance committee, perfectly law-abiding, and acting as one of the instruments of the law. It is also, to some extent, an insurance company, paying within certain limits of value for the property stolen from members and not recovered. It is not difficult to realize how important a field of usefulness is open to an organization of this kind in a rural community; and this one has done a vast amount of good by its energetic and well-directed efforts. The very knowledge of its existence and efficiency is in itself a protection to a greater or less extent.

The company was organized February 6th, 1875, and was incorporated by the Legislature, by an act approved March 25th, 1875. The incorporators were Levi Ballinger, Levi L. Walton, Joshua Hollinshead, Nathan S. Roberts, Eli Sharpiess, William Dunn Rogers, Charles Collins, Samuel C. DeCou, Samuel Brown, Josiah Lippincott, William Dyer, J. Willits Worthington and Josiah D. Pancoast. The first officers were Charles Collins, President; Frank

Garrigues, Secretary and Treasurer; J. Willits Worthington, Corresponding Secretary; and the above named incorporators as a Board of Directors.

The constitution of the company provides that its officers shall consist of a President, Secretary, Treasurer, thirteen Directors and a Correspondent, to be annually chosen by ballot at a general meeting of the company, said officers to continue in office for one year, or until their successors are elected. The offices of Secretary and Treasurer may be held by the same person, as they are now and have been ever since the company was organized. The Board of Directors are authorized to appoint or elect any number, not exceeding twenty, of detectives, or pursuers, and give to each a badge of office. The full number—twenty—are appointed each year. They are selected from the members of the company, the selection being governed by the fitness of the person named for the work imposed upon him; care being taken also to apportion the membership of the pursuing force as evenly as may be over the territory under the company's jurisdiction.

Each pursuer has the power and authority of a constable, so far as it may be necessary to carry out the objects of the company, and may execute warrants for that purpose, issued by justices of the peace and aldermen. While having the authority, they are also held liable to the responsibilities of constables in the exercise of their power, except that they are not liable to perform constables' services save as directed by the by-laws of the company. They are not entitled to any fees or compensation except out of the company's funds. Under the by-laws each pursuer is entitled to four cents per mile, going and coming, as his mileage when in pursuit, and is to have other necessary expense paid, as a majority of the Directors may deem reasonable.

The funds of the company are provided by a system of membership fees, fines, etc. Each member, at the time of admission, pays into the treasury one dollar; and at each annual meeting thereafter he is required to pay a like amount, unless it shall be decided at the annual meeting that the annual dues shall be increased or diminished. Members who do not attend the meetings in time to pay their dues are liable to a fine of twenty-five cents unless excused. Each director and pursuer neglecting or refusing to perform the services required of him under the by-laws is required to pay a fine of five dollars into the treasury. The constitution also empowers the company to increase the fund, if necessary, by assessment levied on the members; and the fees, fines and assessments may be recovered by suit, brought in the name of the company, the same as any other debts of like amount. The annual meetings are held on the first Saturday in

January each year. One o'clock in the afternoon is the hour of meeting. Special meetings may be called by the company or the Board of Directors whenever they may be deemed necessary; and the President has power to convene the Board of Directors at any time in the interest of the company.

The company does not undertake to look after any property except that stolen from members, and its interests lie within a radius of six miles from Moorestown, as any person living beyond that distance is not eligible for membership, and any member removing beyond that limit forfeits his place in the company. A member is required to keep a written description of all the horses and mules he may own, specifying all marks and characteristics by which they may be recognized. Wilful neglect to do this precludes any assistance being given by the company in recovering such animals in case they are stolen. Any member who has had property to the amount of five dollars stolen is required to notify a Director of the fact, and also to give any information in his power respecting the theft and the supposed guilty parties. If such notification is not made within ten days of the discovery of the theft the member forfeits all rights to the protection and property of the company, and his name is dropped from the rolls.

As soon as he is notified by a member of loss sustained, a Director is required to take immediate action, such as he may deem best. Ordinarily the action taken is to call out the pursuer or pursuers nearest to the despoiled member; but he can call all the Directors together for consultation if he thinks such a course necessary. Three of the Directors are a sufficient number to offer any reward, payable out of the treasury of the company, for the arrest of a depredator or the return of stolen property. A pursuer, on being called upon, must at once set to work in his capacity of detective and arresting officer, and use his best endeavors to recover the stolen property and arrest the guilty parties. It is not always convenient, of course, and it is never very pleasant, but he cannot yield to such considerations; he must at once leave his own interests and go whenever and wherever he is ordered to go by one of the Directors. Any member who has been selected as a pursuer must take the necessary affirmation and secure his badge within ten days of his appointment unless excused for good reasons. If he fails to do so, through neglect, or repugnance to the work involved, his name is dropped from the company's rolls.

After all reasonable efforts have been made to recover the property stolen from a member it becomes the duty of the Directors to pay the losing member a certain proportion of his loss. This payment, however, is conditioned on several observances. The owner of the stolen property must be clear on the Treasurer's books at the time of the theft; the stolen property must not be covered by any insurance company that protects property from theft; the member whose property has been taken must have informed one of the Directors of the theft within twenty-four hours of the discovery of his loss, and an application containing an itemized list of the stolen property shall have been presented to the Board of Directors on oath or affirmation on or before the 31st day of December of the year in which the loss occurred. These conditions being fulfilled the Directors assess the valuation of the stolen property and pay the loser a sum equivalent to two thirds of such valnation, provided that the amount to be paid shall not exceed two hundred dollars for a horse, or four hundred dollars for "any and all property that may be stolen from a member at any one time."

The company is a potent agency in the cause of good order and good morals. In the pursuit of evil-doers its constabulary force are empowered to prosecute their work in adjoining counties; and so its power for achieving good results is not restricted. The good work it has done has brought it more and more into favor with law-abiding citizens, and its membership has correspondingly increased. At the present time there are about two hundred members. The list of officers is as follows: President, William Dunn Rogers; Secretary and Treasurer,

Frank Garrigues; Correspondent, Benjamin H. Gillingham; Directors, William Dunn Rogers, Benjamin H. Gillingham, Charles Andrews, John B. Warrick, Joseph H. Cole, Charles Collins, Samuel L. Burrough, Samuel S. Huston, William Dyer, John R. Mason, William T. Lippincott, William R. Lippincott, of Cinnaminson, Frank Garrigues.

MOORESTOWN AGRICULTURAL AND INDUSTRIAL ASSOCIATION.—In an agricultural community there is almost no institution that exerts a stronger influence for material good than the agricultural society in one or another of its modifications. It arouses new interest in the business of life. Its annual exhibitions give a chance for comparing different methods, and for rubbing ideas together. The competition gives a new zest to the work that may result in triumph; and the effort to find the best way is sure to result in the discovery of some good way, even if it is not the best. Moreover, the yearly fair affords entertainment and recreation as effectively, in its way, as the opera, the theater, and the lecture in theirs. The general outcome is that the community is benefitted and does better work in a better way by reason of such organization.

The Moorestown Agricultural and Industrial Society was organized under the State laws, and incorporated in March, 1880. The purpose of its originators and promoters was to establish a society which should be purely local in its character and direct results, stimulating the agriculturists of this part of the county to the improvement of stock and farm products. This purpose has been successfully carried out. The farmers hereabouts, some of them at least, are progressive men, keenly alert to discover and try the best methods and accomplish the best results. Friendly rivalry and competition among such men is sure to effect something worth effecting. In giving the opportunity for such competition, and encouraging it, the association is undertaking and is fulfilling a most worthy mission.

The first Board of Directors of the association was composed of Levi Ballinger, William R. Lippincott, William Dunn Rogers, J. E. Watkins, S. C. Deacon, Josiah Lippincott, Howard Taylor, Thomas J. Beans, Joshua L. Haines, Clayton Conrow and Joseph H. Haines. The first officers chosen were: William Dunn Rogers, President; Howard G. Taylor, Vice-President; J. E. Watkins, Recording Secretary; Thomas J. Beans, Corresponding Secretary; Josiah Lippincott, Treasurer; T. J. Beans, W. D. Rogers, Levi Ballinger, Salmuel C. DeCou and H. G. Taylor, Executive Committee. The stock of the society was divided into four hundred shares, of $10 each. The annual meetings are held on the first Saturday in February in each year. The standard set up by the originators of the enterprise is indicated by an article in the constitution, which declares that "at the exhibitions of this society horse-racing, side shows, and all gambling institutions that tend to demoralize rather than elevate society will not be allowed or tolerated."

Of course an important feature of such an organization is the annual exhibition. The Moorestown Fair is held each spring and autumn, and is an event of interest to all classes of the population. In seeking for suitable grounds whereon to place their buildings and hold their exhibitions the members of the association were so fortunate as to secure a location that combined a large proportion of desirable qualifications. The convenience of the situation for both exhibitors and visitors especially commends it. The ground formed a part of the farm owned by Mrs. Mary Lippincott, whose boarding school was formerly so prominent an institution here. The enclosure is about seven acres in extent and is situated some distance East of the East Moorestown station. It is directly on the railroad, on the North side of the track. A station has lately been built almost at the gates of the grounds, and besides being so accessible by railroad it is equally so by driving roads. The fair grounds are surrounded by a substantial fence, and are well supplied with the necessary buildings. These are of a kind suitable for agricultural, horticultural, mechanical and stock exhibitions. The

Main Building was a donation from the Camden and Amboy Railroad Company, and was formerly the company's repair shop at Bordentown.

At the time this is written a railroad switch is about being constructed close to the grounds, so that all exhibits addressed to Fair Grounds Station can be taken on the cars directly to their place of destination. A steam engine, with shafting attached, furnishes motive power for machinery that depends upon that kind of power; and teams are provided by the society to run the horse-machinery at the trials held at the exhibitions. These trials of various kinds of agricultural machinery have already become events of recognized importance, and the Moorestown Exhibition has taken rank as an important machinery fair. Manufacturers, agents and purchasers acknowledge the fact and govern themselves accordingly.

Growers of small fruits are encouraged to make manifest here the best that can be done in their line, and the exhibitions uniformly attest the high excellence achieved by our local cultivators. The same is true of fruits in general. Garden vegetables are also given due importance in the offering of premiums at the fair, and this part of the exhibition is always of interest. The exhibition of plants and flowers is freely encouraged by the offer of premiums for professional and amateur displays. Dairy products hold an important place, of course;

and all results of farm industry, as well as the appliances for promoting it and obtaining the best returns, are exhibited in friendly and interesting rivalry.

The ladies are given an equal opportunity and encouragement by the institution of the Home Department. Premiums are offered for the most appetizing array of good things to eat; and the young girls are stimulated to do their best in the way of bread-baking. Then, to give a chance to those not included in any of the regularly scheduled classes, special premiums are offered for special kinds of work. Sometimes it is home-made dresses; sometimes a local map; sometimes one thing and sometimes another. By reason of the comprehensive range taken by the society it has established a hold on all classes in the community, and everybody takes a more or less personal interest in its progress and achievements.

The present officers of the society are as follows: President, Levi Ballinger; Vice-President, George L. Gillingham; Directors, Levi Ballinger, Josiah Lippincott, Chalkley B. Zelley, David Roberts, Samuel S. Huston, George T. Haines, Maurice B. Comfort, Benjamin H. Gillingham, Levi Rogers, Frank Garrigues, John M. Lippincott, Samuel L. Burrough, George L. Gillingham; Recording Secretary, Frank Garrigues; Corresponding Secretary, George T. Haines; Treasurer, John M. Lippincott;

Executive Committee, Benjamin H. Gillingham, Chalkley B. Zelley and John M. Lippincott.

THE CHESTER CLUB.—A private club, composed of private gentlemen, and organized for exclusively social purposes is not a legitimate subject for detailed public comment. The Chester club must be mentioned, however, as occupying a position unique among the institutions of Moorestown. It was organized January 1st, 1881, with the sole purpose of social intercourse and recreation. The rules governing the club are very strict. Liquor is rigidly banished from its quarters, and nothing in the semblance of gambling is tolerated. The means of recreation are abundant; and the idea of a high-class social club is put into practise.

The club room is located in the upper part of George Heaton's store, at the corner of Main street and Church Road. It is handsomely furnished, and is amply provided with the appliances of a pleasant reading room and place of recreative resort. The club numbers between twenty and thirty members.

SECRET SOCIETIES.—Of secret societies, beneficial and otherwise, there is a goodly representation here. The Odd Fellows—who came by their very peculiar name no man knows how, and who are no more odd than their fellow men—have two organizations here, an encampment and a lodge. Powhatan Encampment No. 30 has a present membership of over a hundred. The regular conclaves are held on the first and third Monday evening of each month in the hall in the upper part of E. B. Brown & Brother's store building. Pocahontas Lodge No. 107 holds its regular meetings in the same place on Thursday evening of each week. It has a large membership. A very considerable amount has been paid out in benefits to members and their families since the institution of the Lodge, and there is a goodly surplus now in the treasury.

The Order of United American Mechanics—the name for which the mystic letters "O. U. A. M." stand is represented here by two councils. They are the Chester Council and the Moorestown Council. Each has a large membership and both hold regular weekly meetings in the hall over Brown's store.

The Ancient Order of United Workmen also has an organization here, with a large membership; and the Improved Order of Red Men has a Tribe— Mineola Tribe No. 57—which now numbers something over a hundred members. The tribe was instituted in Masonville, and removed to Moorestown in 1883 or 1884.

There is a Grange here, strong in numbers and actively prosperous. Heretofore it has had its headquarters in a frame building on the South side of Main street a little way East of the Friends' Meeting Houses. Recently it purchased the property where the old blacksmith shop stood, on the

North side of Main street, East of George F. Doughten's store. On this property the Grangers are erecting a large brick building, the lower portion of which is to be occupied as a Grange store, and the upper part fitted up for a Grangers' Hall.

The Grand Army of the Republic has its representation in the E. D. Baker Post, which has its meeting hall over A. L. Brock's store on Main street West of Church Road. The Masons have not, as yet, any lodge here, but the establishment of one is now in contemplation.

Chapter XV.

The News of the Day.

IN his very charming "Back Log Studies" Charles Dudley Warner relates how, one day in the dead of winter, when he was snowbound and scant of resources, he discovered a daily newspaper and began the reading of it with keen pleasure. He read the news, foreign and domestic, and felt himself once more in contact with the active affairs of the world. The whole experience was eminently satisfactory until he chanced upon a paragraph announcing the death of a man in the streets of Boston the day before from sun-stroke. That seemed queer winter news, and the reader looked at the date of the paper. It had been published the previous summer! Immediately his satisfaction was changed to disgust, and he read no more of the stale news. What he had read had all been new to him, and was very interesting so long as he supposed the events described had just happened; but with the knowledge that they had happened last summer all interest in them vanished.

He was like all the rest of us; and the little incident he so pleasantly describes illustrates, for one thing, how retentively we read our newspapers. Last summer's news is quite fresh again by next winter, and the Associated Press would be tolerably safe in using year-old dispatches over again. But chiefly the incident emphasizes the universal passion for news. We all want to know what has happened, and are best pleased when there are a multitude of happenings to read or hear about. But that is not all. The events described may be of the utmost importance and interest, and revealed to us now for the first time; but unless they happened to-day, or yesterday at farthest, we have been swindled and are resentful. The news we have must be the news of the day.

The facilities a community enjoys for obtaining and distributing intelligence—for holding communication with the rest of the world—have come to be accepted as a pretty accurate gauge of its character and importance. The greater the number of mails that arrive and depart every day, the higher the rank of the town; if it has a telegraph office it advances an additional claim to respect; if it possesses a telephone exchange it is well abreast of the times; if it has all these and a newspaper besides, it is a place well worth living in. Moorestown fulfills all these conditions and is to be rated accordingly. The mails come and go with convenient frequency; telegraphic messages can be sent and received; telephonic conversations can be held, and the town has its own newspaper as well as such of the city dailies as the people desire.

THE POSTOFFICE.—The Postoffice is a comparatively modern institution in Moorestown. The old town had to wait a hundred years and more for it. So late as 1791 there were only six postoffices in the entire state of New Jersey, and none of them were in Burlington county. Moorestown had to wait until eleven years later than that date for the enjoyment of postal privileges. In the meantime it depended for its share of news on such means as are always in operation. Travelers brought frequent reports from the outside world; the memory of man goeth not back to the time when quilting parties or their equivalent did not exist; and there probably never was a community yet that did not have within its limits some of those mysteriously endowed people who always know everything that happens, and have special facilities for telling it.

Still the systematic and regularly organized machinery for the reception and distribution of outside intelligence was very desirable, and we may well believe that when the postoffice was established here, in the year 1802, it was cordially welcomed and made much of. The first postmaster was Isaac Wilkins, and he held his commission under Thomas Jefferson's administration. But where he established his office seems to be a thing past finding out. It is quite within the range of possibilities that he carried it about with him; for in those days pockets were large and the mails presumably small; and even now, according to report, there are postoffices established in very simply arranged cigar boxes and hat-crowns. It is supposed, however, that the first Moorestown postoffice was kept in a tavern on Main street below Church Road, but of this there is no certainty.

How long Isaac Wilkins served his neighbors as postmaster is not known. Neither is it known who was his successor, or how long he held the position. After a time (how long a time is uncertain) Gilbert Page assumed the duties and responsibilities of the postmastership. He lived on Main street, in the house now owned and occupied by Ebenezer Roberts, nearly opposite the William Penn Hotel. He had a store in one part of his residence, and here he kept the postoffice. We may safely conclude that the postal arrangements did not occupy much room, and that the affairs of the store were not seriously interfered with. When Mr. Page's term of office began, or under how many administrations he served are things unknown; but he was postmaster here for many years—so long, indeed, that going to Page's store for the mail became so much a matter of habit that, after the office was established elsewhere, people frequently walked past the new office up to Page's, from sheer force of custom, and then had to walk back again, from force of changed cirsumstances.

The postoffice passed out of Gilbert Page's hands into those of William Doughten, father of our townsman, George F. Doughten. Mr. Doughten was proprietor of the Washington Hotel, and to that place the office was removed, and there it remained for a term of years, for Mr. Page's successor held the position for a long time, as seems to have been quite the customary thing in those days. Changes of administration did not always bring about a change in the postoffice, but they did sometimes, and when Martin Van Buren succeeded Andrew Jackson in the Presidency there was a more or less general "rotation in office."

Among the events of the time was a change in the Moorestown postoffice. William Doughten was replaced in the position by William Collins. Mr. Collins was commissioned in 1839, by Postmaster General Amos Kendall. He removed the office to the building that stood where Brown's store now stands. A one-story brick building then occupied the site. It had formerly been a blacksmith shop, but had been remodelled into a store. Here Mr. Collins arranged his postoffice boxes. They were by no means so elaborate as they are now. There were no lock-boxes, no boxes for individual holders to rent—no glazed and numbered pigeon-holes at all. A large drawer was divided into compartments, these compartments were lettered in alphabetical order, and when the mail brought a letter for Mr. Smith it was put in the "S" box; if a letter came for Mr. Jones it was put in the "J" box, and so on.

The tenure of office had manifestedly become less fixed than it had hitherto been; for after Gen. Harrison took the Presidency in 1841 Mr. Collins relinquished the postmastership. His successor was George F. Doughten, son of Mr. Collins' immediate predecessor. Mr. Doughten removed the office to his store, and the people had to accustom themselves to seek their mail in East Moorestown, instead of the western and middle sections. But John Tyler succeeded Harrison in a month's time. The postoffice did not change hands so speedily as that, of course, but under Tyler there was a general readjustment, and after serving a year in the position Mr. Doughten was rotated out of office and Mr. Collins, whom he had replaced, was rotated in again and replaced him in turn; so that this gentleman had the rather unusual experience of being the successor in office of father and son consecutively. Mr. Collins received his second commission from President Tyler's Postmaster General in 1842, and continued in office until 1846, when President Polk's administration resulted in another change. He re-established the office in the quarters it had occupied during his first term, and retained it there until his second term was ended.

In 1846 Mr. Collins was succeeded in the postmastership by James Davis. Under the new administration the postoffice was again moved to other quarters, but to quarters that were not unfamiliar to it or the public. It went back once more to the building it had occupied when Gilbert Page was postmaster. Gilbert Page no longer kept the store there, however, but had been succeeded by Mr. Alfred Burr, who had previously been clerk in Page's store. Mr. Davis did not himself attend the office, but employed William W. Leeds as his deputy.

At the end of his official term Mr. Davis was succeeded by this same William Leeds, who had attended the office for him, and who retained the office through several terms, still retaining it in Burr's store. Mr. Leeds continued to hold the position until the beginning of President Lincoln's administration brought about a change in postmasterships, as in most other things. By this time Mr. Burr had erected his present store building on the North side of Main street. Elwood Stratton had kept a drug store in a small frame building that had previously occupied the site, and in the new building erected by Mr. Burr he still had accommodation. The building was arranged as it is now, with a drug-store beside the store kept by Mr.

Burr, and Mr. Stratton continued his business in that part of the building where Walter Reeve now has his drug-store.

Under President Lincoln Mr. Stratton was made postmaster, to succeed Mr. Leeds, and he established the postoffice in his drug-store; so it was still in Burr's building, and altogether Mr. Burr furnished postal accommodations for the town for a good many years. Mr. Stratton continued in office through the administration of Presidents Lincoln and Johnson, and through President Grant's first term. Then he was succeded by his son, Henry Stratton, who retained the office in the same place. He only held the office one year, or a little over.

On the 9th of December, 1874, J. Willetts Worthington was appointed postmaster. His commission was issued by Marshall Jewell, Postmaster General during President Grant's second term. Moving day had come again for the postoffice, and it was established in the new postmaster's drug-store, where it has ever since remained. Mr. Worthington at the beginning of his term arranged the box window and lock boxes as they are at present, and made adequate provisions for transacting the increased business of the office. He served during the remainder of Grant's administration, through the term of President Hayes, and through the tragically ended administration of President Garfield.

In July, 1882, the office was raised to the rank of a Presidential appointment, and Mr. Worthington was reappointed to the postmastership by President Arthur. His second commission bears date July 6th, 1882, and is signed with the autographs of Chester A. Arthur, President, and T. O. Howe, Postmaster General.

In the autumn of 1883 Mr. Worthington resigned the postmastership, his private business making it inconvenient for him to attend to official duties. His resignation took effect September 30th, 1883. Thomas M. Pancoast was appointed his successor, and on the 1st of October, 1883, assumed the duties of the position. President Cleveland on coming into office did not disturb the Moorestown postoffice, and Mr. Pancoast still remains in charge of it, to the satisfaction and advantage of the community.

This was made a money order office July 1st, 1869; and on July 1st, 1883, the first postal note was issued by the office. Three mails are received and three are sent out each day. Things have changed mightily since the time of Postmaster Wilkins; and if that public functionary could step into the postoffice to-day to see how things were going he would be sorely tumbled up and down in his mind at the revolution that has been effected. The box window would bewilder him; the number of letters to be handled would appal him; he would be helpless in the presence of a money order, and what on earth to do with a postage stamp would be a thing past finding out.

THE TELEGRAPH.—Wherever the railroad goes, there the telegraph is very sure to go also; and it is never very long in following, even if the wires and the rails do not come along at the same time. The lines of the Western Union Telegraph Company accompanied the railroad on its way through here; but the telegraph did not "stop off" here at first. When the West Moorestown station was established, however, in the early part of 1871, a telegraph office was one of the features of the new arrangement. Mr. Robert Stimus, the station agent, was the telegraph operator also, and he has continued to combine the duties of the two offices ever since.

The primary function of the telegraph station here is to do the necessary work of the railroad company; but in addition to that a large number of private messages are all the time received and sent; and messages received are very promptly delivered at their places of address. So the telegraph is an institution of great convenience to the public, notwithstanding the rather out-of-the-way location of the office. Efforts have been made from time to time to establish an office in a more central and convenient position, for the sole use of the public. The efforts have thus far been unsuccessful; but the desired improvement is only a question of time, and probably not a very long time. In the meantime the telegraph facilities as they now exist are a source of eminent satisfaction to the community.

THE NEWSPAPER.—This is a reading community, and always has been. The literature of the day is kept well in hand, and the magazines as well as the newspapers find a large circle of readers here. The newspapers in particular are liberally subscribed for, and the carrier of the news depot has a long list of subscribers to serve each day with the various Philadelphia dailies, while the postoffice distributes a fair share of the New York dailies and weeklies to the box holders. Not only does this apply to the village population, but the country all around is inhabited by reading people to whom the newspaper is as much a need as sugar for their coffee.

To such a community a newspaper of its own was a thing to be wished for, and to be cordially welcomed when it came. Come it did at last, although not until the opportunity for it had long been ripe. On the 10th day of December, 1879 the first number of the *Chronicle* was issued, with the announcement that it was to be a weekly paper of independent politics. The principal proprietor of the new enterprise was Mr. J. E. Watkins who had for some time been a resident of Moorestown. Mr. W. J. Lovell, a thorough practical printer, came here from Philadelphia to conduct the enterprise. At first the style of the firm was Watkins & Co. That title was retained for a little over a year and on January 1st, 1881, was changed to Watkins & Lovell, Mr. Lovell having taken an interest in the business. On the 18th of June, 1883 Mr. Watkins retired from the firm, Mr. Lovell becoming sole proprietor, as he has ever since remained.

For a time the paper led a wandering life, and circulated in two ways—among its subscribers, and from one publication office to another. It was first issued from a room in the lower part of Mr. James Sankey's old furniture shop—the building that stood on the site now occupied by the Bank building. Before the paper had been in existence three months a fire, caused by spontaneous combustion, broke out in the upper part of the old building, destroying the rear portion of it. Moorestown's volunteer department, with its hand engine, saved the rest of the building, but in the process pretty effectively deluged the newspaper office. The combined effects of fire and water rendered necessary a removal, and the *Chronicle* found temporary quarters in the building owned by Mr. George F. Doughten, now occupied by Worrel's plumbing shop, above Chester avenue. It remained here a few weeks, and then removed to the upper part of what was then A. W. Deacon's store, and is now Charles Evans' flour and feed store. An outside stairway was constructed to give access to the office. This location was not so favorable as could be desired, and after a few months spent there the office was again removed, this time to the upper part of the Post Office building. The business of the newspaper, and the job office connected therewith, speedily grew to such proportions that steam power and manifold other improvements became necessary, to supersede the simpler mechanism with which the work had been begun. Steam power and heavy machinery could not be used in the second story of the postoffice, so at the end of six months that location was abandoned, and quarters taken up in a portion of H. W. Doughten's warehouse building on Chester avenue, just North of the railroad. In the new location steam power was added to the resources of the establishment and adequate machinery put to work. The paper was enlarged and the general facilities for newpaper and job work were increased.

The removal to H. W. Doughten's building was made in January, 1881, and the *Chronicle* remained there until the summer of 1885. That season the *Chronicle* Building on the West side of Chester avenue, just South of the railroad, was constructed. It is a two-story brick building, of ample size, and well supplied with steam machinery for executing the constantly increasing work of the office. The new building was taken possession of the 1st of

August, 1885. The *Chronicle* is entirely independent in politics, but by no means neutral. It has a good circulation, which is increasing; and it is likely to become a more and more important factor in the life of the place.

THE TELEPHONE.—Long-distance conversation is within the resources of the Moorestown residents, as well as the older methods of communication; and any one desiring to do so can stand in the front part of the postoffice building and shout "Hello, hello!" so as to be heard in Philadelphia, or farther away. The telephone took its place among our local institutions in 1885. J. Willits Worthington is manager, and the exchange is located in his drug-store. Connections are made East and West, and through the Philadelphia office Moorestown is within talking range of any place in the circuit of telephone comnmunication. Mr. Worthington was the first subscriber for an instrument, and Mr. H. W. Doughten was the second.

Chapter XVI.

The New Station.

A SUBURBAN town must have a railroad station, of course. Otherwise the town is not suburban but rustic. A railroad station makes it next door neighbor to the rest of the world. Two stations place it on a footing of intimacy with mankind at large. Moorestown has three, and a three-station town that does not take on more or less of metropolitan airs may be considered pretty well balanced. Perhaps it is because she is steadied by the sobering influences of two centuries that our old town does not show any signs of skittishness, even now when she offers three halting places for the trains.

The new station, the third on the list, was erected early in the spring of 1886. It is small, but as pretty a building as one need desire to see. It is a Queen Ann structure of brick, with a tiled roof and and stained glass windows. Its location is about two-thirds of a mile East of the East Moorestown station, near the entrance to the Fair Grounds. A street, called "Fair Grounds Avenue"—which, by the way, is the name given to the station—has been opened from Main street to the railroad, at the end of the station platform, and a plank sidewalk constructed the entire distance.

Thus a new convenience has been given to comers and goers, and a new means of communication established with a very delightful portion of Moorestown. There are many people living at the Eastern extremity of the town who will appreciate the closer proximity to railroad privileges. A half mile walk as the preface or appendix to a day's business or shopping in the city is not always desirable, and not everybody keeps a carriage. Under the new order of things East Moorestown station is not the Hobson's choice of those living towards Mrs. Lippincott's old boarding school when they want to take a train.

With this addition to its facilities Moorestown may freely extend itself to the East as well as to the North. From old times a good many homes have been located well to the Eastward along Main street, and of late more have been established there —some of them elegant and attractive in the extreme. Distance from the center of the town does not involve so much inconvenience now as formerly, for all the dealers in the place send out order and delivery wagons for the convenience of customers. That part of the town is a very choice one for residences, and many who have looked wistfully in that direction have been deterred from establishing their homes there only by the inconvenience caused by the distance from the railroad station. The distance from the town center need not interfere with going and coming if one has time. But to catch a train from there required such a careful and troublesome economizing of time that it amounted to a serious obstacle. That obstacle is now removed, for already trains stop at the new station on signal, and it will eventually have its due place on the time-table.

When the Telford pavement has been completed, this section of the town will be still more attractive and desirable; for then the walk or drive " into town" will be even more of a pleasure than it is now. The drive will also be an attractive pleasure for others than those who live in East End, and the road will much of the time be gay and lively with the turn-outs of pleasurers. This will afford an added satisfaction to the dwellers in the beautiful region along the road, furnishing an animated spectacle which it will be very pleasant to look upon. So, with the railroad and the new pavement as resources, there certainly would be no isolation for the dwellers in the Eastern extremity of the town, and the inconvenience of residence there will be reduced to its minimum.

As was to have been expected private enterprise has seen all these advantages, and is ready to avail itself of them. The only wonder is that the steps now taken were not taken earlier. They have been taken at all events, and as private enterprise is always an important element of public enterprise, this movement must take its place as a matter of history. So much of the farm of Mrs. Mary Lippincott as remained unsold, comprising about thirty-one acres, and including the old residence which was for so many years the boarding school building, has been purchased and laid off in building lots. Fair Grounds avenue has been opened along the Western side of the property, from Main street to the railroad. Other streets, parallel to this, are to be opened, and an avenue constructed through the tract, parallel with Main street. On these street lines the lots are laid out. The conditions of sale prohibit the erection of buildings for purposes prejudicial to health or comfort, and building lines along the different avenues as established. The suggestion is made to set apart a portion of the tract for the erection of a chapel and school-house. Whether this will be done or not is uncertain. If it should be, a still further convenience will be afforded the dwellers in that region.

All things considered—the advantages offered by the new improvement company, and the advantages existing aside from that organization—it seems probable that the new station will become the nucleus of an important and most desirable extension of Moorestown; an extension that will in time assume as important relations to the older portions of the place as those now held by the extension North of the railroad.

Chapter XVII.

In Later War Times.

NORTH, South, East or West, there is not a hamlet so remote that it has not some link of association connecting it with "war times." Every community has in it at least one or two men—they are gray-headed and grizzly-bearded now, probably, and are apt to be a little stooped as to the shoulders—who make an occasional remark beginning: "When I was in the army." This one has a bullet hole somewhere about him; that one "came out without a scratch," but finds himself a good deal older now than he would have been if he had spent those three or four years in houses instead of tents and bivouacs; and another one is short in his account of legs or arms. There is pretty certain to be one or more of these men to remind the generation that is going down and the generation that is coming up of the terrible episode that grew into one of the world's mightiest tragedies. Other reminders make mute signals from every country grave-yard, no less eloquent than those from stately cemeteries and national burial places. The green mound behind a country church shows as distinctly as the most elaborate monument where a sleeping soldier has his place in the "bivouac of the dead." Other reminders, again, stir and cry out in the hearts that have not, after all these years, forgotton to ache for the soldier who never came back, even to the quiet rest of the church-yard grave.

That later war sent the eddies of its fierce tide into quiet Moorestown, as into every other place, quiet or unquiet, great or small, near or remote. Little fluttering flags in every grave-yard in the place, mark to-day where "the silent tents are spread" of some of the great army of soldiers whose warfare is all accomplished. Even in the Friends' Cemetery the fluttering signal is seen, and the sleep that follows the health of peace has fellowship with the sleep that ends the fever of war. There is nothing strange in such fellowship to those of us who remember those wonderful years. The furnace heats in which the nation was moulded anew softened the elements of every community and welded them into a closer brotherhood.

The Friends are a war-condemning people, but to country and to principle they are loyal through and through. So when the Civil War burst upon us in 1861 the Friends, here as well as elsewhere, were placed in a very trying position. They could not sanction the doing of evil that good might come, but the good that was sought through the evil of war was as dear to them, and was as earnestly and zealously hoped and striven for by them, as by any man who drew a sword or shouldered a musket. They must deprecate the means which were employed, and which they were powerless to change or modify, but they could not but hope and pray for the result that was striven for. The cause of the Union had no more loyal adherents than they; the *war* for the Union was, in their estimation, bad, as all war is bad. If any war could have seemed right to them this war would have seemed so; and since war was the means appointed to accomplish the purpose in view, and the saving of the Union depended on the successful issue of the war, they must hope for that issue.

The position of the Friends was appreciated and fully respected by both President Lincoln and Secretary Stanton. Their principles as non-combatants did not, in the minds of these men, conflict with their standing as thoroughly loyal citizens, and were entitled to the utmost consideration. This consideration they received. In some instances Friends who were drafted for the army were held exempt, and in others they were assigned to non-combatant duty. The volunteer service they rendered in hospitals and in the promotion of sanitary enterprises, needs not the telling. Its record is preserved in the grateful recollection of many a sick and wounded soldier.

In those later war times Moorestown and the region around it were not so exclusively populated by the Friends as in the Revolutionary days. They still constituted a large and a strong element; but there were other elements here that were also strong and active. A large proportion of the community gave to the war the sympathy and sanction which the Friends reserved for the object of the war; and among these the war fever burned hotly and without intermission. A goodly number put on the blue, took sword or musket and marched away to the front; and straightway that part of the front where "our boys" were became the center of interest for those who staid at home. With but few exceptions—just enough to emphasize the rule—the community was a unit in its steadfast and enthusiastic endorsement of the National cause; and this remained true all through the war. Victories were greatly rejoiced in; reverses were grievously deplored; the news of the doings at "the front" was eagerly snatched at and earnestly discussed; excited and enthusiastic meetings were held as special points of interest commanded attention; a battle in which "our boys" suffered— and such battles were many—was mourned over as if the soldiers who were stricken had shared kindred with the entire population instead of with single families in it; and the while the quiet work of aiding and cheering the soldiers in material ways went on, and some in the community, more particularly the women, actively co-operated with the larger work that was doing in Philadelphia. In short, as it was in almost every city, town and hamlet throughout the North, so it was here. The war and the issue for which it was fought constituted the one great interest of life; and the daily hopes and fears of every individual were shaped and colored by its ebb and flow, as the sand is influenced by the coming and going of the ocean's tide.

But the hoarse echo from Sumter swelled quickly into a loud rallying cry for soldiers. Its note penetrated to the remotest recess. and everywhere it was heeded and answered—can any of us every forget with what tumultous eagerness? Here, as elsewhere, the answer was prompt and emphatic. The interest in the war was not of a kind to expend itself wholly in good wishes and anxious hopes. It must have its active part in the great chapter of history the country was writing. Moorestown was a much smaller place then than it is now; but it was large enough, with its immediate neighborhood, to furnish its share of "boys in blue." A company, made up almost wholly of men from this town and the close vicinity, was organized here, amid great enthusiasm. The company, when fully made up, comprised ninety-seven officers and enlisted men. It was when the war was new, in that never-to-be-forgotten summer of 1861, that this band of soldiers was recruited. For several weeks before their departure for the scene of active service they were quartered in the Town Hall, and were in the heartiest and most cordial fashion the guests of the community. Everywhere the soldiers were the aristocracy then; and the Town Hall was not so much the barracks as the reception room of the soldiers. And how bountifully they were supplied! The best from every household was generously contributed to the soldiers. Housewives baked noble batches of fresh bread daily for the "boys in the hall"; and every substantial and delicacy that stomach could crave was freely sent in from far and near. The soldiers uniformed themselves before leaving here, and money contributions to help them do this were freely tendered. Indeed there were almost none in the entire community, of whatever denomination or belief, who did not in some way give practical expression to the cordial sentiment that prevailed.

Toward the middle of August the company left here for Trenton; and there on the 15th of August, 1861, it was mustered into the United States service for three years. It was attached to the Fourth Regiment, New Jersey Volunteers, and was Company "E" of that regiment. The commissioned officers chosen before the company left here were: Charles Hall, Captain; William H. Eldridge, First Lieutenant and Samuel Ellis Second Lieutenant.

George Brooks was Orderly Sergeant on leaving here; but not long after he was promoted and Thomas Maxin became Orderly and held the position until the term of service expired. On the 21st of August the regiment arrived in Washington and went into camp at Fairfax Seminary, Va., with the First Second and Third New Jersey Regiments. They formed the First Brigade, First Division of the First Corps of the Army of the Potomac. The Brigade was commanded by "Gallant Phil Kearney" of the Regular Army. Gen. McDowell was the Corps Commander until the Peninsula Campaign when the Division was made the First Division of the Sixth Corps, commanded by Gen. Franklin.

During its term of service (which lasted until the end of the war, for it re-enlisted) the regiment took part in the following engagements, exclusive of numerous skirmishes of which no mention is made: West Point, Va., May 7, 1862; Gaines' Farm, Va., June 27, 1862; Second Battle of Bull Run, Va., August 27, 1862; Chantilly, Va., September 1, 1862; Crampton's Pass, Md., September 14, 1862; Antietam, September 17, 1862; Fredericksburg, Va., December 13, 1862; Gettysburg, Pa., July 2 and 3, 1863; Williamsport, Md., July 6, 1863; Rappahannock Station, Va., November 7, 1863; Mine Run, Va., November 29 and 30, 1863; Wilderness, Va., May 5 to 7, 1864; Spottsylvania, Va., May 8 to 11, 1864; Spottsylvania

Court House, Va., May 12 to 16, 1864; North and South Anna River, Va., May 24, 1864; Hanover Court House, Va., May 29, 1864; Cold Harbor, Va., June 1 to 11, 1864; Weldon Railroad, Va., June 30, 1864; Snicker's Gap, Va., July 18, 1864; Strasburg, Va., August 15, 1864; Winchester, Va., August 17, 1864; Charlestown, Va., August 21, 1864; Opequan, Va., September 19, 1864; Fisher's Hill, Va., September 21 and 22, 1864; New Market, Va., September 24, 1864; Mt. Jackson, Va., September 25, 1864; Cedar Creek, Va., October 19, 1864; Hatcher's Run, Va., February 5, 1865; Fort Steadman, Va., March 25, 1865; Capture of Petersburg, Va., April 2, 1865; Sailor's Creek, Va., April 6, 1865; Farmville, Vs., April 7, 1865; Lee's Surrender, Appomattox, Va., April 9, 1865.

At the battle of Gaines' Farm on the 27th of June, 1862, the entire regiment, together with the Eleventh Pennsylvania Reserves, were captured and taken to Richmond. There they were kept as prisoners of war till about the middle of August, when they were exchanged and returned to their brigade, which was at this time lying at Harrison's Landing on the James River. The regiment rejoined the brigade on August 15, 1862, just one year from the day the boys were mustered in at Trenton; and also just in time to participate in the second battle of Bull Run, on the 27th of August.

Who has forgotten—who can ever forget—that

wonderful month of April, 1865? The capture of Petersburg, the fall of Richmond, the surrender of Lee, set the nation wild with the gladness of victory and the assurance of peace. Then all the gladness was suddenly quenched in the horror of Lincoln's assassination. The lamentations over this tragedy were still sounding when they were drowned in a peal of laughter that rang from ocean to ocean at the absurd capture of Jefferson Davis. Moorestown, like all the rest of the country, has never been so shaken to and fro as she was that month; and like the rest of the country she had added to the other excitements of the time the anticipation of welcoming home the soldiers who had helped to achieve the grand consummation. They came at last. Did they? Alas! So few of them. It was but a remnant that received the welcome of those who had given the parting God-speed to all. Thirty-two battles, with the sore experiences of camp and hospital had thinned the ranks to a pitiful extent. Some had come home in advance and been laid to rest in quiet church-yard nooks; more had been left behind, resting as quietly in less quiet places. Others had brought life home with them, but life so bruised and shaken that suffering must be one of its conditions through all the years to come. But the war was over, and the ending was such as all those living and all those dead had striven for.

Chapter XVIII.

Old Houses and Landmarks.

OF course anything in the way of antiquities that Moorestown has to show—or any part of America, for that matter—must necessarily be new and raw compared with the hoary landmarks of the Old World. To be sure some of our newer possessions are ancient indeed beside some of the old relics sold to tourists in Egypt and India; for oftentimes these are sticky with the recent varnish of the English workshop; but in the way of genuine old age, almost any little place in England or Germany or Italy, to say nothing of Egypt and China and Japan, can boast structures that were historic long before our oldest landmarks were thought of; unless, indeed, we choose to fall back upon the works of the Mound Builders or the Aztecs, and they can hardly be said to be ours. But after all, old age is only a relative result, and must be estimated by different standards in different places and circumstances. If a house or a tree is as old as its opportunities permit it to be, that is all that can be asked or expected of it. Judged by that standard we have some very creditable antiquities in Moorestown.

The oldest relics hereabouts take us back to the Indians, as might be supposed; but how far back into Indian history and experience is not known. The Indian Spring, on the ridge at the Southeastern border of the town, in the neighborhood of Mrs. Lippincott's school, has already been mentioned. It is not now so strongly suggestive of its Indian importance as it was a few years ago, but is still interesting. For very many years it was carefully kept as nearly as possible in the same condition as its aboriginal proprietors had maintained for it when they used to assemble about it from far and near and build their council fires beside it. They had evidently esteemed it very highly, and had given it a degree of care and attention worthy of its importance. Its basin was kept carefully cleaned out and walled up with rude stone work, and its outlet had a well-kept channel prepared for it. Its abundant chalybeate waters evidently stood high in the estimation of our predecessors; and probably for many generations of red men the spring was the object of solemn pilgrimage and popular resort.

Scattered freely about the spring were relics of a a more portable sort. These the school-girls took delight in searching for and bearing away; and many widely scattered homes have among their bric-a-brac to-day stone arrow-heads and spear-heads that must be classed among the antiquities of Moorestown. An uninformed white man is very naturally led to inquire why the Indians were so careless as to leave these manufactured flints so profusely scattered over the surface of the ground. One would suppose that articles which evidently required so much time and labor to make, and which were so useful to their owners, would be kept carefully in possession instead of being reck-lessly strewn about for white men to plough up and white girls to gather into their treasuries of curiosities.

It is not only in the neighborhood of Indian Spring that the flinty traces of the original dwellers here have been found. At various places in and about the town they have been turned up more or less abundantly. Mr. Edward Harris has collected quite a little museum of such articles that have been from time to time discovered on his farm. His collection includes not only such specimens as arrow-heads and spear-heads, but more important and curious articles. One of these is the stone head of a war club. It is of murderous weight and proportions, and has encircling it a carefully made groove by which it was to be bound, with tough fibred withes to its wooden handle. Another specimen is in two pieces and of formidable weight. The two parts are a large, hollowed stone—a kind of petrified chopping bowl in appearance—and a long, heavy piece of stone, larger at one end than the other, with the large end carefully rounded and the small end shaped into a handle. These together formed the mill for grinding the family supply of Indian meal. The bowl was to hold the corn which the rudely formed pestle pounded and ground into meal. The mill would hardly be equal to turning out patent process flour, but is a very curious and interesting affair, notwithstanding.

But all these are relics of a time that passed, probably, long before Moorestown was thought of, and can hardly be said to belong to it at all. That is not the case with the old sycamore tree which stands on the north side of Main street a short distance East of the William Penn Hotel. This old survivor of the past is one of the best known and one of the most conspicuous landmarks of the place. It will be remembered that the original Meeting House of the Friends stood in the enclosure that now constitutes the Friends' Greenlawn Cemetery, with horse and wagon sheds extending towards where the hotel now is. Thomas Warrington, son of Henry Warrington—who was the first of the family to settle in West Jersey—felt the need of a hitching-post in front of the sheds for his own convenience and that of his neighbors

So in the year 1740 he supplied this want by setting out a strong young sycamore tree there, which might serve the present purpose of a hitching-post, and also, in time, afford shade to the horses tied to its trunk. The hitching post so thoughtfully provided in 1740 is the noble old sycamore which Moorestown takes pride in to-day. It must have been some years old when it was placed in its present position; otherwise it would uot have served the purpose for which it was selected. So it is to-day at least a hundred and fifty years old.

Some years ago a large hole appeared on the South side of the tree near its foot, and the old landmark was threatened with a fatal decay which would speedily bring about its overthrow. Mr. C. C. Coles, the proprietor of the hotel, happily remembered that the decay of an old tree in the Friends' burying ground at Mullica Hill had been successfully checked by closing the opening with masonry; so he resolved to try the same treatment with the sycamore. A quantity of bricks and fresh cement were left from some recent work about the hotel premises. Mr. Coles had the bricks placed in the hollow of the tree, causing them to be packed and driven in as firmly and closely as possible. The entire opening was filled in this manner, and then the surface of the brickwork was thickly coated with cement so as to entirely exclude the air from the inside of the tree. The remarkable surgical operation was eminently successful. The decay was checked, on the same principle, probably, that the filling of a decayed tooth preserves it. The old tree regained its health; the opening was gradually hidden by new growth of wood and bark, and now only a scar remains to remind people of the heroic treatment that was resorted to.

An interesting fact connected with the affair is that the tree at Mullica Hill, whose rescue suggested that of the sycamore, was operated on by Lindzey Nicholson, one of whose daughters is the wife of Dr. Joseph Warrington, one of Moorestown's old citizens, and a descendent of the Warrington who planted the "hitching-post" in 1740. Mr. Nicholson experimented successfully on a tree near his residence on Walnut street, Philadelphia, and then extended his treatment to the Mullica Hill tree, in which he took great interest from old association.

Another of the old landmarks of the place is also a tree. This one is a grand white oak, which is now growing where it originally took root in the woods. The woods have disappeared and left the old tree standing out in the sidewalk on the South side of Main street at the end of the line that separates the property of Dr. S. C. Thornton from that of William Matlack's daughters. It is supposed to be about a hundred years old, and is a magnificient specimen of tree-growth. It was utilized by some of the old-time surveyors in their work, being referred to in one of the old conveyances as "a small white oak tree," which marked a corner of the land conveyed. Under the shadow of this old tree the original Methodist church stood—the first house of public worship erected in Moorestown after the Friends' meeting house. To all appearance the tree is now in the prime of life, and it is pleasant to think that it is likely to be spared many years yet as a landmark for Moorestown to be proud of.

One of the old buildings identified with the early times of Moorestown has been removed this spring (1886). This was the old blacksmith shop that stood on Main street a short distance East of Mr. Geo. F. Doughten's store. If old age can make anything venerable, it was evident to all beholders that this old structure was venerable. It was of composite architecture, being partly of frame and partly of stone, and a part of the frame portion standing at an obtuse angle from the rest of it. A queer little after-thought addition, in the shape of a low, square box with a window in it, stood out from the Southeastern corner and formed the Eastern end of the shed that fronted the smithy. To all appearance this was the oldest portion of the building, but it probably was not. The blacksmith shop was sold in 1780 by John Cox to his son, William Cox. It is supposed that either John or William built the stone portion of the structure, and that the business had been carried on in a still older portion of the building for an indefinite time prior to the transfer of 1780. But when that older portion was erected is not known. The old shop and the ground on which it stood were purchased by the Moorestown Grange in the early part of 1886, and the building torn down. A new building is being erected on the site of the old landmark, to be used by the Grange as a general store, with a Granger's Hall in the upper story. The substitution will undoubtedly be a great improvement to that part of Moorestown, even though it does obliterate one of the relics of old times.

Another old building which is associated in history to some extent with the blacksmith shop, is the frame dwelling house on Main street, just East of G. F. Doughten's residence. In 1745 John Cox, who sold the blacksmith shop to his son in 1780, bought the land lying between Levi Lippincott's property and Chester avenue. It would appear that the frame building in question was standing on the ground at the time; for Mr. Cox became tavern-keeper there soon after his purchase. "Cox's Tavern" became one of the notable places of Moorestown and so continued for many years. Mr. Cox died about 1800, and after his death the property passed through a number of ownership's until about the year 1842, when David McCoy, who had purchased the consolidated stage lines from

George F. Doughten and John Courtland Haines, bought the old tavern. He had leased the property some time previous to this, and established stage headquarters there; but after purchasing he put on improvements which bore testimony to a good deal of enterprise on his part. He erected a large barn at the rear of the premises, which still remains there, and constructed a very ample wagon shed which occupied the ground where Mr. Doughten's residence now stands. For a time the business of the tavern flourished; but when the stage line passed out of McCoy's possession and was established elsewhere, the hotel business ebbed away from the old place; then it ceased to be a tavern at all, and for many years now the old building has been rented as a dwelling.

On this same property, purchased by John Cox in 1745, stood one of the very early stores of the town. It was a frame building which occupied the ground where now stands the Store of G. F. Doughten, at the corner of Main street and Chester avenue. Who built it, or when it was built are things unknown; but it was an ancient structure. John Cox sold the portion of the property on which the store was standing, to John Wilkinson Fennimore in 1801. Fennimore sold it to William Doughten, father of the present owner. George F. Doughten returned here, a young man, in 1832, and entered into a business partnership with John

Courtland Haines. They bought the old store and began business there. In 1838 Mr. Doughten bought out his partner's interest in the business, and continued the enterprise independently. In 1849 he removed the old frame building and replaced it with the building he now occupies. The lot adjoining was also a part of the old Cox property. This lot David McCoy tried to purchase before he bought the Cox Tavern; but Mr. Doughten had forestalled him, purchasing the lot himself in 1839. On this he erected his present residence, and while he was rebuilding his store he kept his goods in his dwelling.

The William Penn Hotel, on the North side of Main street, just West of the Friends' grave-yard, is another of the old buildings of the place. Its appearance at this time does not denote its antiquity; for it has seen changes as time went on, notably under the administratton of its present proprietors, Messrs. C. C. Coles & Brother. Fresh paint and other added improvements have made it, to all appearance, an essentially modern building. It is not that, however; and it has a history full of interesting points, if there were only somebody who could remember them. Pretty much the only outward indication of old times now visible about the building is a couple of small holes in the Western end. Into these holes were inserted the ends of the iron rods which formed the support of the old swinging sign, on which was displayed a portrait of William Penn. Under the proprietorship of John West the old house was headquarters for one of the rival stage-coach lines and had its full share of the liveliness that belonged to those lively times.

About 1820 Thomas Porter was the proprietor. He was a well known character hereabouts, and combined the vocations of hotel-keeper, tailor and auctioneer. He is said to have been equally efficient in all, and to have been a jolly soul withal, as a man so prosperous and full of resources may well have been. His wife, Polly, was as important a personage as himself, and her skill as a cook and caterer gave her a wide reputation. It is stated that no wedding or important festival of any kind was deemed a success unless Polly Porter had the management of it and provided the good things.

Thomas Porter was succeeded by John West as proprietor. Then came Daniel Bennett, Benjamin Martin, Nathan Stokes and John West—another John West—in succession. In the winter of 1859 C. C. Coles & Brother, the present proprietors, purchased the place. About forty years ago important alterations and improvements were made in the building, which changed it from an old-time tavern, and gave it a more modern appearance. Other, but less radical changes have been made more recently.

The Washington Hotel, on the North side of Main street, West of Mill street, is said to be a still older house than the William Penn, and it certainly has retained more of its ancient appearance. It was also headquarters for one of the opposition stage lines in the exciting days of stage-coaching; and has always been a prominent feature of Moorestown. William Doughten, father of George F. Doughten, was proprietor for a long time. He was succeeded by Henry Louden, and after him came Abel Small, Jr., Michael O'Neil, Nathan H. Stokes, George Dull, Lewis Wood, Frank Lightcap, and the present proprietor, Lee Stroud. During Dull's proprietorship the hotel barn was destroyed by fire. Alterations have been made from time to time, but they have not changed the appearance of the old place to such an extent as in the case of William Penn.

There is not much in the appearance of the store block West of the William Penn Hotel, on the same side of the street, to indicate antiquity. But Burr's store and Brown's store both occupy sites that were held—and not so many years ago—by very old structures. When A. L. Burr kept his store in the house now occupied by Ebenezer Roberts, a small frame building stood on the ground where his brick store now is. It was a very old structure, but how old is not known. In it Elwood Stratton, who became postmaster under President Lincoln's administration, kept a drug store. He was the last to occupy the old building. The little frame structure was not destroyed when the new building was to be erected, but was purchased and moved off. It is now occupied as a dwelling on French's alley, below Second street.

Where the brick store of E. B. Brown & Brother now stands a blacksmith shop formerly stood. No man knows when or by whom it was erected. Very many years ago it was diverted from its original purpose and became a store. It was occupied successively by a number of proprietors, and for a good many years prior to 1860 John Court-Haines and John Buzby carried on business there under the style of Haines & Buzby. In 1860 Mr. Haines retired in favor B. L. Davis, who had been a clerk in the store, and E. B. Brown bought Mr. Buzby's interest. In 1864 Mr. Brown bought out Davis and took his brother Charles into partnership. In the summer of 1876 the old building was torn down and the present brick store erected in its place. The new building was occupied September 9, 1876.

A very old frame dwelling house was removed to make room for present residence of Mr. A. L. Burr on the North side of Main street. How long it had stood there cannot be told, but it was very venerable. It had belonged to Joseph Matlack, and was said to be considerably over a century old. One of the last to occupy the old house in its old position was Charles Burden, still a resident here.

When the time came to remove the venerable building it was purchased by John Manion, and removed to his lot on Second street in West Moorestown, where he still occupies it as a dwelling. There is a well in the southwest corner of Mr. Burr's grounds, which was probably dug when the old house was built. There is a pump in it now, and the supply of water has never been known to fail in the severest drought. The well is lined with great blocks of iron-stone, and formerly a part of the grounds about the old house was paved with similar blocks. A number of years ago it was decided to clear out the old well, which is used by by the present owner only to supply water for the lawn and shrubbery. In the cleaning operations a jar of butter was brought up from the depths. It had been hung down there unknown years before to keep it hard and sweet, and in some unaccountable manner had been forgotten, with the result of being pretty well fossillized.

Where the Bank Building now stands there was formerly an old building which had occupied the ground from a time when the memory of the oldest inhabitant runneth not to the contrary. It was torn down to make room for the Bank, and its destruction removed one of the most universally accommodating old buildings, perhaps, that Moorestown ever possessed. It had been a cabinet maker's shop on different occasions; a school house from time to time; a store when it came handy; a drug store when the emergency demanded; had given quarters to a newspaper, and had encouraged other industries in the most versatile and impartial manner possible.

When or by whom it was built are points on which there seems to be no exact information. It was an old building a great many years ago. The investigator who tries to get back of that goes into a fog and is lost. Very early in the present century Richard Haines occupied the old shop and followed his trade of cabinet-making there. After his time William Jones, also a cabinet-maker, worked there. He was the father of the late Samuel Jones, the well known citizen who was for so long a term of years Moorestown's only undertaker. Samuel worked with his father in the old shop, and the family lived in a little frame house that stood on the lot adjoining, where the residence of the Misses Slim now is. This little dwelling house is reputed to have been still older than the shop. It could hardly have been called spacious, for it is said to have consisted of only two rooms—one down stairs and another above, which was reached by means of a trap-door and open stairway. A little store was kept in the lower room, and was a favorite shopping place for the lovers of taffy and cream cheese. Samuel Jones succeeded his father as cabinet maker in the old shop, and carried on business there for several years. In those times cabinet makers made coffins when the occasion demanded, and undertaking was not a distinct business, as now. Gradually Mr. Jones was compelled to give more and more of his time and attention to making coffins and attending funerals, and eventually dropped the other branches of his old trade and became a regular undertaker. After a time Joshua Borton built the house now occupied by Ebenezer Roberts, and also the one standing West of it. This one Samuel Jones bought and occupied. He built a shop back of it, and then the old building in which he had so long carried on his business was vacated by him.

It would seem that the old shop was not occupied continuously by the cabinet makers through all these years; for there are recollections of schools that must have been sandwiched in between the wood-working periods. Rev. Daniel Higbee kept a school here sometime about 1820, and had among his pupils some boys and girls who are now living among us as grandfathers and grandmothers. During his experience as teacher Mr. Higbee lived in the little house next door. At a later period Isaac Bunting had a school in the old shop. He had previously taught in an old school house some distance west of Moorestown. This school house had been destroyed by fire, and the old shop was the pedagogue's place of refuge. There is one old lady still living here who has a distinct recollection of school-days passed in the old school house that was burned, while Isaac Bunting taught there; and there are others, many years younger, who were his pupils in the cabinet maker's shop.

In later years Mr. James Sankey purchased the old building and used it for a cabinet shop many years. It was fulfilling that part of its vocation when the ground on which it stood was purchased for a bank site and the old landmark was demolished. In the meantime, however, it did not forfeit its reputation of being the most accommodating building in the place. When Mr. A. L. Burr was about to erect his present store and it was necessary to remove the old frame building that stood on the ground, Mr. Elwood Stratton, who had his drug store in the doomed building, removed his stock to Mr. Sankey's shop and carried on business there until his quarters in Burr's new building were ready for him. So too, when the Brown Brothers put up their present building they removed their goods to Mr. Sankey's shop and kept store there until they could occupy their own building. When the *Chronicle* was started here it had its first quarters in Mr. Sankey's shop, and staid there until a fire which threatened the entire destruction of the building, drove it out. Indeed there seems to have been very few spheres of usefulness which the old structure could not fill.

Another very old building is that in which Mrs.

Esther Stiles has her dwelling and her trimming store, on the South side of Main street, some little distance below the Bank. Its appearance does not indicate old age, for it has been kept in good repair, and has been somewhat modernized by slight alterations; but it dates back to Revolutionary times, and was a spacious and commodious dwelling for the time of its construction.

The Town Hall is not a very antique structure, but it bears a tolerable weight of years, nevertheless. It was built by the township authorities in 1812, and at the time of its construction was held to be an architectural credit to the place. It was then just half the size it is now. When the Moorestown Literary Association was in its heyday of prosperity it became joint proprietor of the little brick building with the township, and built an addition which just doubled the size of the hall. It added other improvements which made the structure notable for its completeness at the time. Since that time the township has been only part owner of the hall. It has always retained the full right to use the building for all township business, so that the hall still serves the purpose for which it was originally intended. Previous to its erection the town meetings were held in the hotels; and as John Cox was the Town Clerk for many years it is supposed that his hotel was used for town meeting purposes during those years until the hall was built.

A notable specimen of the old time mansions is that now owned and occupied by Dr. S. C. Thornton, on the South side of Main street a short distance East of Mill street. Standing far back from the street, fronted by a large lawn, and its white walls gleaming through the abundant green of trees and ornamental shrubbery, it answers fully the idea of a stately country residence of olden times.

The house was built nearly a hundred years ago, by Thomas Ewing, of Philadelphia, for the summer residence of his family. Its beginning is associated with the youth of the grand old white oak which stands in the sidewalk in front of the premises; for the deed conveying the property referred to this tree as a "white oak sapling" marking one of the corners. As originally constructed the building had a decidedly different appearance to what it has now. A broad veranda ran across both ends and the back of it. The front door was sheltered by a narrow little porch or "stoop." The roof of the house was flat, and for many years it was known far and wide as the "Old Flat-Roofed House."

The original veranda is still retained at the Western end of the house, and very quaint and pleasant it is, with its wooden "settle" fastened to the wall the entire length of it. The remainder of the veranda was removed years ago to make room for additions and improvements; and the little front stoop has been replaced by a roomy piazza, so designed as to harmonize with the rest of the building. The front of the house gives the impression of spacious roominess inside, but originally the building had but two rooms on each floor—one room on each side of a broad hall running from front to rear. A large back building has been added, so that the promise of the imposing front is more fully kept now. A feature which is singular among old houses is the staircase, which instead of running up from the hall, is enclosed, and ascends from the back at one side of the hall. The clapboards are of cedar, tongued and grooved, and all the timbers are of solid oak, strong enough to withstand a cyclone.

For many years the title to the property was in dispute; and during that time the old house stood empty, and the grounds were the resort of all the idle youth in the neighborhood. Many of them cut their names in the house-walls, and there they remain in spite of much paint. In 1838 Dr. Samuel Thornton, father of the present owner, saw an opening through the legal entanglement, and bought the property. He added to and improved the house and brought it up to the condition in which his son has since maintained it. A noble orchard formerly stood back of the house set with apple trees that came from England. All but one of the old original trees have died out. So also have all the cherry trees which came from England,

and the rows of Lombardy poplars which once stood sentry all about.

Dr. Thornton erected the present back building, remodelled the roof, replaced the little front stoop with the present piazza and expended a vast amount of paint upon the battered ontside of the house he had purchased. But the changes he made were such as harmonized with the original character of the house, and its individuality as a type of the fine old mansion house has never been impaired.

A short distance West of the head of Mill street stands one of the most interesting of all the houses that remain as mementos of the remote past. It is the old Smith or Harris mansion, of which mention has been repeatedly made. It stands some little distance south of Main street and looks off toward the northeast, with one shoulder partly turned toward the street. When it was built it fronted squarely on the King's Highway; but years ago that thoroughfare was straightened, and although the general course of Main street is the same as that of the old road, still there are places where the little change that was made produced a very noticeable effect, as when this old mansion was put back in comparative seclusion. Until a few years since it stood alone, with quite a grove between it and the street; but now most of the great taees have been cut down, and the handsome residence of Mr. J. C. Hopkins occupies the foreground of the immediate neighborhood of the old farm house, as it has been known of late years.

The ground on which the house stands formed part of one of the extensive purchases made here at the beginning of Moorestown's existence. On the 13th of May, 1682, Robert Clinton sold the property to Thomas Martin; on the 25th of September, 1686, James Martin, brother of Thomas, under a letter of attorney given by the latter, sold it to Thomas Rodman; Thomas Rodman died at his home in Rhode Island, and in his will left the New Jersey property to his son Clark Rodman; on the 13th of October, 1730, Clark Rodman sold the property to Francis Hogsett; he, on the 1st of April 1734 sold a part of his possessions here to Nehemiah Haines; in March, 1738, Nehemiah Haines sold to Joshua Humphries, and on August 2, 1766, Joshua Humphries and Increase, his wife, sold the land and whatever buildings were on it to Samuel Smith.

Samuel Smith kept the place until his death; and by his will, which bore date December 23, 1775, left it to his son Richard Smith. Richard Smith, by his will, dated April 30th, 1796, directed that the property, with such other lands as he possessed, should be sold after his death, and appointed Hannah and Joseph Smith to execute the provisions of the will. Accordingly on the 18th of May, 1798, Hannah and Joseph Smith sold the

Moorestown property to Edward Harris, of Philadelphia.

The property remained in the Harris family for many years. On the death of Edward Harris, the purchaser, in 1822, his son Edward inherited the estate, and lived upon it until his marriage, when he made a protracted visit to Europe. On his return he purchased the homestead now occupied by his widow and his son Edward, on Main street some distance above the old mansion. He still retained possession of the original estate, but after some years sold it to Dr. Haines. The old property was subsequently in the possession of Samuel Farvour, and after his death came into the possession of Deacon William Mead. He retained it until a few years since when it passed into the hands of its present proprietor, Bartholomew Sutton.

The historic old house is said to have been built by Joshua Humphries shortly after his purchase of 1738. If so the building was altered and added to by Samuel Smith and his son Richard. In their time the mansion was one of the most considerable in this region. Richard Smith was the owner and occupant during the Revolution; and it was here that his niece, Elizabeth Murrel, had her memorable experience when his house was the headquarters of the retreating British commander.

The liberal hospitality of Edward Harris rendered the house still more notable after it came into his hands. Here ministers of every evangelical denomination were made welcome, and here in the absence of regular church buildings, they were invited to hold services. In the parlor and on the veranda of this mansion preachers of various creeds have from time to time delivered sermons in the hearing of interested congregations. When the original Methodist church was built the dwelling house was no longer needed as a place of public worship, but the memory of its old time usefulness in that direction still clings to it.

Old age does not seem to have told upon the venerable structure with any damaging effect; and it is still a comfortable and commodious dwelling, as pleasant to live in as it is picturesque to look upon and interesting to think about.

A short distance below Union street, on the South side of Main street, stands a house with a history extending pretty far back into the past. It is the house now occupied by Ebenezer Roberts' daughters. It was built before the King's Highway had become Main street, and before the old road was straightened. When the straightening process had been completed the old house found itself standing on the opposite side of the road form that on which it had originally stood. It was built on the North side, and fronted South. It was left standing on the South side, and had to make an exchange of front and back doors to accommodate its new situation.

A still older building formerly stood in the same yard with this house. It was in this building that one of the first stores in Moorestown was kept. Numerous store-keepers served customers here through a long term of years, the last proprietor being Joseph Wood. He left the old place to set up business in the ancient building which formerly stood on the site now occupied by E. B. Brown & Brother's brick store. After his removal the original store was occupied as a school house; for some years a boarding and day school was kept there by Darling Lippincott and Ezra Roberts.

Until a few years ago an exceedingly interesting group of old houses stood nearly opposite the Roberts house just alluded to. It was here that one of the first tan-yards of Moorestown was located. It extended some distance West from Union street, and from the King's Highway North, to where Second street now is. It was within these boundaries that Thomas Moore, the man who gave his name to Moorestown, had his abiding place and kept his hotel.

The entire premises may originally have been devoted to the tannery, but in the later years of the business the tan yard proper, with its vats and bark mill occupied the Northern part of the ground, and dwelling houses stood fronting the highway. Just West of Union street and facing Main street, stood one of these old houses. It was last occupied by William Gottbier. West of this stood what had formerly been the curry shop of the tan-yard. It had been changed into a dwelling many, many years ago, and during the last seven years of its existence on the old ground, was occupied by William Rexon and his family. It was a story and a half high, and stood with its side to the street. It had two rooms below and two above. There was a window in each end of the house for the up-stairs rooms, and there were two windows on each side down-stairs. The windows had only a single sash which disappeared from view in the walls when the windows were raised. The fastenings of the doors were the old-time wooden latches, and the "latch-string hung out" through a gimlet hole in the door.

The Gottbier house was somewhat larger than this one, and had a good sized barn back of it, apparently as old as the house. Notwithstanding their great age and the primitive manner in which they were fitted up, these old houses were comfortable and convenient homes, and their former tenants have pleasant recollections concerning them. The solid manner in which they were built was shown at the time of the terrible hail and wind storm about the year 1874. The hurricane had such force that Main street was fairly blockaded with great branches of trees that had been twisted off; and the tin-roofers were kept busy repairing the damage done to modern roofs by the wind and the hail.

But beyond the breaking of windows by the hailstones, these venerable houses suffered no damage whatever.

No wells could be dug on the premises because of the old tan vats; and water had to be brought from a distance, which is the one inconvenience remembered against the old homes. But there was full compensation for this in the exceeding richness of the garden soil. The fertilizing effects of the leather scrapings were still felt by the ground, and everything that was planted grew with wonderful vigor.

The property belonged to the widow of Joseph Stokes, and that portion of it on which these two old houses stood was sold to Mr. Albert C. Heulings. In 1880 the old buildings were removed to make room for modern residences. The Gottbier house was torn down; but the old curry shop was bought by Samuel Cranmer, the pump manufacturer, and removed to his premises on the corner of Third street and Church Road, where it now serves him for a shop. The residence of Mr. Ambrose Risdon now occupies the lot where stood the curry shop; and on the corner lot adjoining stands the residence of Mr. Cameron.

Just West of the curry shop stood a building which, at the time of its destruction, was said to be the oldest house in Moorestown. It was this old house which the best authority that can be obtained declares Thomas Moore built and occupied as a hotel. If this be so the travelling public must have spent most of its time at home in Mr. Moore's days; for his "hotel" consisted of just four rooms, all told. Two were on the ground floor, and two were upstairs under the roof. These latter were so unambitious that a man could stand in the middle of either of them and touch the peak of the roof with his finger tips; from which it may be inferred that no very massive furniture was at the disposal of Mr. Moore's guests. The manner of getting up stairs, too, was somewhat different from going up in a modern elevator. The stairway was open at the back, like ordinary cellar stairs, and led up to a trap door in the floor of one of the upper rooms. At the foot the stairway was unattached, but at the top it was fastened to the beam by a pair of hinges. In the day-time, when people were not supposed to have any use for their bedrooms, the stairs were swung up against the ceiling and fastened there by an iron hook, so that they were quite out of the way. As bed-time approached, the hook was displaced and the stairs made available.

As in the other old houses, the doors were furnished with wooden latches and leather latch-strings; but the front door was made secure by an extra and unusual attachment. This was a bolt, elaborately whittled out of tough hickory wood. It was held against the door by two heavy wooden clamps, and slid into a wooden socket fastened to the door-casing.

The building stood with its side to the street, and had but a narrow strip of ground between it and the sidewalk. This was very different from its first estate however. When it was built the highway ran some distance to the South of its present course, and then there was a broad stretch of ground in front of the hotel. When the road was straightened the door yard was annihilated.

How many years the old house offered accommodations as a hotel is not known; any more than it is known what name was borne upon its sign, or what became of Thomas Moore when he retired from the hotel business. In the course of events the old house and the ground it stood upon came into the possession of Mrs. Susan Simpson, who lived there until her death. Her daughter, Mrs. Rakestraw, lived with her, and after Mrs. Simpson's death continued to occupy the old house until death ended her occupancy also. Mrs. Rakestraw's daughter, Mrs. Blackwood, succeeded her as the occupant of the old homestead; and Mrs. Blackwood's daughter, who is now Mrs. George Bracebridge, and lives in the immediate neighborhood, resided with her mother in the Moore house until her marriage. So the ancient roof sheltered four succeeding generations—great-grandmother, grandmother, mother and daughter.

Mrs. Bracebridge claimed to inherit the property under the will of her great-grandmother, Susan Simpson, but her claim was disputed and a prolonged litigation resulted. The end was adverse to the claim of Mrs. Bracebridge, and the homestead passed into other hands. The last owner of the old house before its final sale and destruction was the widow of Joseph Stokes. Joseph Lippincott, Justice of the Peace, purchased the property in 1878, and the old house was torn down to make room for Mr. Lippincott's present residence.

After the property passed out of the hands of the original owner, an addition was built on the Western part of the house. This addition extended back, so that the original structure formed a kind of front wing to the completed building. The well now in the side yard of Mr. Lippincott's premises belonged to the oldest portion of the house, and was directly back of it, in the angle formed by the older and newer parts.

When the old house was torn down Mrs. Bracebridge collected and preserved a number of relics belonging to it, including all the wooden latches of the doors. But the keep-sake she treasures with special pride is the hickory bolt of the front door. There is but one heirloom she prizes more highly than this piece of wood, and that is a silver teaspoon which she traces back through seven generations of fore-mothers. And these successive owners, as she declares "were all Susans but one."

An old house that saw the Revolutionary War begin and end, stands on the South side of Main street some distance below the old tan yard. It is at present the residence of Mr. Elisha Barckelow, and stands well back from the street, in a large yard beautifully shaded by old trees. Years ago it was occupied by William Roberts, and he built a brick addition at the Eastern end of the building. The older portion is a frame structure, and is quite an ideal "old house" in the way of quaint nooks, unexpected angles, high mantels and odd little cupboards. It is in the immediate neighborhood of this old house that the cabins of the first white settlers here are supposed to have been built. At the bottom of the ridge on the South of Mr. Barckelow's dwelling is the spring which is said to have been the inducement for home-seekers to settle there. Its abundant and unfailing supply of good water had long attracted the Indians to its neighborhood, and the white men's cabins sprung up among their wigwams. Formerly traces of the Indian occupation of the ground were found in the the shape of arrow-heads and other relics.

Opposite Mr. Barckelow's house is a little whitewashed building that looks as if it might have been built by one of the first squatters in the place. It probably was not, but it is certainly very old. Its small windows are protected by solid wooden shutters which are single instead of double, like modern shutters; and the clap-boards of the house look as if they had been the product of the first saw mill. George French, the great-uncle of Mrs. Barckelow, formerly owned the building. It is now in the possession of non-resident owners.

Mr. French also owned the double house West of this, in one portion of which Rev. Mr. Algor now lives. This, too, is a very old building, but it has grown old very gracefully. It has been kept in excellent repair, and is as cosy and pleasantly situated a home as any one need desire. Its antiquity only gives it the added charm of quaintness.

To go back, now, to the extreme Eastern part of the town, the old building in which Mrs. Mary Lippincott's boarding school was kept claims attention. This was originally a stone house—when or by whom built is not known. The records show that Jacob Hollinshead owned the property some time previous to 1817, and by his will, dated in that year, left it to his son, Thomas Hollinshead. It passed successively into the hands of Thomas Stiles and Alfred Small, and finally, in 1842, into the possession of Isaac Lippincott, husband of Mrs. Mary Lippincott, whose name is so closely identified with it. In 1858 Mr. Lippincott died, leaving the property, heavily encumbered, to his wife. By her energy and enterprise she not only cleared off all the debts, but added to the original property. When Mr. Lippincott bought the place he enlarged the house by putting a large frame addition to the original stone structure. It is remembered that when this was completed a keg of beer was tapped upon the roof of the new building, and the contractor christened the place "North Bend." The name is still sometimes heard, but Mrs. Lippincott repudiated both it and the ceremony by which it was conferred. In the latter part of 1885 the property was purchased by the Moorestown Land Company, and the frame building was remodelled into the present Rosamond Inn. The original stone house was torn down, and in the process of removal a stone was taken out of the foundation, on which was the date 1757, and the initials "I. M. H." in letters about three inches long. The letters were scattered, and may have belonged in a different order. Mrs. Lippincott is under the impression that a family of Moores lived in the old house before Jacob Hollinshead owned it, but there are no authentic accounts previous to the Hollinshead ownership.

Trinity Church is not a building old enough to be classed as venerable; but it has among its belongings two which perhaps antedate any of the old landmarks that have been mentioned. They are the Communion service, and the bell. The

Communion service is that which was given by Queen Anne to St. Mary's Church, in Colestown. When Trinity Parish, the child of St. Mary's, was established here, the consecrated vessels came, by right of inheritance, into the possession of the new church; and apart from their sacred character they are treasured for their association with the remote past. The service consists of two pieces—a paten and a chalice. Both are of solid silver, and the paten, or plate, in particular is very heavy. The chalice is gold-lined, and has engraved on its foot: "St. Mary's, Colestown." The same inscription is on the bottom of the paten; but instead of having been engraved it would appear to have been scratched—very carefully—by some pointed instrument in the hands of a prudent officer of the old church. Other pieces have been added to the service, but they are new in comparison with these two which Queen Anne sent to her loyal subjects in West New Jersey.

The bell which calls the worshippers to service is old and has a curious history. Unlike most old things in Moorestown it has been a wanderer. It has crossed the ocean at least three times, and has spoken its summons to worshippers in the Church of Rome no less loudly than to those in the Protestant Church. It is a Spanish bell, and there is a tradition that it once did duty in the belfry of a Spanish convent. Be that as it may, it eventually found its way to Canada and there served for many years to call the inmates of a French convent to their various exercises. One statement is that before it went to Canada it had hung for a time in the belfry of an English church, but that is doubtful. About fifty years ago the bell, through some unexplained circumstances, was taken from Canada to England. There it came to the notice of Mr. Edward Harris and Dr. Spencer, who were abroad together. Both these gentlemen were greatly interested in the new church in Moorestown. They knew it was in want of a bell, and there was something pleasant in the thought of its having a bell with so interesting a history. Therefore the old Spanish bell was purchased and sent from England as a gift to the Moorestown church and in its belfry it still remains.

Chapter XIX.

A Dish of Old Gossip.

IT is well known that nothing but the flavor of antiquity makes gossip at all endurable. No man or woman could be expected to patiently regard a chapter of *recent* gossip. But having accumulated material for a little chit-chat concerning people and events of a previous time I feel emboldened to retail some of it here.

Perhaps nothing—not even the Revolutionary War—seems more remote and shadowy to us of to-day than slavery. I do not mean the slavery that existed South of Mason and Dixon's line—although it is pretty difficult to believe in that now—but the slavery that existed here in New Jersey, in Burlington county, in Moorestown. There are many who will find it difficult to realize that negro slavery ever was known here, where we live; but it was, and not so great a number of years ago as might be supposed. There are persons still living among us who remember the last of the old slaves.

The Manumission Act, abolishing slavery in New Jersey, was passed February 24th, 1820. By its provisions the children born of slave parents after July 4th, 1804, were to be free, the males on reaching the age of 25 years; females at the age of 21. Slaves who had reached a certain age before the law went into effect were to be provided for and taken care of by their former owners until their death, as it was held that old age incapacitated them for providing for themselves, and justice and humanity required that those whom they had served through their years of vigor should take care of them at the last. So late as 1844 there were still colored people in New Jersey who under the terms of this law were yet technically slaves. In 1840 there were 674 slaves in the State.

Long before the Manumission Act was passed, or thought of, the Society of Friends had borne testimony to the wickedness of slavery, and had in their discipline prohibited members of the Society from holding slaves. Previous to that action, however, slaves had been held in Friends' families here as well as elsewhere. Traditions still linger of old colored men and women who had once been the slaves of Friends here, and who were still cared for by their former masters and mistresses. In some instances they still lived on as paid servants in the families where they had once been slaves, knowing no difference except that now they got wages and could go away if they wanted to—which they apparently did not.

Sarah Elkton was the great-grandmother of Miss Hannah Warrington, a very aged Friend, now living in West Moorestown, and probably the oldest person in the place. When Sarah married John Roberts and went to live near Haddonfield, her father gave her, as his wedding present, two slaves. One of the children of these slaves was named Candas, and she married another slave named Jethro Gungas. When the daughter of John and Sarah Roberts married, her father gave her Candas as a wedding present. When "freedom time" came Candas and Jethro were too old to be freed, and were cared for by their owner, Miss Warrington's grandmother. They were still alive in Miss Warrington's youth, and her brothers gave them a sum of money sufficient to support them until their death. They had one son named Noble, who, although practically free, was technically a slave. He had a wife and children, and had accumulated some property. As a matter of precaution he requested that his freedom be formally given him, so that no unforseen change of fortune might interfere with the interests of his family. His request was granted and he and his were made secure.

Among the recollections of an aged inhabitant here, is that of an old slave who was left by the Manumission Act in the hands of her owner, being too old for freedom. When at last the poor old creature broke down utterly under the weight of years, she was put into the smoke house and kept until she died. Then she was buried in the corner of a "worm" fence, so that her grave might not spoil any serviceable ground.

An old couple who had been slaves, and whom aged people here still recollect, were Frank Vanderbeck and Lydia his wife. After they became free they lived in the family of Commodore Truxton, East of Moorestown. They had a son who was noted throughout the region as a fiddler. Tab Still and Daphne, his wife, were another pair of ex-slaves who are well remembered by some of the older inhabitants here. "Billy" Bassett, an old negro who had once been a slave, died in the neighborhood of Moorestown many years ago, but his memory is still alive among some of the old people here. He was over eighty years old when he died, and was known among his people as an eloquent preacher.

There are some living who still remember "Old Romy." He was a well known character in his day, and was a relic of slavery days. He was an imported specimen, however, and represented foreign slavery. A great many years ago a family named Haines, living on the Fellowship Road, became in some unexplained manner the guardians of a group of liberated slaves sent here from Barbadoes. They were sent by friends or relatives of the Haines family living in Barbadoes, and the request was made that the family here would look after the interests of the humble strangers, and help them to help themselves. The new-comers included "Romy" and his wife and children; an old woman named Dinah, and a man named Tony. Dinah was given a home in a neighboring family, and the others were given some ground, were helped to build cabins, and were given a good start toward supporting themselves.

One of the oddest things about "Old Romy" was his name. His former owner had evidently been an admiring, if not very discriminating, reader of Shakespeare, and had named his dusky man-servant Romeo-Juliet! Of course the name had to be shortened in practice, and the first name instead of the last was the one retained. The closest estimate I have been able to obtain of the age of Mr. Juliet is given in the assurance that "he must have been about as old as the everlasting hills." He was a wool-comber by trade, and travelled from house to house throughout the region, combing the wool the house-wives had provided for their spinning and weaving. With the proceeds of his trade and of his little patch of ground the Shakspearian refugee was able to make a very comfortable living.

The old man took an annual holiday, and went on a little excursion all by himself. There lived at Mt. Holly a gentleman, occupying an official position, who had removed thither with his wife from

Virginia. There had been some kind of association between this gentleman's family and the friends who had sent Romeo-Juliet from Barbadoes, and after his arrival here the old negro cultivated the acquaintance, keeping it up until the year of his death. Each year, when sweet potatoes were in their prime, "Old Romy" selected a number of the finest from his home garden. Then he killed and dressed a chicken which had been carefully fattened for this special occasion. These preliminaries attended to, the old man dressed himself in his best, completing his toilet by putting on an old, long-skirted overcoat which somebody had given him. Into one of the immense side-pockets of this garment he put as many sweet potatoes as it would hold, and in the other the chicken was deposited.

Thus freighted Romeo-Juliet started on his yearly excursion. All the way to Mt. Holly the faithful old fellow trudged, on a pilgrimage of affection. To the house of his Virginia friends he would go, and present the good things he had brought in his pockets to the lady. She always accepted the offerings in the most appreciative spirit, and made her visitor welcome in a pleasant and hearty fashion. She always knew when to expect him, and was never unprepared for his visit. When he started for his homeward jaunt he invariably received a bundle of old clothes, which the lady had selected for him, and the gift was often accompanied by a little hard cash. A curious feature of the transaction was that the old fellow was always surprised at receiving his bundle. He never expected any such thing.

Tony, the other man of the Barbadoes party, was given a piece of ground a considerable distance from the home of his fellow-refugees, and some of the white people helped him to build a cabin. He lived quite a hermit's life there for a time, for he was the first and only settler. Gradually white people established their homes in his immediate neighborhood, and he found himself the founder of a community. In honor of the sable pioneer the new settlement was called "Tonytown." At length the name seemed hardly genteel enough to suit the more fastidious residents, and the place was formally christened Fellowship. But to this day Tonytown is the name that comes most readily to the lips of some of the old people hereabouts when Fellowship is the place spoken of.

Another extinct institution which is remembered by more people than have any recollection of slavery, is the public whipping-post. Its day ended somewhere about sixty years ago, but it had been a pretty long day. A certain specified class of crimes and misdemeanors were made punishable by a greater or less number of lashes publicly scored on the bare back of the offender by the constable. The mode of punishment yielded to the sentiment of the age, and was abolished; but in recent years a reaction against the softer sentiment has begun to manifest itself. The whipping-post has been re-established in some places, and it may be that Moorestown will yet see its revival. In the old time the whipping-post here was the great sycamore tree just East of the William Penn Hotel. Culprits were fastened to the trunk that had originally been intended to secure the horses of worshippers in the old Meeting House, and the sentence of the law was marked with the lash upon their backs. One of the last whippings administered there had a most tragic sequel.

Between sixty and seventy years ago the old Cox Tavern, East of William Doughten's store, was kept by Joseph Bright. He was not only hotel proprietor, but constable also; and a part of his official duty was to administar punishment to offenders at the whipping-post. One day he whipped a couple of men at the old sycamore, and it was the last whipping he ever inflicted. A day or two afterward he drove out of town in his sulky on a business errand. He had not returned at dark, but in the night his horse was heard to enter the hotel premises. When some of the household went out, there stood the horse, still attached to the sulky, and there, with his foot fast in the wheel, and his battered head upon the ground, hung poor Joseph Bright, stone dead. His horse had run, and he had been dragged an unknown distance by the foot. He was dreadfully mangled, and the first theory was that he had been thrown from his seat by the runaway, and had been caught by the foot and dragged to his death. But a further investigation led many to believe that his death was not the result of accident, but of murder. It was declared his foot could never have got into the wheel by accident in the peculiar manner in which it was fastened there, but must have been placed there by design. Physicians also asserted that there were injuries on the dead man's body which could not have resulted from being dragged by the foot, and these in themselves would have produced death. At length the belief became general that Joseph Bright had been waylaid and murdered, and his dead body fastened by the foot to his sulky, after which his horse had been lashed into a run. If so the murderer was never caught and punished.

The Cox Tavern under Joseph Bright's administration, as under the administration of those before and after him, was the headquarters of the war-like citizens who participated in General Training. There is nothing in our time that takes the place of "Training Day." The circus does not come within a long way of it; and the encampments of our State Militia bear no more resemblance to it than the service of the Paid Fire Department bears to a "run with the machine" under the escort of an old Volunteer Company. What elderly man will ever forget the training days of his youth, with their "fuss and feathers," their gingerbread and beer, their dreadful din of fife and drum, and their motley gathering of all the elements from near and far? If he should forget all the rest he never can forget the bloody fights which the day inevitably brought. The occasion seemed to breed the ferment of war in the blood of some of the most peaceful soldiers; and when the whisky liberally furnished in the bar-room of the Cox Tavern had had time to take full effect there was very sure to be blood in the eyes of at least half a score of men; and such fights have never been seen since in Moorestown as were always seen on Training Day. Altogether it was one of the institutions that will do very well in memory and tradition, but nobody need wish to see revived.

Mention has been made of the tribulations of the people hereabouts in Revolutionary times because of the predisposition of the British soldiers to assume the ownership of whatever property came within their reach. The owners of live stock had a particularly hard time of it, because of the difficulty of hiding horses and cattle. The grandfather of Miss Hannah Warrington, being fully aware of the risk his good horses ran of becoming some other man's horses, took timely precautions in his own way. Every day he and his men would go into the field and chase the animals about, throwing their hats at them and making the most unearthly hullabaloo that could be devised. The result was that the horses soon became as wild as the wildest specimen then ranging the prairies of the West. The owner of them had his reward. The British came, and all the neighbors saw their horses driven off; but in the field of this prudent man there was much racing and chasing and swearing, all with but slight effect. There was one young horse which the soldiers were specially ambitious to catch. They chased him until they were tired and discouraged. They went away, but some of them came back after marching a considerable distance, and renewed the attempt. Their second effort was no more successful than their first, and they finally withdrew, leaving the horse to prance undisturbed. How long it was before this enterprising Friend was able to catch any of his own horses is not related.

A woman living in the same neighborhood had a very serviceable inspiration when the British came and her family silver was in danger. There was not time to bury it, even if she had been so minded. There was barely time to tie it up in a bundle. This was done, and then came the inspiration. The precious bundle was plumped into a tub of soft soap. Accustomed as they were to searching in all sorts of unlikely places for valuables, none of the soldiers thought of exploring the bottom of a soap tub, and the lucky owner had an opportunity of scouring her own silver bright again.

Captain Murrel, of Burlington, the grandfather of the late Reuben Stiles, has been mentioned as a daring and successful scout in the Revolutionary army. When the Americans had regained possession of Burlington a council of officers was held one night to decide on the fate of a prominent and active tory of the place. He had fled from home when the Americans got possession of Burlington, and had since been with the British. At this time, however, it had become known that he was secretly visiting his family in Burlington. At the council it was decided, after much consideration, that he should be caught and hung. The man was a neighbor and had been a friend of Captain Murrel, and that officer could not bear to think of his dying an ignominious death if an effort of his could save him. So he slipped unperceived from the council room, ran to the tory's house, saw his wife, and told her that, if her husband was at home and valued his life he had better be gone in five minutes' time. Then he ran back to his companions before his absence had been noted. His thoughtful bravery—for if his action had been discovered he himself would have fared but ill—saved the life of his tory neighbor. When the searching party reached his house he was gone. He was heard from next in Philadelphia, and in a way that might well have made Captain Murrel repent his kindness. The tory refugee sent a letter to the man who had saved his life, not to thank him for his service, but to assure him that the writer had a halter for his rebel neck, and would put it there when the opportunity offered!

Some seventy years ago a tragedy occurred which made a profound and lasting impression, not only in Moorestown but in a wide circle outside of it. In the latter part of the winter a party of four well known persons, comprising Henry Warrington, Esther Collins, Ann Edwards and Nancy Stokes, left Moorestown in a carrage to visit friends across the river in Pennsylvania. They drove Northward to the river, intending to cross on the ice. The winter had been a very severe one; the ice had formed to a considerable thickness, and there had been a great deal of travel upon it. Too many heavy vehicles had traversed it for the safety of those who now wished to cross the river. Deep ruts had been cut in the ice, and recent warm weather had weakened the whole mass.

Unconscious of any danger Henry Warrington drove his horses upon the frozen bridge. They had gone a considerable distance from the shore, and Mr. Warrington was making a jesting remark to his companions, when, without any warning, the ice broke under them and horses and carriage were in the water. Henry Warrington and Mrs. Stokes were on the front seat of the carriage, and their escape was easy. He assisted Mrs. Stokes to step upon the unbroken ice, and followed her without any difficulty. This seemed the only way to assist the others, who were on the back seat of the carriage, where the closed curtains prevented their getting out. As soon as the front seat was vacated Mrs. Collins stepped over it and endeavored, with Mr. Warrington's and Mrs. Stoke's help, to reach the ice. But she was a large and heavy woman; the edge of the ice broke under her weight; she fell back into the water and was swept under the ice before her friends could make any further effort to save her. Mrs. Edwards was apparently stunned by the suddenness of the accident, and made no effort to leave her seat. The others urged her to come within their reach; but in a moment the swift current had drawn the carriage under the ice with the unfortunate woman still in her seat.

The body of Mrs. Collins was recovered shortly after the accident, not far from where she had been drowned, and her funeral took place at the house of David Roberts on the Fellowship road. She had been a well and widely known woman, highly esteemed as a preacher in the Society of Friends, and greatly respected far and near as a person of superior character. Her death under any circumstances would have been generally lamented; and the terrible manner in which it came made it doubly impressive. Her funeral was the largest that any of the old inhabitants remember in this vicinity. People came from Burlington, Philadelphia and from many other places to be present at the services.

An old citizen now resident here, was then a boy living with David Roberts, and with a boy's curiosity he counted the vehicles assembled at the place on this occasion. There were one hundred and sixty-seven carriages, and thirty-five gigs and chairs. The carriages—or wagons as they were called—were of the old fashioned style, capable of holding six or seven persons, and all had come filled with occupants. When the train started for Moorestown the boy climbed out upon the roof of the house to watch the procession. When the head of the line had reached Moorestown the rear of it had not yet turned out of the Fellowship Road.

The body of Mrs. Edwards was not found until the following summer. Some fishermen found the carriage lodged in a cove near Camden. The body of the drowned woman was still in it, and almost in the spot where she had been sitting before the accident. Her funeral took place in Moorestown on the Sunday following, and is said to have been even more largely attended than that of Mrs. Collins.

The "Log Cabin and Hard Cider Campaign" of 1840 brought more political excitement to Moorestown than the old town had ever known before. Whether any time since has exceeded it is very doubtful. The flame that over-ran the whole country was as fierce here as elsewhere, and people indulged in excesses of enthusiasm which it is difficult to comprehend in an "off year." The largest meeting of the campaign, and at that time the largest political meeting ever held in Burlington county, was held at Gilbert Page's place, opposite the William Penn Hotel. Wagons loaded with men and boys came pouring in from all the surrounding country. Log cabins, trees with coons among the branches, typical cider barrels, flags, torches, transparencies, brass bands, men hoarse with shouting, boys wild with excitement, all combined to make that particular night one that is still vividly remembered by some of those who then lived here.

The principal feature of the display was an immense log cabin, mounted on wheels. It had been dragged by four horses from Medford, and was inhabited by a crowd of enthusiastic men and boys. This particular cabin was afterwards taken to Baltimore to help out a big meeting there. The fervor of those who participated in the meeting at Gilbert Page's was kept up through a great part of the night, being re-inforced in numerous instances by fluids that were even more potent than hard cider. The next morning there was less enthusiasm, but a good deal more serious reflection.

Gilbert Page seems to have been a man of many parts in his time. He was postmaster, storekeeper, politician and prominent citizen generally. He not only kept a store and kept the postoffice, but he also kept geese. Between the Friends' Meeting House enclosure and the House which served Gilbert Page as residence, store and postoffice, there was a shady lane, as there is now. Down that lane Mr. Page used to drive his geese, that they might forage along its pleasant length.

His flock of geese numbered about thirty, and the owner took much pride in his web-footed tenantry. But one night some miscreant stole every goose of the flock, leaving an old gander as the sole representative of what had been. The theft was bad enough, but the circumstances attending it made it especially exasperating. In a little bag the thieves had put a penny for every goose stolen, and placed the parcel in a conspicuous position in the immediate neighborhood of the gander's resting place. To the outside of the bag they had pinned a piece of paper on which had been written the following lines, to serve as a specimen of the talents possessed by these literary brigands:

"Dear Mr. Page,
　Don't be in a rage;
But if you do it's no wonder,
　For I bought all your geese
　For a penny a piece,
And left the money with the gander."

As the old-school novelists used to say, Mr. Page's feelings may be more easily imagined than described when he perused these lines and comprehended their full import. From all accounts he was not a man who was much given to disguising his emotions. On the contrary he always gave them the most emphatic expression he could master. On this occasion he is reported to have exhausted a tolerably extensive vocabulary of vehemence. Accordingly no long time had elapsed before everybody knew just what had happened, and just how Mr. Page felt about it.

Unhappily the perpetrators of this double crime were never discovered. It would be a pleasant thing to know that they had been suitably punished for stealing the geese, and twice punished for dropping into such poetry as that quoted.

Another thieving enterprise that is still told of by some of the old people, had a different ending. Sixty years or more ago a store was kept in the building which is now a dwelling at the Southeast corner of Main street and Church Road, opposite George Heaton's present store. The ground where the Episcopal Church stands was at that time covered with a growth of bushes and small trees capable of affording a good hiding place for skulkers.

One afternoon a couple of suspicious-looking fellows were seen lurking about the vicinity of the store; and their actions and appearance set the proprietor to thinking that mischief was intended. He determined to set a watch for that night; for there were no special policemen then, and he must needs depend upon his own resources. A shoemaker, noted for his fleetness of foot, lived on the opposite side of Church Road, and he agreed to watch with the store keeper. In the night the two watchers heard noises in the store, and took prompt and decisive action. They acted in the wrong way, however. Instead of going out at the back door and entrapping the intruders at the front door, they came into the store from the rear room where they had been posted, and the thieves made an easy exit at the front door by which they had entered.

The volunteer police were armed with guns, so that things were not quite so bad as they might have been, after all. Both of them fired just as the fugitives took refuge in the bushes on the opposite corner. They hit one of the fellows and captured him; but the other one got away. However, they felt that it was better to catch one burglar than none at all.

For so old a place there is a surprising small amount of legendary treasure buried beneath the surface of Moorestown. No "Treasure Tree," or "Miser's Cave," or "Robbers' Rock" is known to exist anywhere about here. People seem to have acquired property and disposed of it in regular, humdrum fashion, except in the Revolution; and the treasure that was buried then seems to have been all dug up again by its rightful owners.

But the matter-of-fact old place is not quite bereft of money mystery. There is here what, in some places, would be considered an excellent chance to dig for treasure; but only a few know about it, and nobody at all knows where to dig. A good many years ago an old lady—long since dead and buried—dreamed a dream. It was a very vivid dream, and its clearness of detail convinced the dreamer that "there must be something in it." One of her ancesters, or else a neighbor of one of her ancestors, had done what a great many other people did in the time of the Revolution—buried money and valuables to keep them out of the hands of the British soldiers. In the dream this individual was seen to dig a hole at the foot of a fence-post at the rear of the old tan-yard below Union street and bury something; she was not seen to dig it up again; therefore she never did dig it up, and it is there yet. The exact location of the post was noted by the dreamer, even to counting the number of posts between it and the corner, so that the particular post could be readily identified.

No attempt was made to follow the leadings of this dream, for a very good reason: The dream was delayed until after Second street was laid out and opened, and consequently the entire fence seen in the dream had disappeared, and the buried treasure was astray somewhere in the middle of Second street.

Some forty or fifty years ago an old house, long, high and narrow, stood on the South side of Main street, just West of George Haverstick's present residence. Whatever it had been originally, it had at this time become a tenement occupied by a number of colored families. The inhabitants of the old barracks are described as having been decidedly undesirable members of the community. There was good deal of brawling and disorder about their premises, and a good many petty depredations that were committed were charged to their account. It was decided that they must move, and a sort of Vigilance Committee was organized to carry the decision into effect. The committee was composed of young men, but who they were of course nobody knows. The tenants of the old house were notified that another and a distant place of residence was what they must hunt for and find within a given time. They heeded the warning and got out. Then, in order that no other like tenants should occupy the house, it was decided that the building itself must go. Accordingly, one night chains and ropes were hitched to the timbers; numerous strong hands tugged at the chains and ropes in silence, and the old structure came to the ground.

It is related that a magistrate of that day, who lived in the neighborhood, got wind of what was going on, and sympathized heartily with the movement. It would not do for him to openly countenance so unlawful a proceeding, but he sought out one of the young fellows whom he judged to be interested and said to him: "If thee wants any ropes or anything at any time, there are some in my barn. The barn is not locked, so thee can help thyself and say nothing to me about it." His ropes helped pull down the old building, but they were in their place in the barn the next morning.

Chapter XX

Some Old Reading Matter.

A GOOD deal of important literary work was done by some of the earlier citizens here, which but few people have ever had the opportunity of reading. Perhaps but few people would care for the opportunity of reading some of it; for, while it had a great deal of meaning it had a still greater amount of words, and a good deal of patient effort is required to shake the ideas out of the wordy entanglement in which they have been caught. Still some of the old documents which, like the names of newspaper correspondents, had to be given, "not necessarily for publication, but as evidence of good faith,"—the conveyances of real estate, and the like—have an interest of their own, at least for some readers; and therefore it may not be amiss to offer a sample or two here for perusal.

The first is a deed for certain property on Penisauken Creek, conveyed in the year 1695, by Charles Reade to Robert Stiles, one of the ancestors of the ate Reuben Stiles, for so many years Assessor of Moorestown. The document is written out with great care on sheepskin, the upper edge of which is left untrimmed. Elaborately illuminated lettering at the head introduces the text of the instrument, and a quaint little square seal of red wax in the center of the bottom edge testifies to the regularity and authority of the transfer described. The handwriting is clear and beautiful, with many flourishes, and the lines of writing are as straight and even as if ruled. There is an untrammelled freedom in the use of capitals that is charming, and some of the abbreviations, as well as some of the spelling are calculated to startle the reader of to-day. Following is the full text of the document:

THIS IDENTURE made the Twenty seventh day of the fifth month called July in the year of our Lord one thousand six hundred ninety and five BETWEEN Charles Read of the Town of Philadelphia in the Province of Pennsilvania Taylor af the one part AND Robert Stiles of the same place Sawyer of the other part WITNESSETH that the said Charles Reade for and in consideration of the full sum of Sixty pounds current money of the said Province to him in hand pd or secured to be paid by the sd Robert Stiles at or before ensealing and delivery of these presents the receipt whereof and every part and parcel thereof he the said Charles Reade doth.

acknowledge and thereof and of every part thereof doth acquit Release exonerate and discharge the sd Robert Stiles his Heirs Executors & Administrators And every of them forever by these presents HATH Given granted bargained and Sold Allyon'd Enfeoffed and confirmed and by these p'sents doth fully clearly & absolutely give grant bargain & sell Allyen Enfeoff & confirm unto the sd Robert Stiles his Heirs & Assigns forever four hundred & twenty five acres of land situate lying and being between the two branches of Pensauken Creek in the Province of West New Jersey bounded on the East with William Clark's land and on the west with the land of John Rudderough excepting two small parcels of meadow and swamp land wch lyes before the land of the sd Rudderough fronting the creek the one parcell lying below the sd Rudderough's house beginning at an oak for a corner by the creek side runs east south east seven chains to a marked corner thence north five chains to the creek again and so down the severall courses of the same to the first mentioned oak Surveyed and laid out for six acres the other parcell lying above the sd Rudderough's house begins at the lower end of the meadow by the creek side adjoyning to the upland and runs by the same seven chains to a corner thence east to the creek and so down the same to the first station layd out for four acres (as the Surveyor's draught thereof more fully may appear) Which said land and meadow was purchased by the sd Charles Reade the one three hundred acres thereof from Joseph Adams and Mary his wife by Indenture bearing date the thirteenth day of August Anno Domini 1694 and one hundred and twenty five acres of it (wch makes up the Compleat Quantity of 425 acres above granted) from George Hutcheson by Indenture bearing date the Twenty sixth day of September Anno Domini 1694 (as by their said Indentures Relation thereunto being had more largely may appear) Together wth all the Edifices and improvemts thereupon and all and every the mines mineralls woods meadows pastures feedings hawkings huntings ffishings fowlings & all other the Royalties and privilidges Profitts Commodities and appurtenances whatsoever to the same belonging or in anywise appertayning And all the Estate Right Tytle Interest Possession claime & demand whatsoever of him the said Charles Reade in Law and Equity or either of them in or unto the sd granted promisses or any part thereof And the Provisions & Remainders thereof & of every part and pareell thereof To HAVE & To HOLD the sd four hundred & twenty five acres of land & meadow wth the appurtenances and every part thereof unto the sd Robert Stiles his Heirs & Assigns forever To the only proper use and behoof of him the sd Robert Stiles his Heirs & Assignes forevermore And the said Charles Reade doth for himselfe his

Heirs Executors & Administrators covenant promise & grant to & with the sd Robert Stiles his Heirs & Assignes by these p'sents that at the time of the ensealing and delivery of these p'sents he stood Rightfully seized of the land and premises above granted and that he had good Rightfull power and Lawfull authority to sell and confirm the same unto the said Robert Stiles his Heirs & Assignes in maner & form afforesd And that he hath not wittingly or willingly committed suffered or done any act matter or thing whatsoever whereby or by reason whereof the sd granted premises or any part or parcell thereof is or shall or may be charged burthened or encumbered in any Style Charge Estate or otherwise howsoever (other than the Quit Rents thereout Issuing to the Chief Lord of the Soil wth the arrears thereof if any be) but the same against him the sd Charles Reade & his Heirs ag'st the Heirs of Joseph Adams & Mary his wife aga'st the Heirs of Hutcheson and against all their Heirs and against all person & persons whatsoever claiming or to claim from by or under him them or any of them their means privity consent or procurem't shall and will warrant & forever defend by these p'sents And further that the sd Charles Read his Heirs or Assignes shall and will at all times hereafter during the space of seven years next ensuing execute such further & other Lawfull Acts for the further confirmation of e above granted premises wth the appurtenances unto the sd Robert Stiles his Heirs & Assignes as by him or them shall be reasonably Required so as such further assurances containe no other Warranty than is above Expressed IN WITNESS whereof the party first above named to this p'sent Indentures hath set his hand and Seal the day and year first above written 1695.

CHARLES (SEAL) READE

The outside of this elaborate instrument is endorsed, with much involved flourishing, as follows:

"Sealed and delivered in p'sence of
    WILLIAM ALBERSON,
    WILLIAM HEARN,
    WILLIAM ALBERSON, JUNER.

A further endorsement reads:
"Be it remembered that on this twentyeth day of April Anno Dom: one thousand seven hundred and twenty-six p'sonally came and appeared before me Daniel Cox Esquire one of the judges of the County Court for holding pleas for the County of Hunterdon in the Pro. of New Jersey William Hearn one of the witnesses above signed being one the people called Quakers who on his solemn affirmation according to law doth declare that he was present and saw Charles Reade the grantor

w'thin named sign seal and deliver the within written Instrument of bargain and sale to the uses therein mentioned and that at the doing thereof the two other subscribing witnesses were p'sent.

WILLIAM HEARN.

Affirmed before me
DANIEL COXE."

The matter is finished up with the following final endorsement:

"Burlington April 20th 1726
Recorded the within written deed ing' Publick Records of the Province of West Jersey in Lib. D. Vol. 94, 95.
SAM'L BUSHKILL,
D Sec'y."

The next of these old writings is about seventy years younger than the preceeding but has more immediate reference to Moorestown affairs, as it is a deed transferring the property on which stands the house that has been referred to in these pages as the old "Smith Mansion," and the "Harris Mansion"—the historic house in which some stirring Revolutionary scenes were enacted, and in which the first public religious services in Moorestown, outside of the Friends' Meeting Houses, were held. The document is a parchment sheet of formidable dimensions. It is executed with but little of the elaborate ornamentation that characterized the older one already given; but although the ink has paled with time, the writing is clear, and follows carefully ruled lines across the ample width of the page. There is a reckless liberality in the use of capitals that is compensated for by the extreme parsimony shown respecting punctuation marks. The deed bears date August 2, 1766, and is as follows:

THIS INDENTURE Made the Second day of August in the Year of Our Lord One Thousand Seven Hundred and Sixty Six Between Joshua Humphries of the Township of Chester in the County of Burlington and Western Division of the Province of New Jersey Yeomen and Increase his Wife of the One part, and Samuel Smith of the City of Burlington and Province aforesaid Esquire of the Other part WHEREAS Robert Clinton by Sundry good Conveyances in the Law heretofore had and Duly Executed became Seized in fee of and in One full Equal and undivided Sixth part of a Propriety to Lands in West Jersey and being thereof Seized Did by Deeds of Lease and Release Dated the Twelveth and Thirteeth Days of May Anno Domini 1682 Grant and Convey the said Sixth part of a Propriety Unto Thomas Martin in fee as by said Deeds recorded in the Secretarys office in Burlington in

Lib B fol 109, will appear. And Whereas the said Thomas Martin being so Seized by Letter of Attorney Dated the Twenty Ninth of August Anno 1684 impower his Brother James Martin to Sell and Convey all his Estate in West Jersey as by the said Letter of Attorney recorded in the said Office in Book B aforesaid fol 78 will appear. And Whereas the said James Martin being Impowered as aforesaid Did by Deed Dated the Twenty fifth day of September Anno Domini 1686 Grant and Convey the said Sixth part of a Propriety unto Thomas Rodman of Rhode Island in fee as by said Deed of record in said office in Book B aforesaid fol 109 will appear And Whereas the said Thomas Rodman being So thereof seized Caused part of the said Share to be Surveyed in the Townships of Chester and Evesham as by a Survey thereof remaining and on Record in the Surveyor Generals office in Burlington in Lib A fol 1 will appear, and being thereof Seized as aforesaid Died having first made his last Will and Testament and therein Did Give and Devise the Said Land with other Lands unto his son Clark Rodman in fee Who being Seized thereof Did by Deed of Lease and release Dated the Twelveth and Thirteenth Days of October Anno Domini 1730 Grant and Convey three Hundred acres part of the Said Lands to Francis Hogsett in fee as by Said Deeds Recorded in the Secretarys office in Lib E fol 207 will appear.

And Whereas the said Francis Hogsett being so Seized Did by Deed of Bargain and Sale Dated the first Day of April Anno Domini 1734 Grant and Convey One Hundred and Eighty acres and three rood part of the said three Hundred acres unto Nehemiah Haines in fee as by said Deed recorded in the said Office in Lib E aforesaid fol 166 will appear. And the said Nehemiah Haines being So thereof seized Did Together with Ann his wife Grant and Convey One Hundred and Seventy nine acres and three rood of the Same unto Joshua Humphries the partie hereto his heirs and assigns as by said Deed Dated the Twenty eight Day of March in the year of Our Lord One Thousand Seven Hundred and Thirty Eight refference being thereto had will appear. And Whereas the said Joshua Humphries being seized of rights unlocated Land Caused to be Surveyed the Quantity of Seventeen acres two rood Situate on a branch of of the Mullica River called Mechescatuxing in the County of Gloucester as by the Survey thereof remaining in the Surveyor Generals Office it will appear. NOW THIS INDETURE WITNESSETH That the said Joshua Humphries and Increase his Wife for and in Consideration of the Sum of Nine Hundred and Sixty three pounds Current money of Said Province to the Said Joshua Humphries in hand paid by the said Samuel Smith at or before the Ensealing and Delivery of these presents the receipt Whereof he the said Joshua Humphries doth hereby Acknowledge and thereof and Every part and parcel thereof Doth Clearly Acquit and Discharge the said Samuel Smith his Executors and Administrators and Every of them by these presents Have Granted Bargained and Sold Aliened Enfeofed Conveyed and Confirmed And by these presents Do Grant Bargain and Sell Alien Enfeof Convey and Confirm unto the said Samuel Smith and to his heirs and assigns two pieces of Land the one being All that his Farm Plantation and Tract of Land Situate Lying and being in the Township of Chester aforesaid and is part of the Land above recited being Bounded as followeth Beginning at a Stake Standing on the North side of the Road Leading through Moores Town which Stake is Corner to a Lot of Land belonging to Joshua Humphries Jun'r and stands One Hundred and thirty foot from a stone Corner to Joshua Bisphams Land then by the said Humphries Lot South thirty five degrees fifteen minutes East fifty two Chain to a Stake Standing in William Hootens Line then by the same South fifty nine degrees West thirty two Chain and forty links to Stake near a Water Oak Bush marks Corner to John Middletons Land then by the same North thirty two degrees West forty five chain and twenty three links to the Corner of a Lot Sold by the said Humphries to Thomas Lippincott then by the same North Sixty Seven

Degrees East two Chain and Six Links to a Stone Corner to the Same then still by Said Lot North Twenty One Degrees thirty minutes West Ten Chain and twenty five Links to a Stake in the Line of Charles Frenchs Land on the North Side of the said Road, then along the Said Frenchs Line North Sixty Six Degrees thirty minutes East Twenty Six Chains and thirty eight Links to the place of Beginning Containing One Hundred and Sixty acres and two rood of Land The Other being the One Equal half part of all that piece of Cedar Swamp above recited to be at the said Samuel Smiths choice TOGETHER with all and Singular the Houses Edifices Buildings Orchards Pastures Commons Woods Woodlands Water Water Courses Mines Minerals profits Commodities Hereditaments and Appurtenances Whatsoever to the said two parcels of Land belonging or in any Wise appertaining or therewithal used Occupied or Enjoyed or Accepted reputed taken and known as part parcel and member thereof And all the Estate right Title Interest use Trust property Possession Claim and Demand Whatsoever of them the Said Joshua Humphries and Increase his Wife of in and to the Premises and Every or any part or parcel thereof And the Reversion and Reversion Remainder and Remainders Yearly and other rents and profits of the premises and of Every part and parcel thereof Together with all and Singular Deeds Evidences and Wrighting

Touching and Concerning the Said Premises only *To Have And Hold* the Said Farm Plantation and Tract of Land as above Bounded and Described as also the one half part of the Said Cedar Swamp and all Singular Other the premises hereinbefore mentioned meant or intended to be hereby Granted Alienated Released or Confirmed and every part and parcel thereof With their and Every of their appurtenances unto the Said Samuel Smith his heirs and assigns To the only proper use benefit and behoof of him the said Samuel Smith his heirs and assigns forever. And the Said Joshua Humphries for himself his heirs Executors and Administrators and for Increase his Wife Doth Covenant Promise Grant and agree to and With the Said Samuel Smith his heirs and assigns and Every of them by these presents in Manner and Form following That is to Say, That the Said Joshua Humphries at the time of the Ensealing and Delivery of these presents is Seized of and in the Said Farm and Tract of Land and also the Said Cedar Swamp and all and singular Other the premises in and by these presents Granted Bargained and Sold With all Every their Rights members and appurtenances Of a good sure perfect and absolute Estate of Inheritance in fee simple Without any Condition Reversion Remainder or Limitation of any use or uses Estate or Estates in or to any Person or Persons whatsoever to Alter Change Defeat Determine or make

Void this present Grant. And that the said Joshua Humphries at the Time of Ensealsng and Delivery of these presents Hath full power Good right and Lawful authority to Grant Bargain Sell and Convey all and Singular the before herewith Granted or Mentioned to be Granted premises with their and Every of their appurtenances unto the said Samuel Smith his heirs and assigns in Manner and Form aforesaid And Further the said Joshua Humphries Covenants and agrees to and with the said Samuel Smith and his heirs and assigns as followeth that is to Say that it shall and may be Lawfull for the said Samuel Smith his heirs and and assigns at any Time hereafter to Cause a Division of the said Swamp to be made and to take his their choice of the part they see fit. And Lastly the said Farm Plantation and Tract of Land With the One half of the said Cedar Swamp in the Quiet and Peaceful Possessions of him the said Samuel Smith his heirs and assigns against the Lawfull Claims of All Persons Whatsoever he the said Joshua Humphries and his heirs shall and Will for Ever Warrant and Defend. In Witness Whereof he the said Joshua Humphries and Increase his Wife have to this Indenture Set their hands and Seals the Day and year above Written 1776.

    Jos'a Humphries   (SEAL)

    Increase Humphries   (SEAL)

Sealed and Delivered   In presence of
                                  Jos Imlaye
                                  Danl Ellis

Rec'd August the Second 1766 of Samuel Smith Esq'r the Sum of Nine Hundred and Sixty three pounds In full of the Consideration money above mentioned I say Rec'd by me
                                  Jos'a Humphries
  Witnesses
        Jos Imlaye———Dan'l Ellis

I think the reader will agree with me, that if it was as hard work to write these specimens of old time literature as it is to read them, the composers of them earned a goodly share of all the property they conveyed.

Chapter XXI.

An Old Neighbor.

MOORESTOWN enjoys the friendly acquaintance of a good many old neighbors who settled in the wilderness and began to grow up with the country about the same time that she did. Some of them are near and some remote, but they are all on familiar speaking terms, and have a bond of fellowship in the common memory of the old times whose hardships and whose rugged enjoyments they shared. Among them all perhaps there is none with which Moorestown has so intimate a relationship as with Colestown. If it were possible for one old town to drop in on another for an afternoon chat, we can well imagine that these two old cronies would grow garrulous together in recalling the events both have known and the experiences they have shared. Many of their dead slumber together; and many of their living worshipped together for years. The ties of association are numerous and strong.

Colestown is the older of the two. Indeed it is older by a century than the Declaration of Independence; for Colestown was founded in 1676. The place was named for Samuel Coles who located a large tract of land near there in the early days of the place, and who became a person of much prominence and consideration. His descendents for very many years were prominent and influential in the affairs of the neighborhood, the family being specially distinguished for patriotism in the Revolutionary times. For a long time Colestown was a leading community hereabouts, and held its own bravely in the way of active prosperity. With the construction of new lines of communication, however, its importance vanished. It was left on one side of the grand highways. The tide of travel flowed past it at a distance, and it ceased to be an active business center. Gradually it fell further and further back in the race until now in its old age it sits quietly in its place and thinks of what has been. It has shriveled up with age, and the outlines that were well rounded and plumply filled out in youth are now but vaguely defined and show but very meagre substance.

Colestown lies between three and four miles from Moorestown, on the road to Haddonfield. The road is not long; but in the bright summer weather, with the dust laid by recent rains, which yet have not been sufficient to accomplish mud, it is a way of delight. Indeed it would be difficult to select a more exquisitely beautiful drive. There is no dead level, but on the other hand there is no rugged abruptness. The landscape stretches away in pleasantly satisfying variety. The surface undulates in smoothly rounded swells, so that there is variety everywhere. Fields of grass and of waving grain, with their limitless variations of color lie spread out on every hand. Trees of many growths are grouped in pleasant fashion here and there. Farm houses, some of them a century old, stand along the road; and between them are spaces of country solitude so quiet and undisturbed that wild rabbits and squirrels are encouraged to indulge in their antics there. Now and then a rustic lane or a country cross road takes its way among the fields, and invites the traveller to come away into even quieter seclusion than he finds on the road to Colestown.

No, it is not a long road but it suffices to take one quite away from even the echoes of city and town life. The railroad might be the breadth of a county away for all you see or hear of it. If you have taken your drive in the right time of the day you will encounter the stage on its way from Camden to Fellowship, for you have got into a region where the railroad is a convenience for other people, and where hurry and racket seem to have no place in the economy of life.

If this is your first excursion in this direction you will be at a loss to know when you get to Colestown; and in any case the demarkation between the town and its suburbs is but vague and dimly defined. Indeed there is no village, in the sense of a close cluster of houses, with stores, hotel and shops. There used to be such in the old, old times; but Colestown, in the village sense, is but a memory; and now the name is floated indefinitely over a rural neighborhood. But what a lovely neighborhood it is! It is difficult to believe that the old place could have been half as pretty as it is now, when it was a thriving, ambitious town with a future before it, as well as a past behind it.

Seeing the beauty of it, and the lovliness of the country around it, it is easy to understand how it came to be a favorite place of resort for invalids and pleasure-seekers in the days gone by. The instinct to seek health and recreation away from home was as strong then as now, and the difficulties in going very far for such purposes were infinitely greater. So it was a capital thing to have a thorough-going watering place right here within easy reach.

Here was a copious mineral spring, with an unfailing supply of water that smelled and tasted bad enough to commend it to the most exacting invalid. Science had given a diploma to the enterprising proprietor of the spring in the shape of an analysis of its waters; and the enterprising proprietor aforesaid had the record of the analysis cut in artistic letters on a marble tablet and the tablet set up beside the spring for all to read and be convinced. He moreover built a hotel, or sanitarium on the ground, and reaped the harvest from the good seed he had so wisely sown.

Sick people came in numbers to drink the waters; and whether it was because the waters were potent, or because the place was so lively and pleasant, or because the marble tablet was so convincing, or because of all these things, many who came got better, and therefore many more came. It is a curious fact that almost any place which attracts invalids also attracts well people and speedily becomes a place of popular resort and fashionable gayety. So Colestown became, in a small way, a center of pleasant social dissipation. The Fountain Hotel, as the sanitarium was called, was a frame structure of moderate proportions, but for that time was considered rather large than otherwise; and in "the season" it was filled to overflowing with guests. Its rooms were all taken by people who came for a regular campaign of greater or less duration. But aside from these, there were frequent incursions of transient parties who rode or drove from some of the neighboring regions for a day's pleasuring. To go to Colestown in those days meant very much what going to the sea-shore means in these.

It is a pity that such good times should come to an end, but they did. The Fountain Hotel ceased to be a place of resort, and not only that but it disappeared utterly from the face of the earth, and now there are not many who remember that there ever was such a place. The marble tablet, too, has long since gone, and nobody can now tell what potent elements that water contained. One old lady who visited the hotel and drank from the spring before the popular tide had been diverted from it, says the water "was bad enough to be good," and people who once drank of it were not likely to forget it. With this generalization we have to be content. It is said that one or two antiquarians know just where the old spring was located, but if so they keep the knowledge to themselves, and nobody else seems able to tell. About a quarter of a century ago a Philadelphia visitor had the place pointed out to him by an old resident; but a recent attempt of his to rediscover the spring was entirely without success. The old guide of the former occasion had passed away, and nobody could be found who knew where to look for what used to be a spot of great and lively importance. An almost forgotten tradition is all that remains of what was once a happy fact for very many of the young and old in Moorestown, and in the region round about.

Colestown still retains one monument of the past which associates it very intimately with Moorestown —St. Mary's Protestant Episcopal Church. Reference has been made in a previous chapter to the age of this venerable building, and to the parental relation in which it stands to Trinty Church in

Moorestown. It is not only one of the oldest churches in New Jersey, but for many years it was the *only* Episcopal Church in this region, and was the place of worship for all the Episcopalians in Moorestown, and in the surrounding country as well. Trinity parish, the child and successor of St. Mary's, was established—how and when have been fully described elsewhere—but the old church still remains; and there is not, within many miles, a more interesting place to visit than is St. Mary's Church at Colestown.

It is not an imposing edifice. Those who imagine that an episcopal church must have stone walls pierced with pointed windows and thickly overgrown with clinging ivy, and that a hoary tower of ancient masonry must point Heavenward from at least one of its corners, will find their imaginings rudely upset at sight of this one. No Friends' meeting house could be more severely plain and simple than this old church. It is of wood, and not the slightest attempt has been made at ornament in any direction. Even paint has been withheld, and the weather beaten boards show only the soft gray color that the winds and the rains bestow upon whatever wood is left for them to decorate.

The building is of moderate size and rather low. It stands with its gable end to the street, and the door is in the side toward the South. Above the door projects a little roof, like a square shelf, with no support save what it gets from the timbers in the wall behind it. There it has hung for generations, without post or brace to hold it up; and it is as straight and level to-day as ever, a good example of the "sincere" work that was done in the good old times.

There are six windows, two on each side and one at either end; and not one of them is arched or pointed or anything else than uncompromisingly right-angled. These are protected on the outside by solid wooden shutters, fastened by strong and quaint old fashioned latch-bolts; while the door is secured by a lock so solid and massive that it might almost protect a bank vault. A little chimney of red brick sprouts up from the middle of the roof-peak, and that chimney is the nearest approach to a tower that is visible about the church.

But it is not until the visitor has entered the building that he gets the full flavor of its quaint old age. There are no carpeted aisles stretching forward between ranks of closely ranged pews; no arrangements anywhere for cushioned comfort; few attempts at anything like beauty or elegance, and no signs of any purpose to use space to the best advantage. Not only does the place and everything in it look old, but in fashion and arrangement it all speaks of the simple tastes and habits of a primitive people.

The first and strongest impression on entering is of old unpainted wood. It is pretty nearly everywhere. The rounded ceiling, close under the roof, is plastered and whitened, and there is a narrow strip of plastered wall running around the building under the gallery, and a space of white plaster shows at the side of the room opposite the entrance door; but all the rest is wood, and for the most part unpainted. The floor is bare and the walls are wainscotted to within a short distance of the gallery. At the gallery floor the wainscotting begins again and is continued to the ceiling.

At the left of the door, as you enter, is the robing room. A wooden partition with a door in it, juts out into the church space for a distance, then turns a right angle and goes off toward the left. There is no ceiling to the little room, so the occupant has air to breathe. He also has light, for the partition encloses the window at the left of the entrance; but he has not much space in which to stand up, for the gallery stairs slope across the top of the enclosure, converting it into a stairway closet.

Two of these staircases lead up to the gallery from the opposite ends of the Southern front, and each is guarded, not by bannisters and rail, but by a solid board screen which extends from the floor to the gallery, and which is high enough to conceal all but the shoulders and head of the person who goes up or comes down. A peculiarity of the arrangement is that the stairs instead of starting near the door, begin the ascent as far from the door as possible, so that the worshipper who seeks a gallery seat has to travel half the length of the building before he reaches the foot of the stairs. The gallery itself extends along the front and across both ends of the building, and is boxed in by a high, solid board screen that extends along its entire front.

Over the front door, between the heads of the two staircases, is the choir, which is separated from the rest of the gallery by a board partition at each end. Here as well as in the rest of the gallery, rows of wooden benches, rising gradually toward the wall, furnish seats for the gallery occupants. Down stairs, also, wooden benches, furnished with comfortable backs and arms, but with never a thought of cushions, are arranged in rows across the floor, with a broad aisle through the middle of the church. The whole arrangement of seats shows utter carelessness as to economy of space.

Of course all these details do not present themselves at first; but the impression of old wood emphasizes itself so strongly that the observer has to analyze it first of all, and so he takes note of all the solid, unpainted masses—the partitions of the robing room, the high-screened stair-cases, the bottom and front of the gallery, the uncovered floor and the rows of benches. But he does all this with the consciousness that the effect which he is analyzing is heightened by a vivid contrast, and as soon as he can he gives his attention to the first object that presented itself to him in clear individuality as he entered. This is the pulpit.

It is placed on the North side of the church directly opposite the door and looms up, high and white, in front of the visitor as he enters. It is a round box, painted a clear white, and is so high that it must be entered by ascending quite a flight of stairs. The occupants of this pulpit whether they were learned or otherwise, must always have "preached far above the heads of their congregation." Above the pulpit hangs a quaint, round sounding board, also painted white. The reading desk below is another white object. The chancel rail, projecting far into the body of the church, is of mahogany surmounting white banisters. The space inside the rail is carpeted, and this is the only portion of the floor redeemed from bareness, as the pulpit and its accessories show the only paint to be seen in the building.

High above the pulpit and on either side of it, are two little square windows to afford light to the clergyman, and they must be rather trying to the eyes of the congregation on a bright day. The six large windows of the church are not so very large, but each of them contains twenty-four panes of glass, twelve in either sash. The panes are very small and the sashes are very large, giving the impression of a great deal of wood to not very much glass.

These eight windows afforded sufficient light for the day service, but what provision was made for evening service? On one of the smooth, round, unpainted columns which support the gallery is nailed a little shelf. On this shelf was set a candle-stick and the solitary candle that burned therein is said to have given the light enjoyed by the congregation on night occasions. A couple of candles placed on the pulpit and the reading desk gave the clergyman what light he needed; and these scant appliances for illumination were the substitute for chandeliers and candelabra.

Warmth seems to have been better provided for than light. In the very center of the church stands a stove which, while it is a good deal younger than the building, is itself in the enjoyment of a hale old age. It is of a pattern long since obsolete, and was made when wood was the accepted fuel and anthracite had not assumed the place it now holds. Straight up from the top of the stove ascends a slender, black column of stove-pipe, its summit disappearing in the bottom of the little chimney. The stove-pipe is held in position by a heavy iron rod, either end of which is made fast to the gallery.

It was certainly not because the old church was falling into decay that it was given up. There is no trace of decay about it, and there seems no reason why it should not last in good condition for another century or two. Certainly it is as sound and robust now as many buildings that have not seen a quarter of its years. And it is not correct to say that it has been given up for it has not. On the second Sunday of every month the building is opened and service held. No evening service is ever held now, and so the candle-sticks have no modern successors.

To visit Colestown and not walk through the old church-yard that lies back of St. Mary's is to miss one of the most impressive experiences our old neighbor has to offer. The original church-yard is comprised now within the wider limits of the present cemetery, but it keeps its individuality intact; and the rows of closely ranged graves show that those who sleep after the conflict far outnumber those who still wake and carry on the struggle of life. Generations of Colestown's dead lie here, some of them in graves so old that all means of identifying the sleepers have disappeared.

Many of the tombstones that remain are quaint enough with their unpretending, old-fashioned sculpture, and their equally old-fashioned epitaphs One of them bears the date of 1764. Another was erected to the memory of "Hannah, Wife of Benjamin Van Leery," who died in 1766. Another, still older, is a broad, low marble slab, inscribed: "In Memory of Humphrey Day, Who Died January 16, 1760, Aged 75 years."

A number of the graves have head-stones of the simplest and most primitive type. These are not of marble, chiselled or unchiselled; but are simply large flat stones in all their original roughness. No attempt has been made to smooth the surface or even to make the edges less sharp and rough. The gray stone, just as it came from the quarry, is set up to indicate that here some one lies, asleep. Some of these have, rudely scratched upon their surface, the initials of the sleepers. That is all; no name, no date, no record of age or time of death. All of them originally had some letters scratched upon them it is said, but some are so old that time has effaced even the little they formerly had to tell.

Probably the strangest and most unique monument in the old churchyard is one of the smallest. It is a trifle over a foot in height, is five and a half inches broad, and of about the same thickness; it is rounded into an arch at the top; its edges are straight and its angles tolerably true, and it is made of—brick, red brick! The clay was evidently moulded, by no unskilled hand, into the shape required, the letters of the inscription were scratched into the soft surface, and then the monument was baked, like any other brick. The inscription borne by this singular head-stone is as follows:

IN · MEMORy
OF · JOHN · FLE
AGO · WHO · DEPAR
TED · THIS · LIFE · DE
CEMBR · THE · 20
1791

With the reading of this quaint memorial it is as well to conclude the church-yard walk, and with it in our minds, we bid farewell to our Old Neighbor.

Chapter XXII.

Moorestown To-day.

AND what is the net result of all the elements and processes that have been touched upon in the preceding chapters? What is the product of their combination? In orderly and natural sequence of development Moorestown, as it is to-day, appears, the fruit—still growing and ripening—from the seed whose planting was in the far-away "old times" we have peered into; and whose growth was shaped by the influences we have considered. It is a fruit that is goodly to look upon, and still more goodly to contemplate in its future completeness. The stock that bears it has made a healthy progress, and the fruit itself is sound from core to rind.

In describing Moorestown as it is to-day, the first and most obvious thing to say of it is that it is a place of homes, and a place for homes. Its other characteristics range themselves about that one, as about their natural centre. The first impression the stranger receives on entering the place is of cosy and pleasant homes set in the midst of beautiful surroundings. On every street, in whatever direction a walk or drive is taken, the leading impression is still of the many charming homes. They are in many styles, from the fine old mansion of a hundred years ago, fronted by its wide lawn and shaded by its grand old trees, to the ornate modern house with its trim enclosure and its bewildering combination of unexpected lines and angles; from the modest little cottage with its honeysuckles and rose bushes, to the many-roomed structure with all the modern improvements. But they are all homes and not merely "residences." One somehow feels sure of that at the first glance.

And this most desirable characteristic will grow with the growth of the town; in fact its development will *be* the growth of the town. It is as a place for homes that Moorestown will widen its borders and add to its figures in the census tables; and nowhere is the opportunity for such growth more pleasantly suggested. The place has room to grow on every side; and on every side—and even within the present limits—the locations for more charming homes present themselves. More and more people are all the time availing themselves of the opportunities so presented, with the result that the old town is widening its borders year by year, and more and more people are becoming interested in its characteristics and resources.

The easy facilities for communication with Philadelphia commend the place strongly to those seeking homes, no less than to those whose homes are already established here. The distance by rail ranges from something over ten miles, to about twelve, depending upon which of the three stations is the point of arrival and departure. More than a dozen trains going to the city, and as many more coming from it, are at the disposal of the traveller every week-day the year round; and on Sundays there are church-trains for such as desire to use them. Going from Moorestown to the heart of Philadelphia is a matter of less time and trouble than going to the same point from many portions of the city itself. The time required to get to the foot of Market street is from thirty to forty minutes.

But the railroad is not the only means of communication with Philadelphia. The turnpike offers a capital drive, during a good share of the year, to such as prefer that method of travelling and have the means at command to gratify their preference. It is much in favor for pleasure driving, and it would be difficult to make a better selection for that purpose. The road is well kept; it runs through a pleasant country; the surface is varied enough to avoid monotony, and is not broken into troublesome hills; the distance is not so great as to be wearisome, and there is not much of it that is not interesting in one way or another.

This readiness of passage to and from Philadelphia constitutes one of the great recommendations of Moorestown as a place to set up a home. The man whose business is in the city, be he proprietor or clerk may have his home here and go back and forth daily to his business with scarcely more inconvenience than if he dwelt in some of the city's wards. The man who has retired from business may still, in his retirement, keep up the contact with the activity of city life. The ladies of the household can readily go on shopping expeditions, or other errands of pleasure, and as readily return to home surroundings. The younger members of a household for whom special city instruction is required, can avail themselves of the school-tickets issued by the railroad company, and so have home-life and city instruction. In short Moorestown is practically a rural suberb of Philadelphia.

So much for its relative position. Another and still more important matter for thought and inquiry relates to the physical welfare of people after they get here. It is pleasant to give the assurance that the old town is as healthy as it is beautiful, and that is saying a great deal. The ground on which it stands is high, forming a ridge; the air is pure and has free circulation; there are no streams in the immediate neighborhood, to overflow and leave pools of water to stagnate and grow green; the soil is a sandy loam through which the rain readily percolates, leaving the surface dry in a remarkably short space of time. As a result of this combination of characteristics malaria is not one of the accompaniaments of life here; and there are no diseases characteristic of the place. Indeed so far as health is concerned Moorestown is as greatly favored as any region in the Middle Atlantic States. To find much improvement on it one must go West or South into a totally different climate.

The convenience with which the details of living are managed here is another thing that commends the place to housewives, particularly. The lively writer who was "twelve miles from a lemon" was more than twelve miles from Moorestown. Easy as it is to get to Philadelphia, it is by no means necessary for residents here to go there in order to secure the necessaries, conveniences and many of the luxuries of daily life.

There are half a dozen general stores here; four or five meat markets; two or three bakeries; trimming and furnishing stores; shoe stores and tailor shops; livery stables, carriage and blacksmith shops; furniture stores and cabinet shops; plumbers, tinners and stove-dealers; carpenters in plenty. Milk wagons, bread wagons and meat wagons furnish daily supplies at the doors of the citizens. The stores send wagons to the houses of customers to receive orders and deliver goods, so that distance from the store causes but slight inconvenience; and local express wagons make daily trips to the city, carrying and bringing parcels at slight cost. So far as material conveniences are concerned Moorestown is pretty well provided.

The higher requirements of the dwellers here are also met to a great extent. Each branch of the Friends' Society has a meeting house, and of churches there are six—the Protestant Episcopal, the Baptist, the Methodist Episcopal, the Methodist Protestant, the African Methodist and the Roman Catholic. Regular services are held in each, and each has a well conducted Sunday School connected with it.

The importance of education is fully realized and and adequate provision is made for it. Besides the well conducted and thoroughly equipped public school, there are the Academy and the High School, under the control of the two branches of the Friends' Society. In either of them a thorough mastery of the higher branches may be obtained. Competent private teachers impart musical instruction to those desiring it. A well provided library offers excellent opportunities to intelligent readers and current literature, in the shape of daily newspapers, the magazines and the last new books, is obtainable at any time. The postoffice distributes three or four mails each day excepting Sundays, and by means of it and the telegraph and telephone, contact with the outside world is fully maintained.

The medical profession has always maintained a high rank in Moorestown. Eminent names appear in its annals—names that carried weight and authority far beyond the sphere of their immediate activity. The profession still maintains its high standard here. Skilful practitioners in both the leading schools of medicine and in surgery and dentistry are in active practise, and render sickness and pain as little formidable as doctors may. There are lawyers also well skilled in the intricacies of legal requirements, and with their learning at the command of any who may need it.

Moorestown, like most other places, is not an ideal abiding place. It lacks some things which it might well have, and has some things which it well might lack. To say that its good qualities far outnumber the other kind is to say very little, and is to state a fact already abundantly proved by the rapidity with which strangers have established homes here in recent years, and by the number of other strangers who are all the time following their example. A fair way to state the case is to say that the virtues of Moorestown are positive, and its faults negative. Its sins are mostly sins of omission. Enough has been told in the preceding chapters of this book to show that the old town has a reserve of wholesome and well directed energy sufficient to supply all important omissions. She has done a good deal in that direction, and is all the time doing more. The process is not a rapid one, but perhaps that is as well. What progress there is is in the right direction, and a carefully considered step, once taken, does not have to be retraced. After a journey of two centuries any town may well fall into a leisurely pace. So that the step is vigorous and firm it may be all the better for not being rapid. Stumbles are avoided, and stumbles are awkward things.

Chapter XXIII.

Moorestown in 1900.

MAY we all live to see what Moorestown is like in the year 1900! It is not a very extravagant aspiration although it sounds a little as if it were. Closing accounts with one century, and opening a new set of books for business with another century seems like a very momentous transaction which must necessarily be a long way off in the future. But, when we consider the matter, the Nineteenth Century cannot possibly hold out more than fourteen years longer.

But a great many things can happen in the space of fourteen years; and it is interesting to speculate on the character of the happenings in Moorestown in the interval. Judging from the past and the present the old town will occupy the time in going forward from good to better, and at an accelerated pace. Things that are desirable will be more readily brought to pass, and things that are undesirable will be more promptly done away with. The community will more and more fully realize the capabilities of the place, and will be more and more ready to develop them in the right way.

In the year 1900 there will be a good deal larger town on the Moorestown ridge than now occupies it. Its Western limit will have been pushed a goodly distance below the Forks of the Road, and its Eastern bound will be considerably above Fair Ground Avenue. Between the two extremes the space on Main street, Second street, Third street and the cross streets will have been filled up. The Eastern end of the town in particular, will have developed in a manner to surprise the resident who goes away now and comes back then. Not only will Main street be lined with homes, but other streets will have been opened and built upon, and the fields of to-day will be the lawns and door-yards of 1900.

North of the railroad an equally noticeable change will have been effected. Not only will the filling-up process keep on East of Chester avenue, but it will spread to the Westward; and a goodly share of the space between Chester avenue and Church Road will be laid off in streets and the streets for a considerable distance to the North will be well built up. Not all the space will be occupied, but a good deal of it will be.

In the year 1900 Main street will no longer form the Southern limit of the town. By that time people will have invaded the slope of the valley to a far greater extent than now. It will have been discovered that even steep places can be terraced, and that the smooth and level places in the world are not always and necessarily the best.

A community of such proportions and such expansive force will strongly desire to manage its own affairs, and the desire will have crystalized into an act of incorporation. Moorestown will have its own local government in the year 1900, and will no longer be merely a well built up part of Chester township. This result will not be attained at once, or without much balancing of opposing considerations. In the end, however, the considerations for will outweigh those against, and the thing will be accomplished.

The Telford pavement is already on its way, and when Main street has demonstrated to the rest of the town what a thoroughly desirable thing a well paved streeet is, the other streets of the place will emulate its excellence and have good pavements of their own, of one sort or another. The sidewalks, also, will declare their independence of mud, and "falling weather" will leave but a slight and transient record under foot. Some portion of this improvement—not all of it—will wait for local self-government to carry it into effect; but the year 1900 will see it accomplished.

Streets and sidewalks are for use in the evening as well as in the day time. Here and there a public spirited citizen recognizes that great truth, and honors his conviction by hanging a reflecting lamp on the front of his house, or setting up a lamp-post at his front gate. Every wayfarer whose feet these beacons save from stumbling blesses in his heart the man who lighted that lamp. And there are many such wayfarers, every night in the year; for the times have changed since those leisurely years when all legitimate business that was not concluded by sunset could wait until the next day, and when all respectable people were expected to be in bed by nine o'clock. By the year 1900 the community as a whole will have recognized this fact, and will have proclaimed its recognition of it by having all the streets lighted by some adequate public system of illumination. The system adopted may involve the use of the electric light; it may require only oil lamps, or it may make use of some agent not dreamed of now—so rapid is the advance of practical ideas. But whatever the means employed, the public streets will, without doubt, be publicly lighted.

Another public want will have demanded and obtained public recognition. It may not have been fully met and satisfied by the end of this century, but progress will have been made in that direction.

A community of such proportions as Moorestown is to attain cannot always depend on wells and rain-filled tanks for its water supply. A system of general distribution from some source will be devised and carried into effect.

One potent influence that will work toward this end will be the necessity for an adequate and reliable source of supply in case of fire. For by the year 1900 we shall have got beyond depending wholly on Providence and a hand-engine for protection against the flames. Some organized method of defense will have been adopted, and adequate appliances will be at command.

It would be a blessed world if every man could afford to own the home in which he desires to shelter his family. Unhappily every man cannot, so very many must pay rent. Unhappily, again, a large proportion of these cannot afford to live in large houses and pay large rent for them. And the class so unfortunately circumscribed as to money resources includes a goodly number of intelligent, educated and refined men and women; people whom any community is the better for having among its elements, and whose coming any community would do well to invite and encourage. This state of things will be more thoroughly realized here in the year 1900 than it now is, and more complete provision will have been made for the accommodation of the class of people referred to. The owners of property, and the men having money to invest will see that a safe and profitable thing to do is to erect moderate sized houses—prettily designed, conveniently arranged and pleasantly located —and to offer them at a moderate rental to the men who draw small salaries but who nevertheless object to living in ill-contrived and badly placed homes.

With the increase of population there will be an ever increasing pressure of the strong necessity, common to human nature everywhere, for relaxation and entertainment. Individuals and communities must have varied opportunities for pleasure, and will find or make such opportunities. In times past the Moorestown Literary Association demonstrated how ready this community was to welcome and pay for good intellectual recreation a quarter of a century ago. It would welcome the opportunity still more eagerly to-day, if the opportunity were offered it. For the most part people are not disposed to ride to the city for an evening's entertainment, pay car fare in addition to the admission fee, hurry out to catch the train before the end of the lecture or performance, and get back to their homes after midnight. So they go without their evening's entertainment. But they want it all the same.

Before the year 1900 they will have the opportunity for it afforded them here at home. Neither opera nor theatricals will be among the resources presented; but there will be good lectures, good concerts, good readings and good scientific demonstrations. These are all available for Moorestown, and these Moorestown will surely have, to its great enjoyment and advantage.

Of course an adequate and fitting place for such entertainments will have been provided. Business enterprise and public spirit will have combined to produce a public hall in which the entertainers can appear with every advantage, and in which the audience can sit through an evening in comfort and enjoyment. It will be commodious enough to accommodate the largest audience the population will contribute. It will be elegant in an unpretentious way, and will be as comfortable as thorough ventilation, good heating arrangements and the best seating contrivances can make it. The audience will be safe from fire, and from the worse danger of panic, because of exits ample for the most pressing emergency; and there will be a thorough protection against the disorderly element. It will be a place to which the most refined can go with pleasure; and through the agency of an association or a public committee, the public will be regularly and frequently invited to an evening's enjoyment there.

Moorestown as it is to-day, with its opportunities for healthful comfort and quiet happiness, is a dwelling place good to see and most good to live in; but with these added advantages supplementing and rounding out its present excellence, what rural or suburban town can surpass Moorestown in.1900?

I. W. HEULINGS' SONS,

DEALERS IN

LUMBER, COA

LIME, FERTILIZERS,

Doors, Sash, Blinds, Shutters, Mouldings,

ESTABLISHED 1841.

YARDS AT

CENTRETON,

MOORESTOWN,

RIVERTON, and

GEO. W. HEATON,

N. E. corner Main and Church Streets, MOORESTOWN, N. J.,
Dealer in

First - Class Groceries, Dry Goods,

NOTIONS, HARDWARE,

BOOTS, SHOES, CROCKERY, ETC., ETC.

Ready Mixed Paints, Oils, Etc., at the Lowest Market Price.

WALTON'S
MOORESTOWN EXPRESS

ESTABLISHED 1876.

All Errands to the City and other Business Transacted Promptly and on Reasonable Terms.

H. P. WALTON.

The Old Reliable Bakery.
ESTABLISHED IN 1851.

JOHN H. EISELE, successor to GEO. P. EISELE, Sr.

BOSTON HOME-MADE BREAD a Specialty.

Plain Cakes and Pies always on hand. All Fancy Cake Made to Order.

Main St., Moorestown, second door above Town Hall.

All Orders Filled at shortest notice. Prices as low as the lowest. Our Goods speak for themselves.

Moorestown Furniture Manufactory
—AND—
HOUSE-FURNISHING STORE.

Upholstering and House-Furnishing a Specialty.

GILBERT AITKEN, MOORESTOWN, N. J.

REEVE'S MOORESTOWN PHARMACY,

IN BURR'S BUILDING, MAIN STREET,

At all times can be found

Pure Drugs and Chemicals, Toilet and Fancy Articles.

Pure Wines and Liquors, for Medicinal Use Only. The preparing of Physicians' Prescriptions a Specialty. Always have on hand a full line of *Pure Spices*, whole and ground. An extensive assortment of Patent Medicines always on hand at MANUFACTURERS' RETAIL PRICES. Orders received and answered with care and dispatch.

WALTER S. REEVE, Pharmacist.

BOOTS AND SHOES

The Best and Most Popular Styles for Ladies and Gentlemen Always in Stock.

CUSTOM WORK A SPECIALTY.

RUBBER GOODS,

Of the Best Quality and in Every Variety.

TRUNKS, VALISES, SATCHELS, ETC.

JOHN LEWORTHY,

Main St., Moorestown, next Methodist Church.

JOHN C. BELTON,

(Formerly with the late Sam'l Jones,)

UNDERTAKER,

MOORESTOWN, - - - - - - NEW JERSEY.

MOORESTOWN
SMALL FRUIT AND PLANT FARM

STRAWBERRIES,	APPLES,
RASPBERRIES,	PEACHES,
BLACKBERRIES,	PEARS, &c.

Steek delivered Free in the Vicinity of Moorestown.

CATALOGUES FREE TO THOSE WHO APPLY.

S. C. DeCOU,

Moorestown, Burlington Co., New Jersey.

Ladies' Furnishing Goods.

TRIMMINGS, PATTERNS, FINE DRY GOODS,

NOTIONS, EMBROIDERY MATERIALS, &c.

Full and complete lines, at reasonable prices, at the Ladies' Furnishing Store of

ESTHER STILES,

South Side Main Street, Moorestown, N. J., between the Bank and th Town Hall.

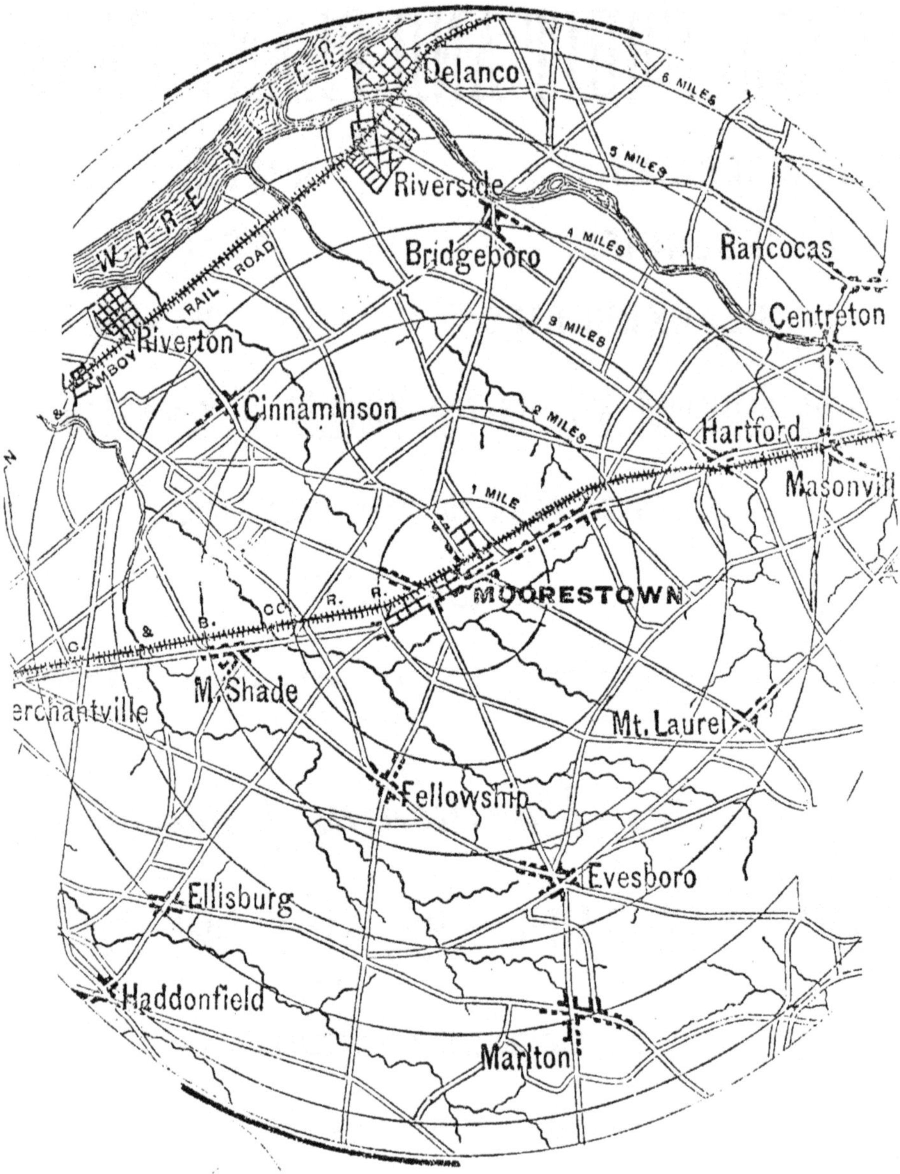
Delanco
6 MILES
5 MILES
Riverside
4 MILES
Rancocas
Bridgeboro
RAIL ROAD
AMBOY
Riverton
3 MILES
Centreton
Cinnaminson
2 MILES
Hartford
Masonvill
1 MILE
MOORESTOWN
C. & B. C. R. R.
M. Shade
erchantville
Mt. Laurel
Fellowship
Evesboro
Ellisburg
Haddonfield
Marlton

CPSIA information can be obtained
at www.ICGtesting.com
Printed in the USA
BVOW08s0117310717
490667BV00011B/74/P

9 781333 644642